Classic KENTUCKY MEALS

Classic KENTUCKY MEALS

STORIES, INGREDIENTS & RECIPES FROM *the Traditional Bluegrass Kitchen*

RONA ROBERTS

Photography by Sarah Jane Sanders

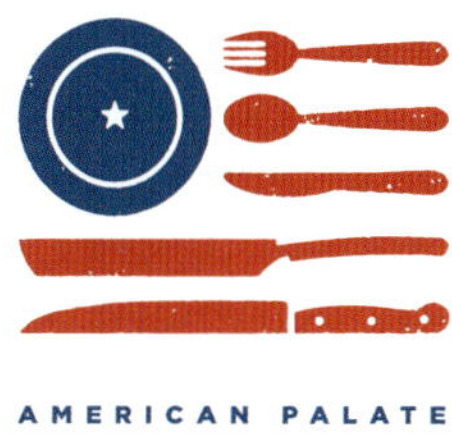

Published by American Palate
A Division of The History Press
Charleston, SC 29403
www.historypress.net

Cover images by Sarah Jane Sanders.

First published 2014

Manufactured in the United States

ISBN 978.1.62619.719.0

Library of Congress CIP data applied for.

Notice: The information in this book is true and complete to the best of our knowledge. It is offered without guarantee on the part of the author or The History Press. The author and The History Press disclaim all liability in connection with the use of this book.

With gratitude to those whose work fills the dishes and makes the meals on Kentucky's many tables

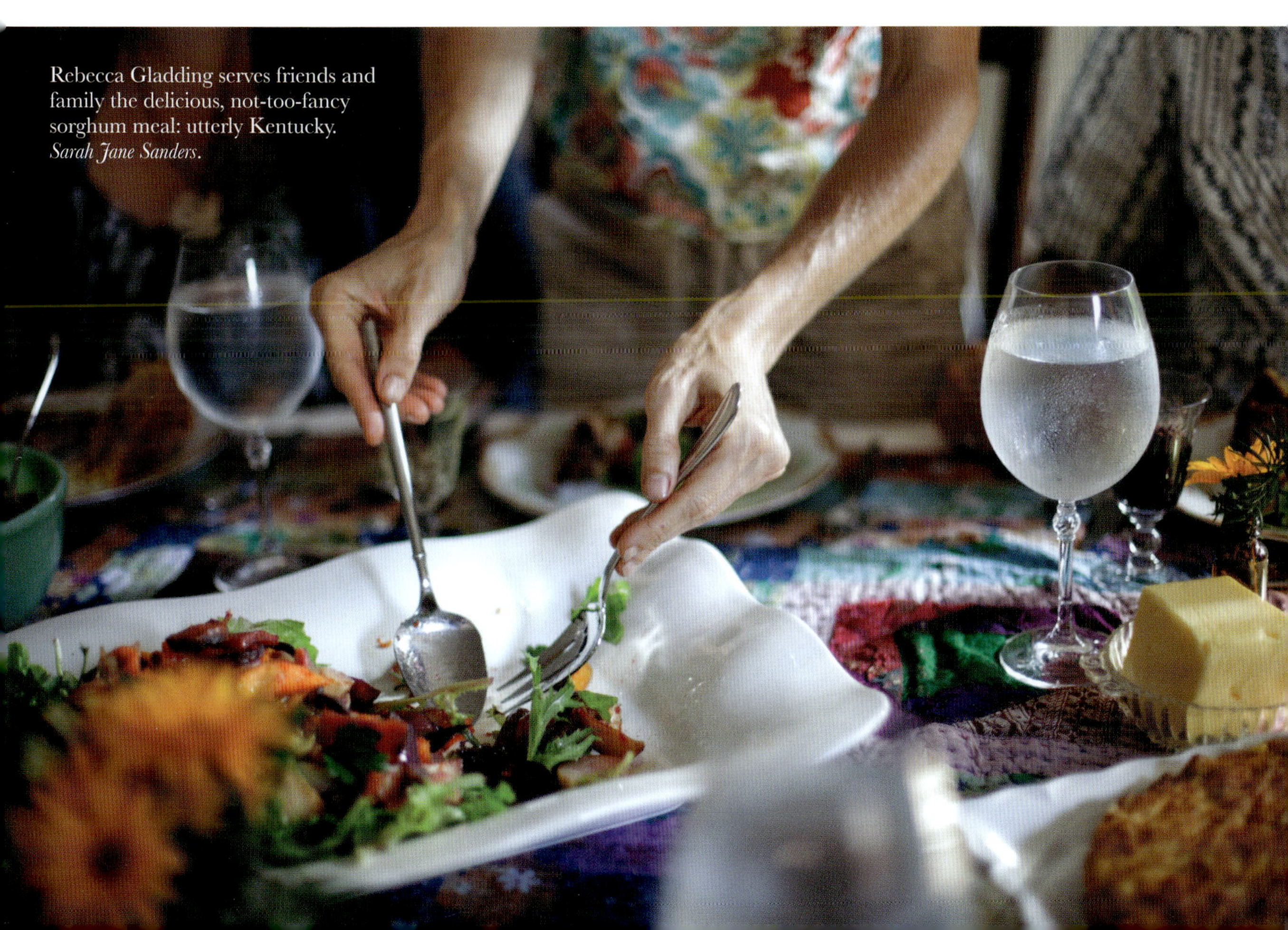

Rebecca Gladding serves friends and family the delicious, not-too-fancy sorghum meal: utterly Kentucky. *Sarah Jane Sanders.*

CONTENTS

PREFACE

On a bright February morning in 2014, I drove through gorgeous central Kentucky with a loyal friend in a car filled with rich cooking smells. I looked forward, at long last, to putting my 4-H demonstration training to good use: I had agreed to do a presentation on how to cook with sorghum to help raise money for the Arts Council of Mercer County.

I had let the mission grow from a simple "Talk about sorghum and tell why you wrote a book about it" into something like the final project for a graduate course I never took: "Cook and serve a meal featuring sorghum nine ways, using as many ingredients from as many Kentucky producers as possible; explain your reasoning and intent."

As we stepped onto the front walk of beautiful, historic Nathaniel Burrus House, Kentucky's sweet winter beauty and fertility surrounded us. We stood above a landscape of rolling fields, and I could almost see Four Hills Farm, the source of the meal's main dish: a savory lamb shoulder, braised with just a touch of sorghum.

Subtract a few utility lines, and the people who built the house in 1830 likely saw much of the same loveliness and promise all around them on a similar February morning nearly two hundred years ago. If we are good stewards, our unknown descendants will stand on that spot in 2230 and sense the same goodness and potential.

At any time across four hundred years, similar savory scents from fine local ingredients might be coming from the kitchen to meet us, drawing us in for conviviality and sustenance. What grows in Kentucky, we trust, will keep growing in Kentucky, giving Kentuckians our best source of wealth in every sense.

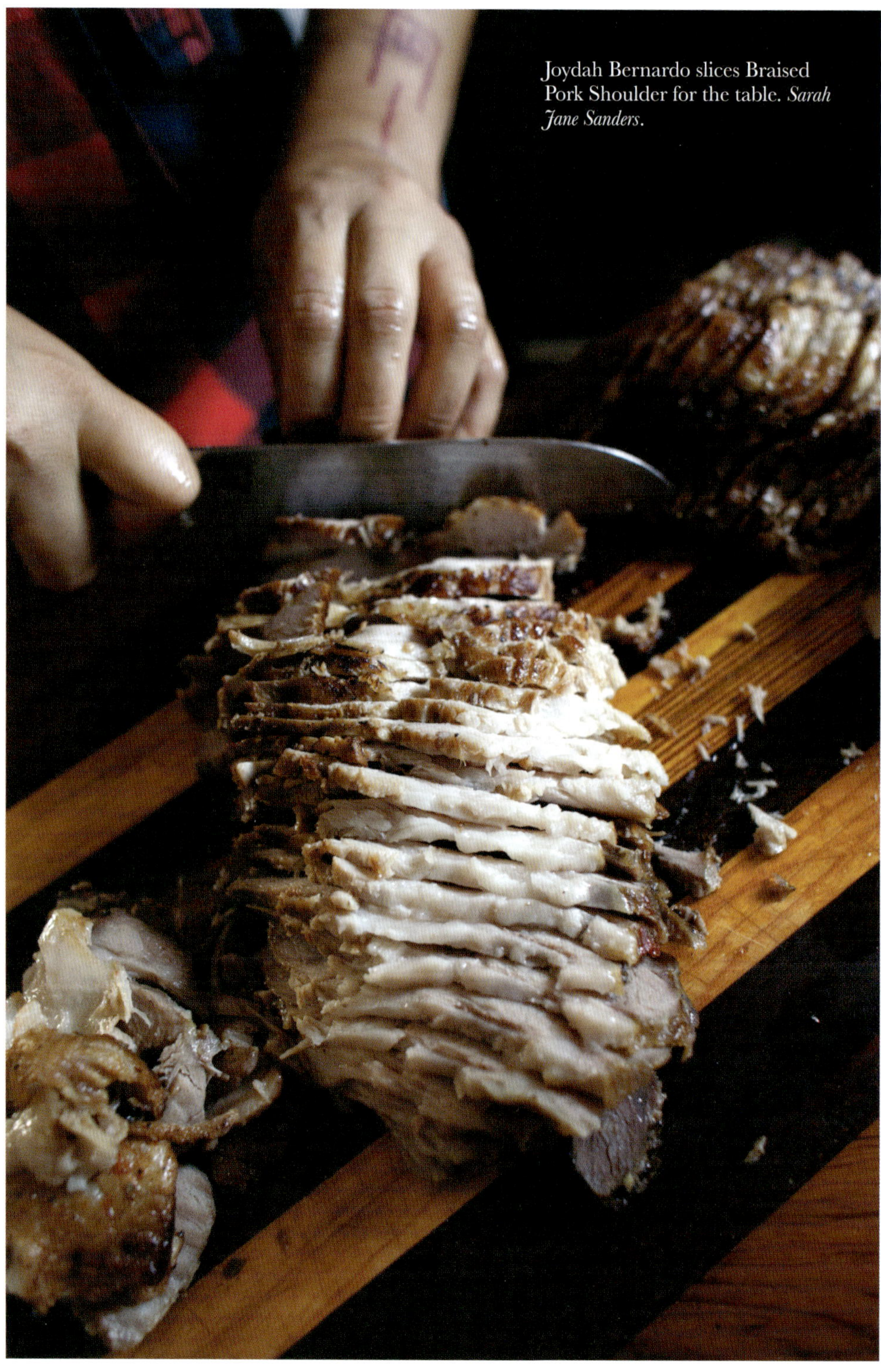

Joydah Bernardo slices Braised Pork Shoulder for the table. *Sarah Jane Sanders*.

Working on that meal brought focus to years of puzzling over several themes that show up often in Savoring Kentucky, my long-running food weblog about Kentucky food and the people who grow it:

- What parts of Kentucky's way of eating are as timeless as our land?
- What ways of eating are distinctively our own?
- How can home cooks make Kentucky-based meals that are good in every way: for our taste buds and our health, for growers as well as eaters, for everyone in all of our communities?
- How can we widen the number of families who eat what Kentucky grows?
- Who gets hurt if we call it a cuisine?
- If we call our way of eating a cuisine, can we still include cornbread?

In *The Third Plate*, legendary New York chef Dan Barber points out that *cuisine* (French for "kitchen") means the foods peasants cooked from what they could grow, wherever they lived around the world. In an interview with Eater.com, Barber said, "All of them were just

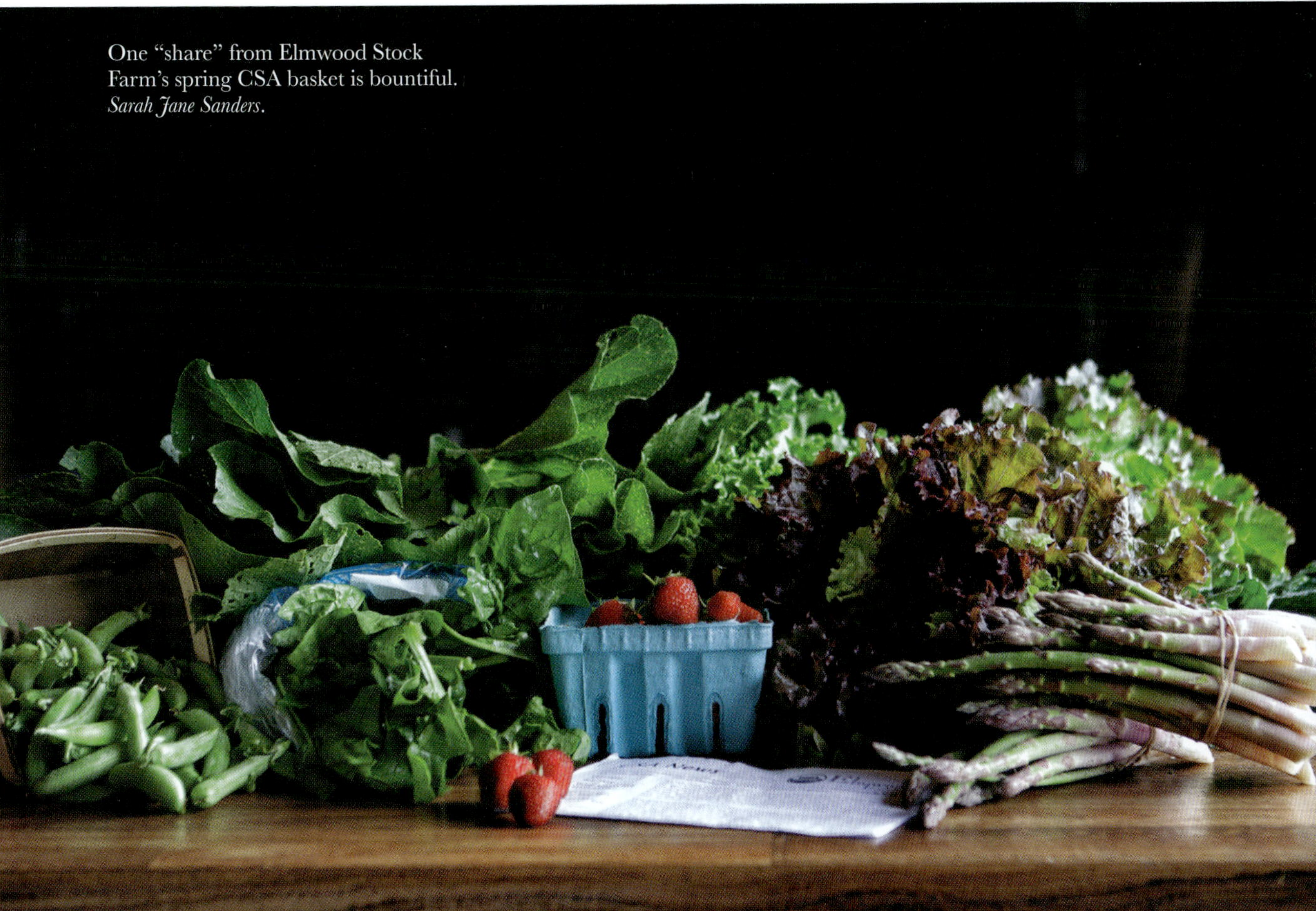

One "share" from Elmwood Stock Farm's spring CSA basket is bountiful. *Sarah Jane Sanders.*

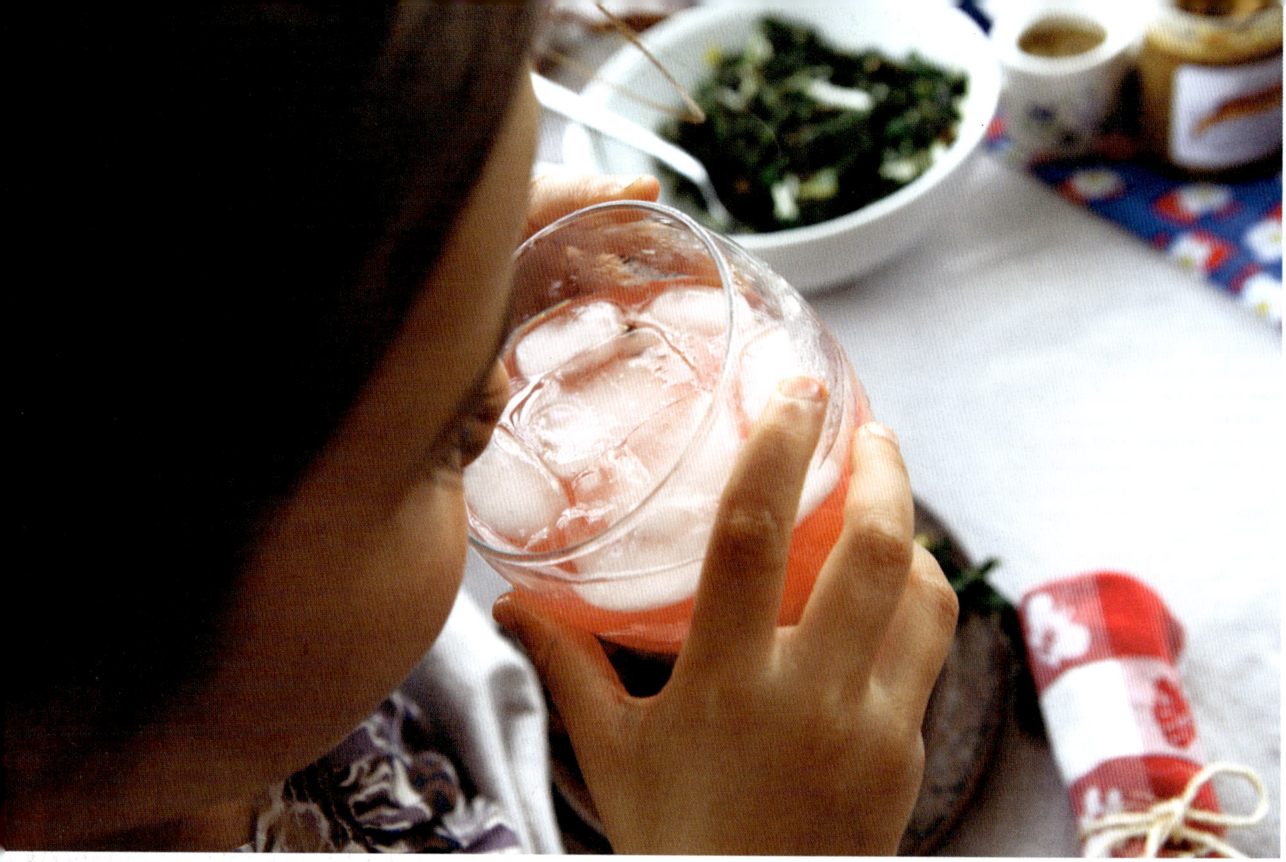

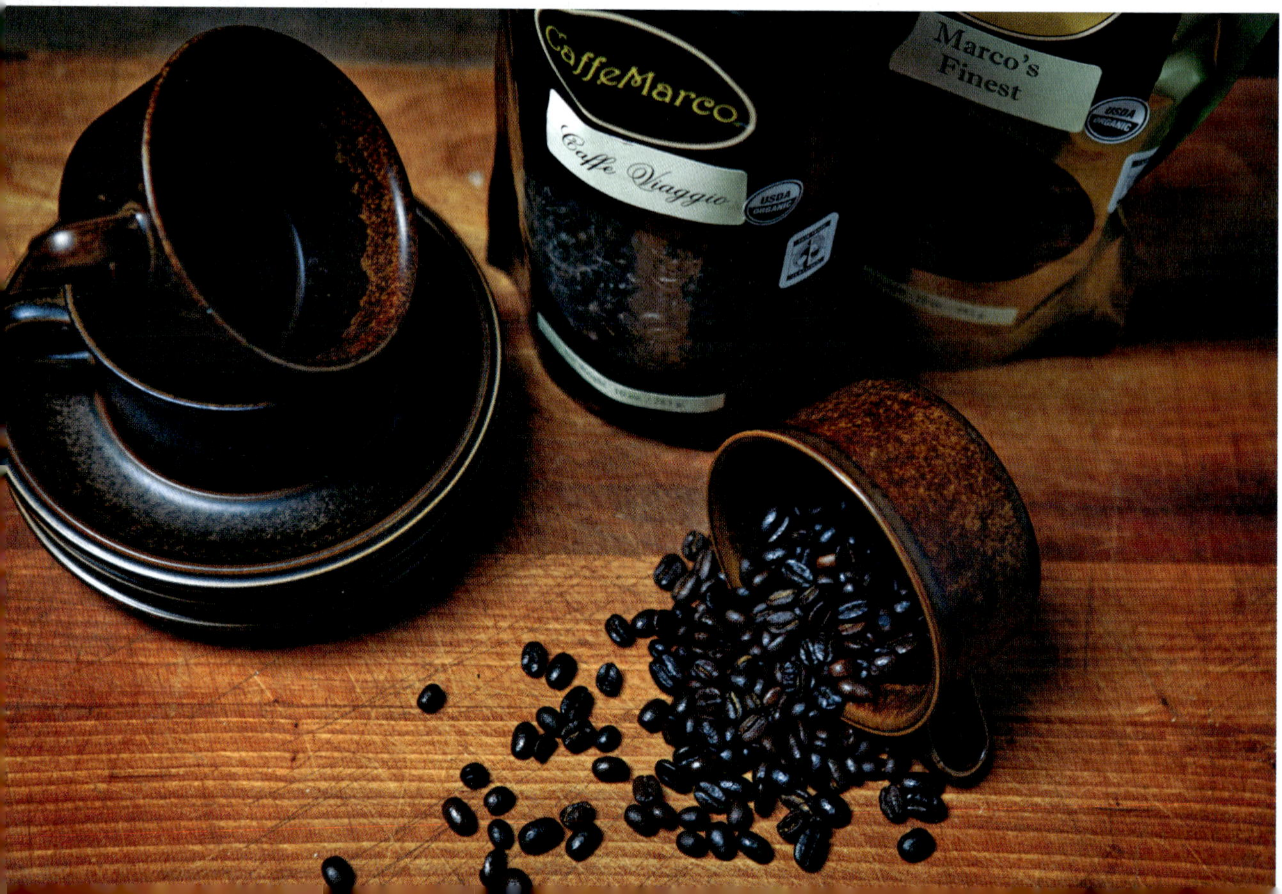

CaffeMarco
Caffe Viaggio
USDA ORGANIC
Marco's Finest
USDA ORGANIC

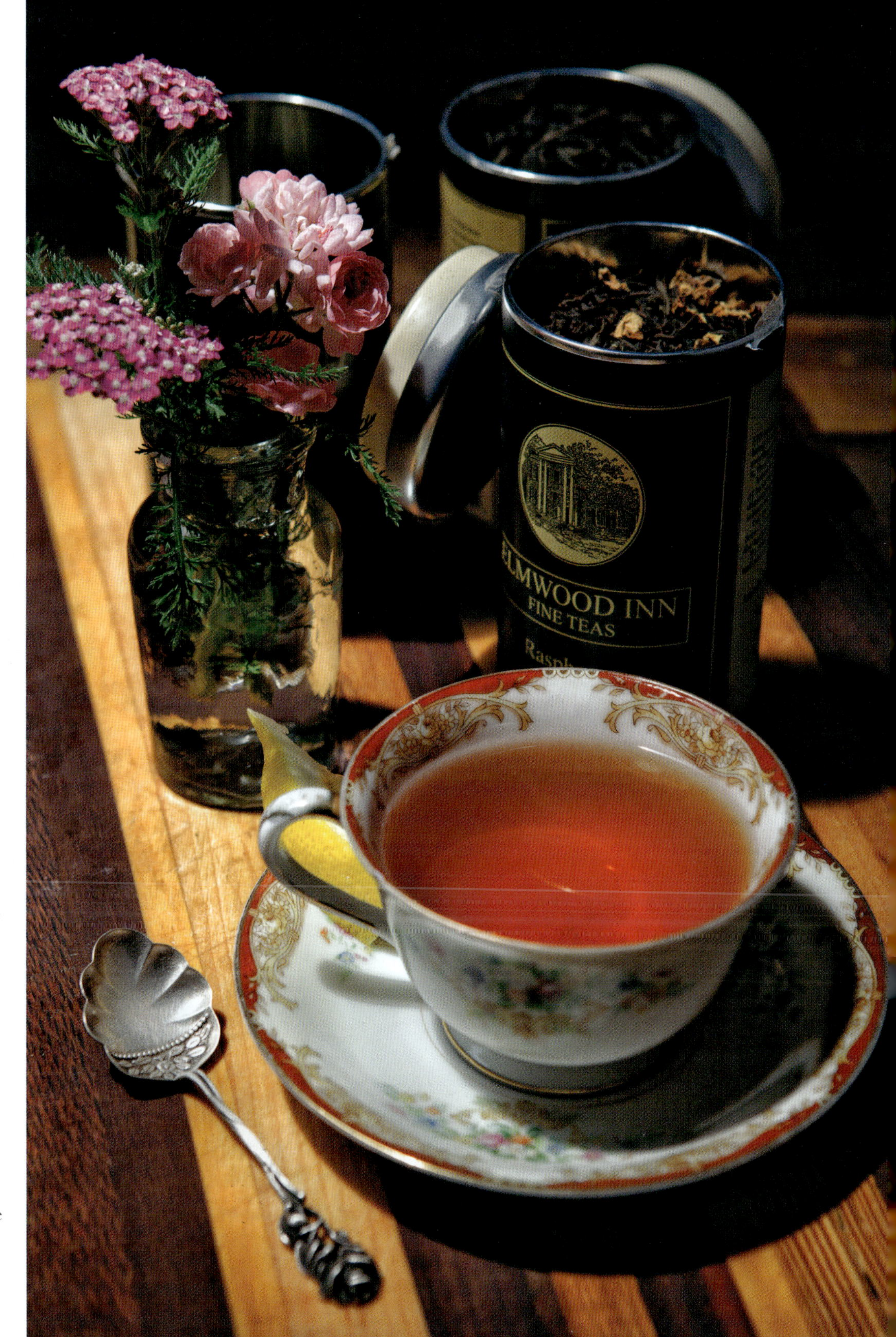

Opposite, top: Sour Cherry Lemonade is perfect for early summer meals. *Sarah Jane Sanders*.

Opposite, bottom: CaffeMarco in Paris is a pioneering Kentucky-based coffee roaster. *Sarah Jane Sanders*.

Right: Tea from Elmwood Inn Fine Teas is treasured around the world. *Sarah Jane Sanders*.

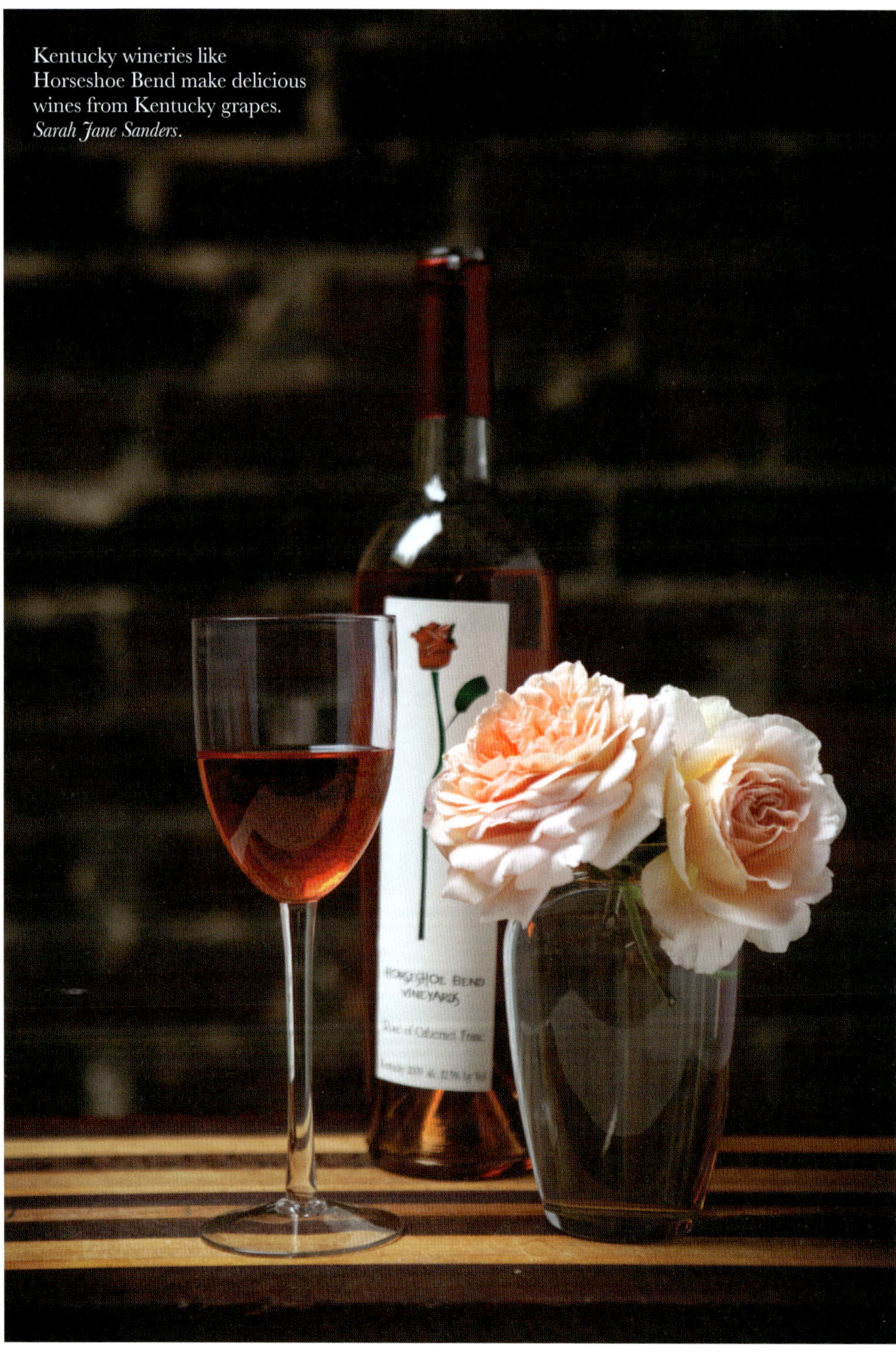

Kentucky wineries like Horseshoe Bend make delicious wines from Kentucky grapes. *Sarah Jane Sanders.*

negotiating, eking out what the land could provide, and then [they] figured out a way to make it nutritious and delicious."

That sounds like turnip greens cooked with leftover pork scraps to me—with some vinegar. And please pass the crusty cornbread. I'll have a little sorghum with mine. I'm eating Kentucky cuisine, so please tell me a good story and keep that Reel World String Band music playing.

Kentucky soil, water, climate and farmers can grow a nearly infinite array of wondrous foods. What would we like them to grow? We let them know the answers by what we buy and eat. We define Kentucky cuisine by what and how we cook and eat at home. By eating what's good from Kentucky's farms and orchards, meal by meal, we steer Kentucky's agriculture toward a positive, permanent capacity to feed Kentucky's people. Kentucky thought leader, entrepreneur and chef Ouita Michel recently called for Kentuckians to embrace "cuisine-supported agriculture." She urges us to grow, buy, cook, preserve and enjoy the foods and ways of cooking that are characteristic of our place. Let's cook and eat what we want grown. Cuisine is too important to leave only to restaurants and professional chefs.

If we want the place around us to nurture us, we can do our part by nurturing it. It means moving other tasks off our daily agenda and putting food in a more central place. We cannot drive through for an order of Kentucky cuisine—at least, not yet.

Cooking the sorghum meal in Mercer County required shopping, cooking, cleaning up and composting scraps. Most of it was memorable, enjoyable time spent cooking with others, doing handwork, smelling, tasting, listening to music and exploring the mysteries of ingredients combining into new foods.

More time like that—cooking daily meals as well as celebratory feasts—means more time shared with loved ones over chopping boards and skillets; more ways to engage children and young people in real, enjoyable work; and more time to use our human senses and faculties to take care of ourselves.

Making meaningful meals and making good local food central to those meals justifies spending some time reading about Kentucky growers and the pillars of Kentucky cuisine. Enjoy planning with a cup of Kentucky roasted coffee or Kentucky blended tea nearby, or relax with a glass of one of Kentucky's new wines close at hand.

This book offers recipes for five meals (plus one bonus), starting with the sorghum meal, that families can vary almost infinitely to enjoy Kentucky cuisine, cornbread included—three cornbreads, in fact.

Welcome to Kentucky cuisine.

Rona Roberts

ACKNOWLEDGEMENTS

Libby Allen
John Bell
Joydah Bernardo
Jodi Chmielewski
Preston Correll
Maury Cox
Janine Damran
Sarah Fritschner
Maggie Gladding
Rebecca Gladding
Sean Gladding
Seth Gladding
Jennifer Gleason
Rudo Greissworth
Leslie Guttman
John-Mark Hack
Travis Hood
Elisha Hopson
Terry Huff
Steve Kay
Eli Kay-Oliphant
Jean Pitches Keene
Leo Keene
Demetria Koch
Ryan Koch
Jim Lally
Rosaline Lobbo
Sherry Maddock
Lois Mateus
Ouita Michel
Alison Oliphant
Noah Oliphant
Sarah Preis
Sarah Jane Sanders
Kirsten Schofield
Becca Self
Marina Squerciati
Ann Bell Stone
Mac Stone
Jennifer Sudduth
Jack Taylor
Norma Taylor
Douglas Vick
Dane Webb
Philip Weisenberger
Carolyn Williams
John van Willigen
Fiona Young-Brown

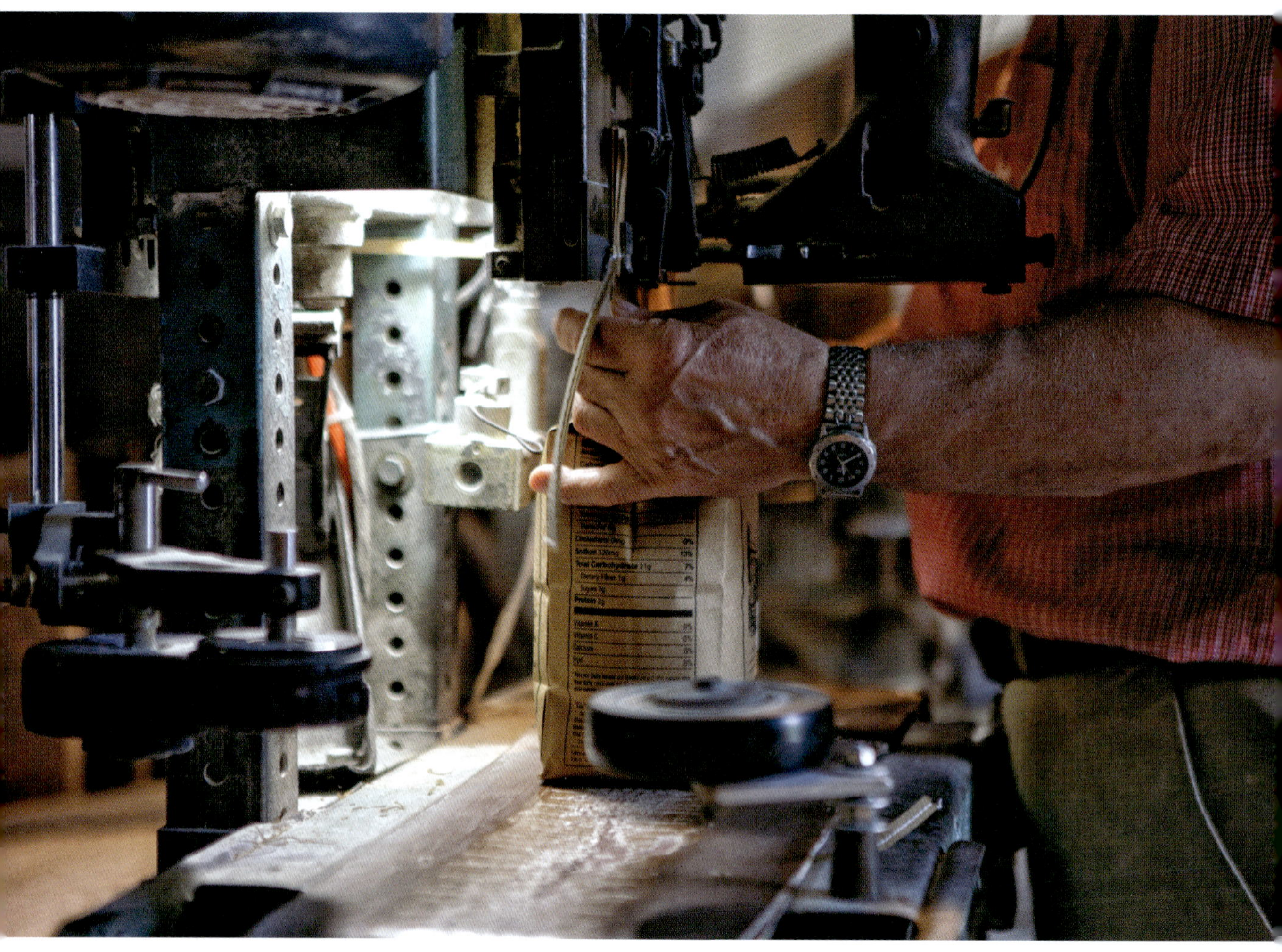

Mac Weisenberger, fifth-generation owner of Weisenberger Mill, packages cornmeal mix. *Sarah Jane Sanders*.

INTRODUCTION

Classic Kentucky Meals centers on meals that come from Kentucky land and ingredients. Each meal includes everyday dishes as well as dressed-up variations for special occasions. Families or friends can cook these meals together. Pairings with Kentucky cocktails, wine, beer, teas, coffees and music playlists help settle each meal more deeply into Kentucky's unique cuisine and culture.

These meals warrant some time and effort, though none is hard to make. Instead, these are meals that affirm what we already sense: growing, cooking and eating food have great value and reward our time and attention richly.

We Kentuckians value being hospitable. We love welcoming people to our tables. These meals help us do what we already love while also supporting the ones who produce our food.

Classic Kentucky Meals introduces dozens of Kentucky ingredients and profiles ten producers, including sixth-generation millers, multigenerational farming families and a heritage hog farmer whose work three years ago involved supervising an Indiana golf course. Each chapter includes a spotlight on one food central to Kentucky's cuisine.

The meals use whole, real ingredients. The flavors lean more toward savory than sweet because Kentucky's land produces savor in abundance. Worry not, though. Kentucky's own sweetness makes plenty of appearances in memorable desserts.

The dishes deliver layers of delicious tastes along with nutrients. The wonderful flavors in these recipes satisfy without the need for oversized portions.

The five meals (and one bonus) included here put Kentucky ingredients to timeless uses. Enjoy in good health!

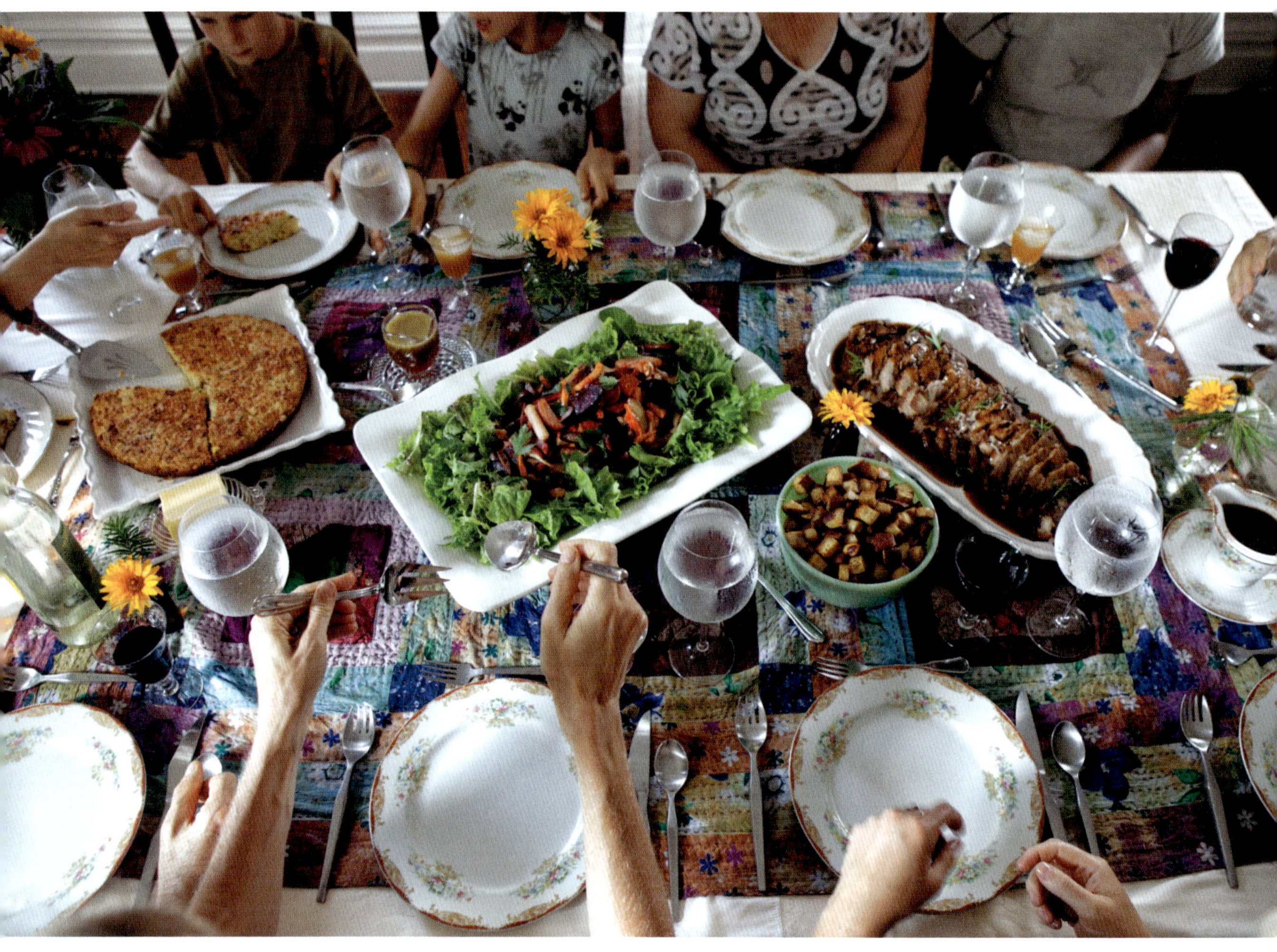

Savory, Slow and Sorghum Sweetened is a warming meal with Kentucky sorghum in every dish. *From left*: Rich and Spicy Kentucky Cornbread, Roast Winter Vegetable Salad with Chef Ouita Michel's Sorghum-Bourbon Vinaigrette, Roast Sweet Potatoes and Braised Pork Shoulder. *Sarah Jane Sanders*.

Meal 1

SAVORY, SLOW AND SORGHUM SWEETENED

Winter likes its table warm and filling. Its rich tastes combine the sweetness of the past summer's gifts with the punch and jab of savor, umami and pan-browned goodness. This meal is all about those deep satisfactions, though to be honest, this meal is good just about year-round.

Everyday Menu

Braised Pork, Lamb or Beef Shoulder
Roast Winter Vegetable Salad with Chef Ouita Michel's Sorghum-Bourbon Vinaigrette
Roast Sweet Potatoes
Plain-spoken Buttermilk Cornbread

For special occasions or holidays, add "fancy" to this meal by amping up the cornbread wattage and adding a warming homemade dessert.

Dressed-up Menu Additions

Rich and Spicy Kentucky Cornbread with Chef Edward Lee's Sorghum-Lime Drizzle
Double Gingerbread with Whipped Half-Sour Cream and Kentucky Pecans

Perfect Pairings

- *Cocktail*: The Worldly Apple, a global Kentucky cocktail (see page 25)
- *Wine*: Up the Creek Chambourcin
- *Beer*: Alltech's Kentucky Bourbon Ale
- *Tea*: Elmwood Fine Tea's Bourbon Black Tea or Assam Tippy
- *Coffee*: Magic Beans Coffee Roasters' Sumatra Mandheling Fair Trade Organic
- *Soundtrack for cooking*: [Some songs on all playlists have adult language and themes.] "Puttin' Up Hay" (Blind Corn Liquor Pickers), "Duel Between a Fiddle and a Banjo" (Lonnie Mack, Rusty York), "Same Ol' River" (Sam Bush), "In the City" (Cunninlynguists), "Dumas Walker" (the Kentucky Headhunters), "Rock-A-My-Soul" (American Spiritual Ensemble), "Same Old Train" (Marty Stuart and many others), "Seasons Are Fun" (Gail Wynters), "Blue Kentucky Girl" (Emmylou Harris)
- *Soundtrack for eating*: "Circuital" (My Morning Jacket), "Closer Walk" (The Swells), "Don't Close Your Eyes" (Keith Whitley), "Keep on the Sunny Side" (the Carter Family), "Kentucky" (Billy Joe and Norah), "Don't It Make My Brown Eyes Blue" (Crystal Gayle), "Every Time You Leave" (Emmylou Harris and Don Everly), "Kentucky Rain" (Elvis Presley), "Kentucky Waltz" (Bill Monroe & His Blue Grass Boys), "This Can't Be Love" (Lou Rawls, Les McCann), "Late October Birds" (Henry Hipkens)

Kentucky Common Cents

Any time you cook at home, you win: Home Cooked: 1, Drive-Through: 0. The wins include money, health and family time.

Good food can come from your farm and garden, your Save-A-Lot or other grocery store, your farmers' market or your CSA (community-supported agriculture subscription) box. When you buy groceries from a chain store owned outside your community, every one dollar you spend has an estimated 13 percent additional local community impact because some of your dollar goes to help pay your neighbors who work at the store. By contrast, when we spend one dollar online, very likely the positive economic impact on our own community is zero; all the money goes to other places.

The goal is not to make perfect choices. We can't do that all the time, and most of us don't need another source of worry about our decisions. My own goals are to cook at home most of the time, buy local ingredients when I can, take pleasure in every meal and let worry go live somewhere else.

For more information, visit Food Tank and Sustain Ontario online.

The Worldly Apple: A Global Kentucky Cocktail

Inspired by an apple-cardamom cocktail from the Union Square Café, this cocktail takes familiar Kentucky ingredients and invents new flavors to layer on top of them.

Yield: 1 tall cocktail

For the Cardamom-Flavored Bourbon

2 tablespoons green cardamom pods
½ cup Kentucky bourbon, such as Four Roses, Wild Turkey or Old Forester

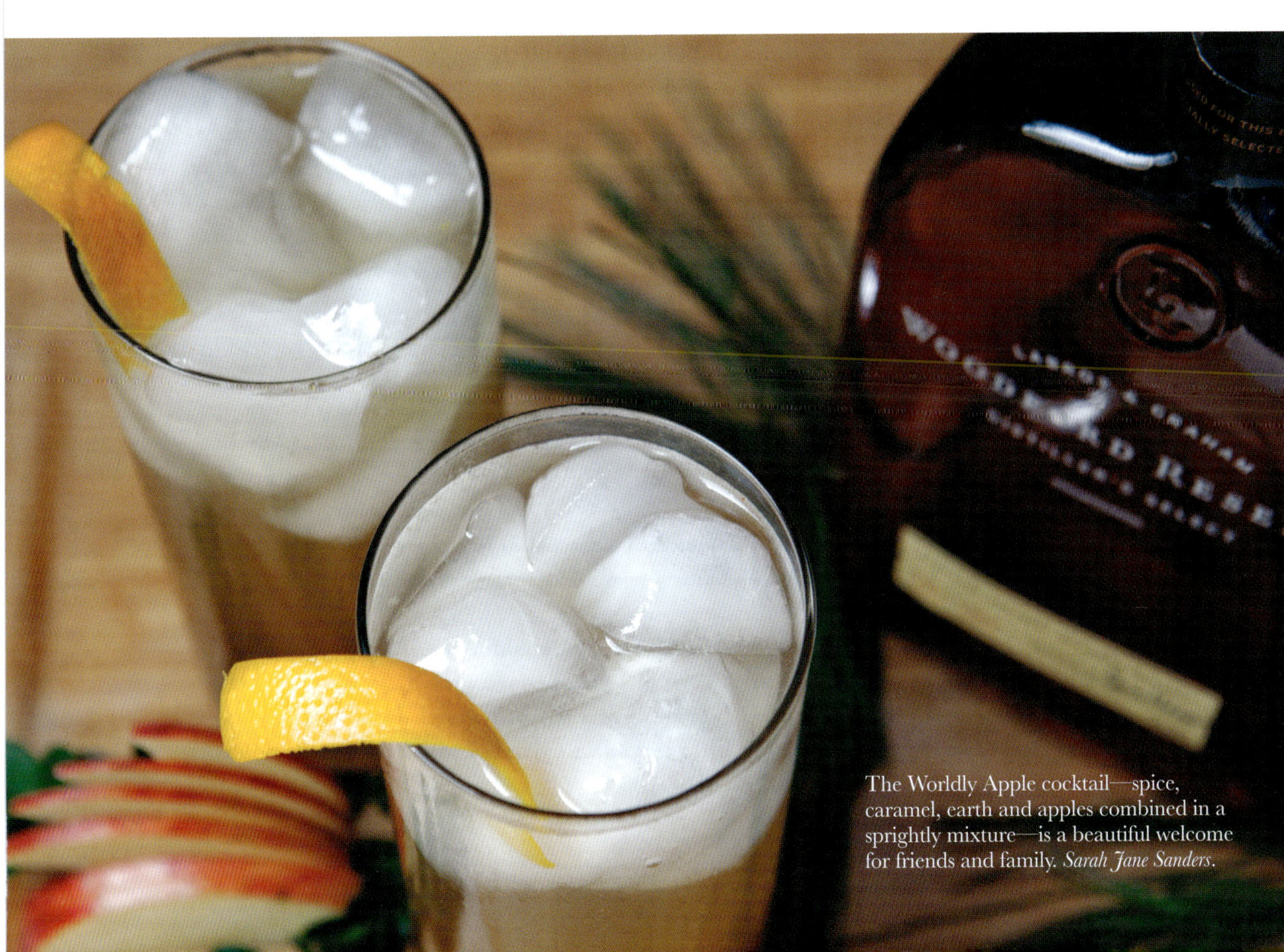

The Worldly Apple cocktail—spice, caramel, earth and apples combined in a sprightly mixture—is a beautiful welcome for friends and family. *Sarah Jane Sanders.*

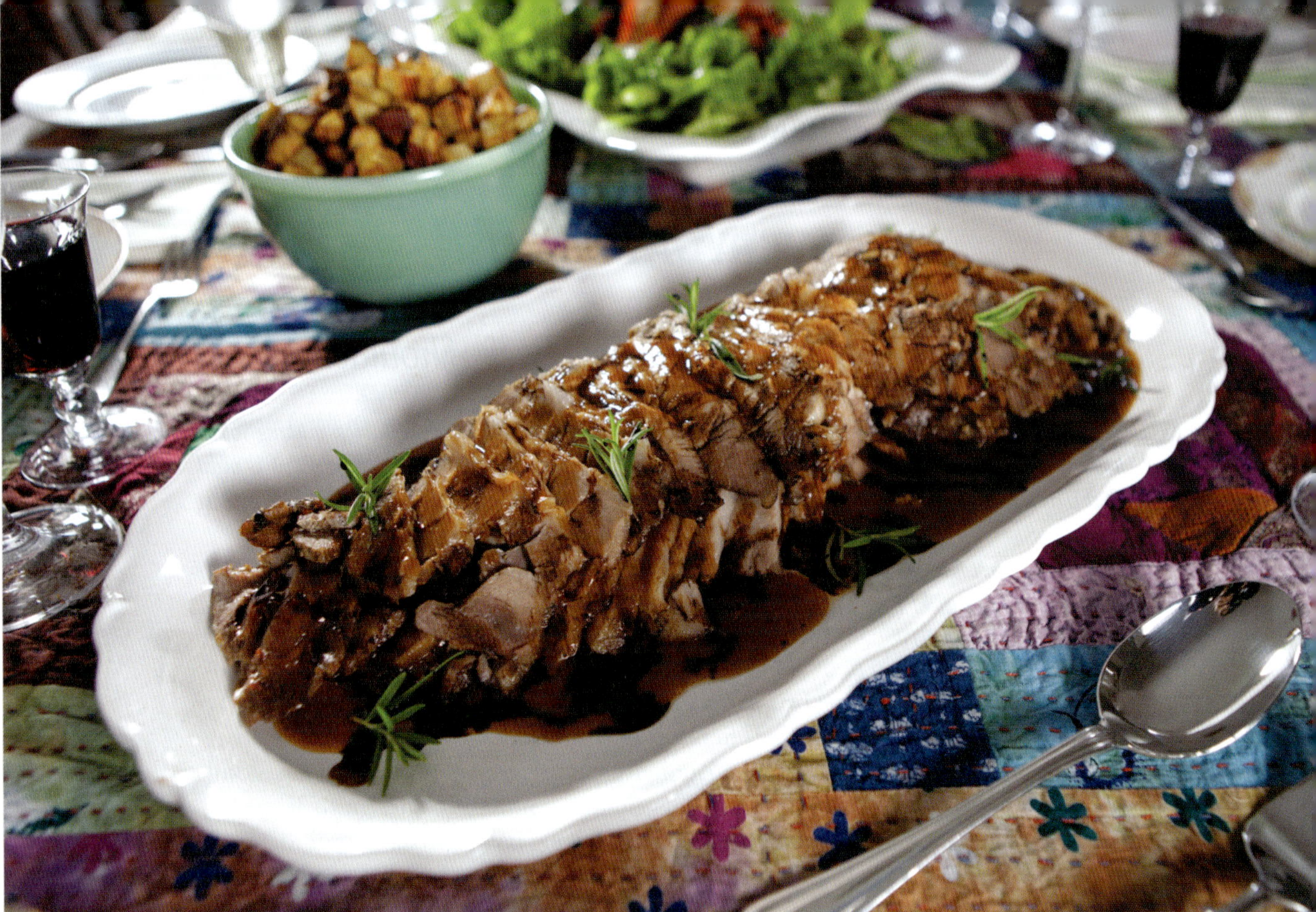

Braised Stone Cross Farm pork shoulders are savory and fork tender. *Sarah Jane Sanders.*

Add the next seven ingredients—carrots, celery, onion, garlic, thyme, bay leaves and whole peppercorns—and stir. Lower the heat to medium-low; cook for about 15 minutes, stirring frequently, until the vegetables begin to brown.

Turn your oven on to 300 degrees Fahrenheit.

Cut the tomatoes into quarters and add them to the vegetables along with the sorghum, bitters and wine. Season with a bit of salt and pepper. Start with ½ teaspoon of each if you need a measure. Bring the mixture to a low boil; stir for about 10 minutes, evaporating some of the wine.

Return the shoulder and accumulated juices to the pot. Add enough stock to come about a third of the way up the meat. Bring the liquids in the pot back to boiling. Cover and place the pot in the oven. Check after 15 minutes to make sure the liquid is simmering (bubbling a little). Cook (braise) for about 4½ to 5 hours, spooning sauce over the meat occasionally. If you have an instant-read thermometer, look for meat temperatures above 190 degrees Fahrenheit.

Move the shoulder from the pan to a cutting board or platter. Cover with foil to keep warm.

For a Kentucky-style pan sauce, use a mesh strainer over a large saucepan to separate the braising liquid from the vegetable solids. Press a little on the solids with a spoon to push the softer solids through—this helps thicken the sauce. Discard whatever is left in the strainer. Skim or use a fat separator to remove most fat from the sauce liquid. Put the defatted sauce-to-be back into the saucepan and bring it to a boil. Immediately lower the heat and simmer to reduce and thicken the sauce. This may take up to 30 minutes. The sauce will become saltier as it reduces. Aim for about 2 cups of sauce. Taste for salt and pepper at the end.

Carve the shoulder into slices about ⅓ inch thick. They will be fall-apart tender. Yummmm!

Arrange on a serving platter; spoon sauce over the sliced shoulder in a pretty drizzle or concentrated band (for dazzle). Garnish the platter with chopped green herbs of choice.

Measuring Salt

Kentucky grocery stores offer Kentucky cooks many salt options from iodized table salt to grind-your-own chunks of sea salt. Chunky or flaky salts add less salt flavor, by teaspoon, than finely ground salts. We use finely ground sea salt for the recipes in *Classic Kentucky Meals*. If you use table salt, the measures should work fine. If you use Kosher salt, you may want to increase the amounts recommended by adding 50 percent more salt, by measure. Taste tests will be good guides to the right levels of salt in Kentucky meals.

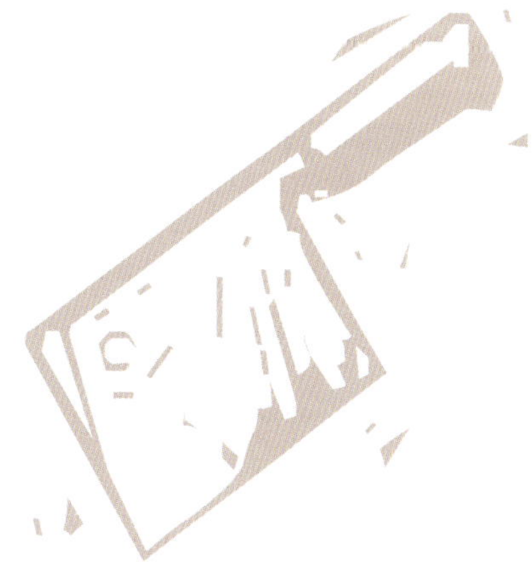

Roast Winter Vegetable Salad with Chef Ouita Michel's Sorghum-Bourbon Vinaigrette

Warm roast vegetables make winter salads compelling; served this way, vegetables become essential, necessary and utterly delicious. Putting Chef Ouita Michel's Sorghum-Bourbon Vinaigrette on any salad or slaw will make salad your favorite course, no matter the season.

Yield: Serves 8 generously; leftovers are scrumptious

5 to 6 cups winter vegetables (use any selection of winter vegetables you have available: sweet potatoes, onions, garlic, winter squashes, fennel, winter radishes, turnips, parsnips, carrots, etc.)
2 tablespoons good olive oil, clarified butter or mild bacon grease
1 tablespoon sorghum
salt and pepper to taste
12 cups or more fresh leafy salad greens
Chef Ouita Michel's Sorghum-Bourbon Vinaigrette (recipe follows)

Preheat oven to 375 degrees Fahrenheit.

Clean vegetables thoroughly. Peel if you like. Cut into spears or wedges.

Place parchment paper or foil on your two heaviest baking sheets. Put half the cleaned, cut vegetables on each sheet.

Add 1 tablespoon oil or fat and ½ tablespoon sorghum to each baking sheet. Mix well with your hands and spread the vegetables as flat as you can get them. Sprinkle with salt and pepper.

Bake, uncovered, until tender. Depending on your mix of veggies, this may take 45 to 60 minutes. Remove garlic early if it starts to brown. Allow other vegetables to brown around their edges.

If you need to hurry the veggies, cover the baking sheets tightly with foil for at least 20 minutes. Then uncover for 10 minutes or so to get a bit of flavor-rich caramelization.

Your choice: let vegetables cool on sheets or use when warm to top salad greens.

For serving, either cover a large platter with salad greens and mound warm or room temperature vegetables in the middle, or make individual salads by placing clean, dry salad greens on salad plates and then topping with a generous serving of roast vegetables.

Drizzle all with Chef Ouita Michel's Sorghum-Bourbon Vinaigrette.

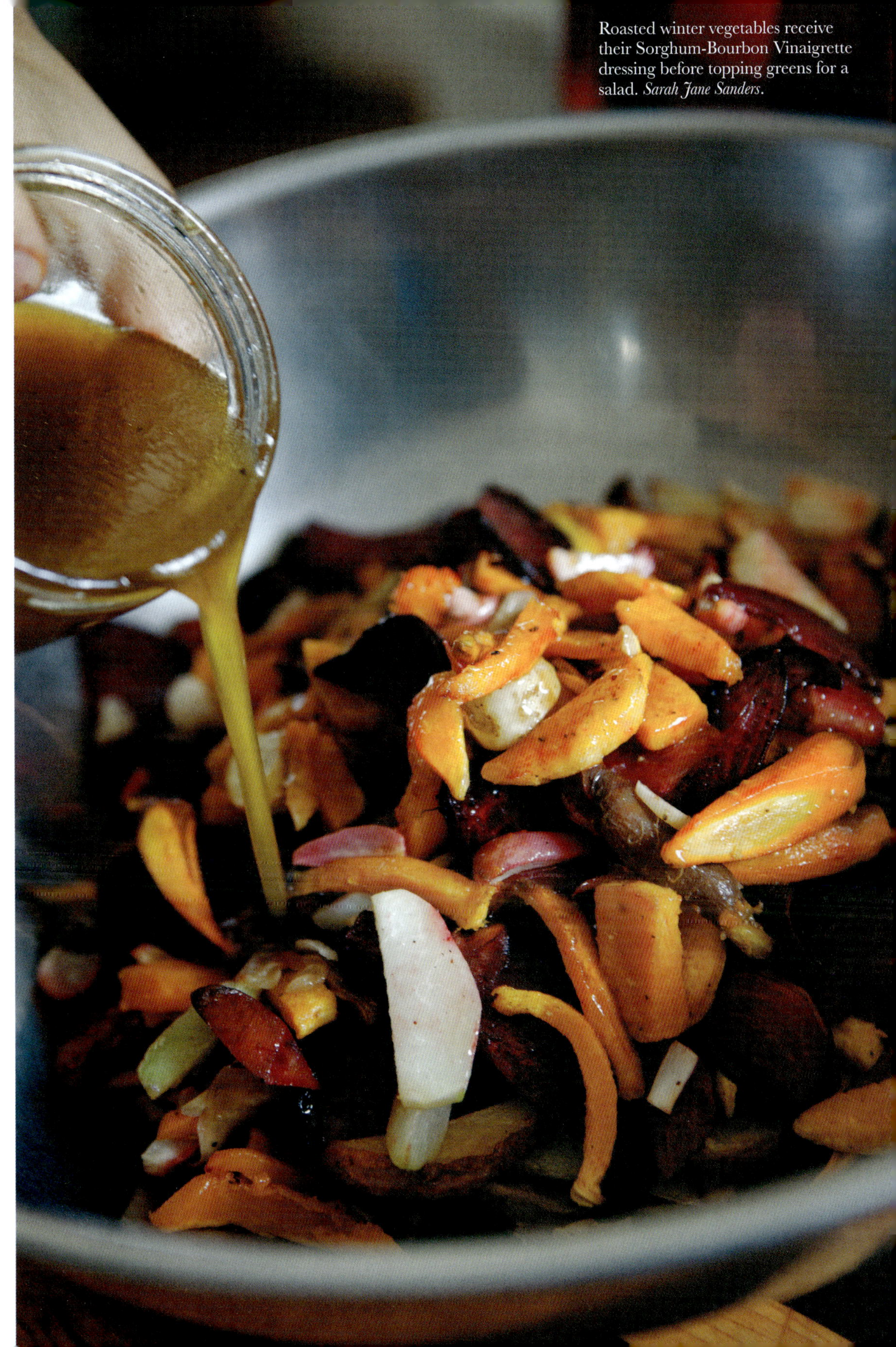

Roasted winter vegetables receive their Sorghum-Bourbon Vinaigrette dressing before topping greens for a salad. *Sarah Jane Sanders*.

Chef Ouita Michel's Sorghum-Bourbon Vinaigrette

Salads and slaws dressed with this vinaigrette transcend the ordinary and reach the sublime. This easily made dressing adds up to more than its parts. Chef Ouita Michel, founder of the Holly Hill Inn family of restaurants in central Kentucky, says, "The bourbon and the grated onion are both imperative." For an even more Kentucky dressing, replace the Tabasco with one careful drop of Sav's Piment, made in Lexington.

Yield: About 2½ cups dressing; keeps well in the refrigerator for one week

½ cup malt or cider vinegar
3 tablespoons Woodford Reserve Bourbon
½ cup pure sorghum
2 teaspoons grated onion
couple shakes Tabasco sauce
1 teaspoon salt or to taste
1 teaspoon freshly ground black pepper
1 cup olive oil

Combine the vinegar, bourbon and sorghum together and stir or shake until dissolved.

Add the onion, Tabasco, salt and pepper.

Whisk in the oil.

Done.

Printed with permission from Chef Ouita Michel, owner, Holly Hill Inn Family of Restaurants, Midway, Kentucky.

Roast Sweet Potatoes

These sorghum-kissed, oven-crisped sweet potatoes bring their own mild goodness to any meal. Their sweetness plays off the savory notes of the braised shoulder in this meal. Maggie Green inspired this recipe with the wonderful Oven-Baked Sweet Potato Fries she included in The Kentucky Fresh Cookbook.

Yield: 8 servings

2 pounds sweet potatoes
¼ cup olive oil, coconut oil or strained bacon or pork drippings
1 teaspoon salt
½ teaspoon ground cumin
½ teaspoon sweet Blue Moon Farm paprika or Bourbon Barrel Foods' Bourbon Smoked Paprika
½ teaspoon garlic powder, or 3 finely diced garlic cloves
⅛ teaspoon cayenne powder
2 teaspoons Kentucky sorghum

Preheat the oven to 425 degrees Fahrenheit. Line a large rimmed baking sheet with either parchment paper or foil.

Wash and scrub the potatoes; trim a tidbit from each end. Pat dry. Or peel if you must.

Cut into your favorite shape. Three good options: round-sliced "coins," about Ð inch thick; 1-inch cubes; or Maggie's style, ½-inch-wide by 3-inch-long strips.

Place in a large bowl. Add the oil, salt, cumin, paprika, garlic powder, cayenne powder and sorghum. Combine thoroughly to distribute the flavorful mixture on all sides of each potato piece. Spread on the prepared baking sheet. Bake for 30 minutes, until the edges are lightly browned and the centers pierce easily with a fork.

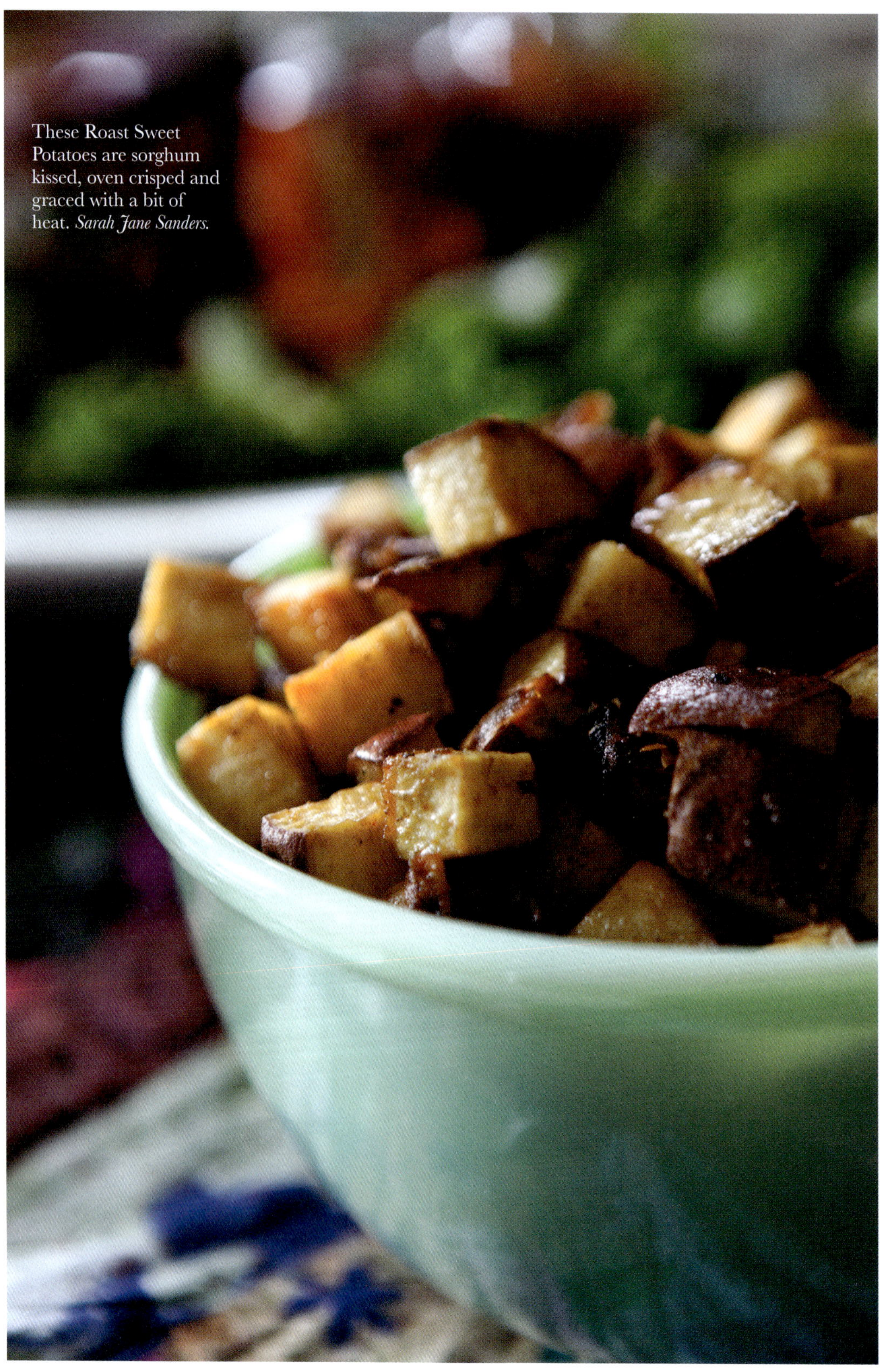

These Roast Sweet Potatoes are sorghum kissed, oven crisped and graced with a bit of heat. *Sarah Jane Sanders.*

Plain-spoken Buttermilk Cornbread

Cornbread graced most Kentucky tables for at least one meal every day for about the first 125 years after Kentucky became a state. (That was in 1792, as you know.) Good cornbread sustains a body like no other bread can thanks to the goodness of that corn-buttermilk-egg triumvirate, all of which came straight from the farm.

Cornbread made sense in working farm kitchens. The cook could step into the kitchen from garden or barn, stoke the fire, stir the batter together in five minutes and—assuming that fire heated up properly—set a steaming skillet of crusty cornbread on the table within thirty minutes.

Note that cornbread, made Kentucky style, has no flour and so is naturally wheat-free.

Yield: Serves 8–10

½ cup plus 1 tablespoon coconut oil or bacon fat
Option: Substitute ½ cup browned butter for the fat in the batter (see "Browned Butter: A Cook's Flavorful Friend," page 39, and see Note below)
2½ cups unbolted white cornmeal
1 tablespoon baking powder
½ teaspoon baking soda
1 teaspoon salt
1 tablespoon coarsely ground black pepper, or other forms of peppery flavor (ground or crushed cayenne, for example), optional
2 cups buttermilk
1 egg
¼ to ⅓ cup boiling water

Note: Browned butter tastes wonderful in this recipe but it can cause cornbread to stick unless you outsmart it. Here's how to have your browned butter and still get the cornbread out of the pan: (1) spray the cold skillet with a good nonstick spray before you add the butter and put the skillet in the oven to preheat; (2) watch carefully for the butter to brown; remove the skillet and add the butter to the cornbread batter immediately; and then (3) add 1 tablespoon of coconut oil or pork fat to the hot skillet after you have poured all the melted butter into your batter and before you pour the batter into the skillet. Those fats should help keep the cornbread from sticking.

Preheat the oven to 425 degrees Fahrenheit. Put your chosen fat in a 9- or 10-inch iron skillet and put the skillet in the oven as it heats.

In a large bowl, combine these ingredients: cornmeal, baking powder, baking soda, salt and pepper, if using. Whisk together.

Add buttermilk and egg; stir well.

Carefully remove the hot skillet from the oven and pour all but about 1 tablespoon of the hot fat into your batter. (Sizzle!)

Set your hot skillet in a safe place or return it to the oven.

Stir the batter thoroughly. The batter will be thick, about like soft-serve ice cream.

Add ¼ cup very hot water and stir. If necessary, add a bit more hot water so the whisk or spoon can move easily through the batter.

Carefully pour the batter into the skillet. (Sizzle again!)

Bake for about 25 minutes, and then check the progress. The cornbread should be golden brown all around the edges and firm to the touch in the center. If you use a thermometer, the temperature in the center should be above 180 degrees Fahrenheit.

Remove the skillet from the oven. Carefully flip the cornbread onto a waiting plate or simply serve it from the skillet.

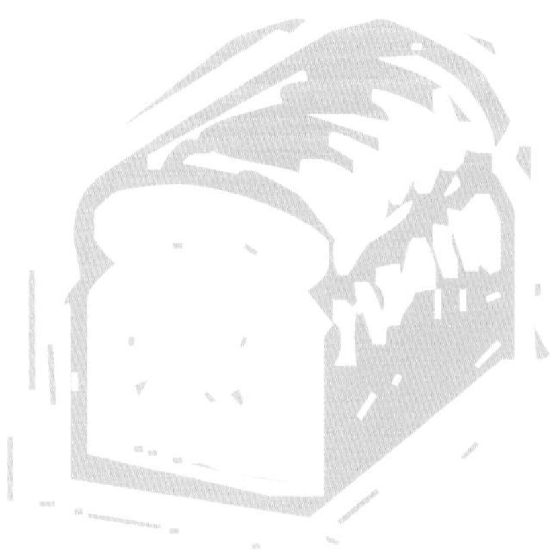

DRESSED-UP MENU

Rich and Spicy Kentucky Cornbread with Chef Edward Lee's Sorghum-Lime Drizzle

Cornbread is simple—when it's the plain-spoken sort just provided. Rich and Spicy Kentucky Cornbread, which lights up special occasion meals, is arduous work by comparison. Yet like all cornbreads worth their buttermilk, this one can be changed, modified, added and subtracted based on what you have. What follows is a good, vegetarian, wheat-free starting point for a decidedly fancy cornbread.

Yield: This recipe serves 8 to 12. It fills one 12-inch cast-iron skillet or a 9-inch skillet plus a 6-inch one.

½ cup butter, melted in skillet (browned butter is especially tasty; see "Browned Butter: A Cook's Flavorful Friend," page 39)
2½ cups unbolted white cornmeal
1 tablespoon baking powder
¼ teaspoon baking soda
1½ teaspoons salt
1 tablespoon coarsely ground black pepper, according to taste, optional
1½ cups buttermilk
½ cup cottage cheese (as tart and as close to dry curd as possible)
½ cup sour cream
2 eggs
1 cup grated or cubed sharp Kentucky cheddar
½ cup grated Kentucky Asiago or Parmesan; hold 2 tablespoons for sprinkling on top
1 medium yellow or extra-sweet onion, cut into small dice
¼ cup finely chopped hot red (or green or orange) peppers (substitute sweet peppers or leave peppers out completely if you wish)
1 cup (or more) fresh or frozen corn kernels
1 teaspoon sorghum (completely optional—it's my good luck charm, and it encourages the naturally sweet tastes of certain ingredients to stand out a bit more in the savory batter)
Chef Lee's Sorghum-Lime Drizzle

Next page: Rich and Spicy Kentucky Cornbread loves butter and wows with Sorghum-Lime Drizzle. *Sarah Jane Sanders.*

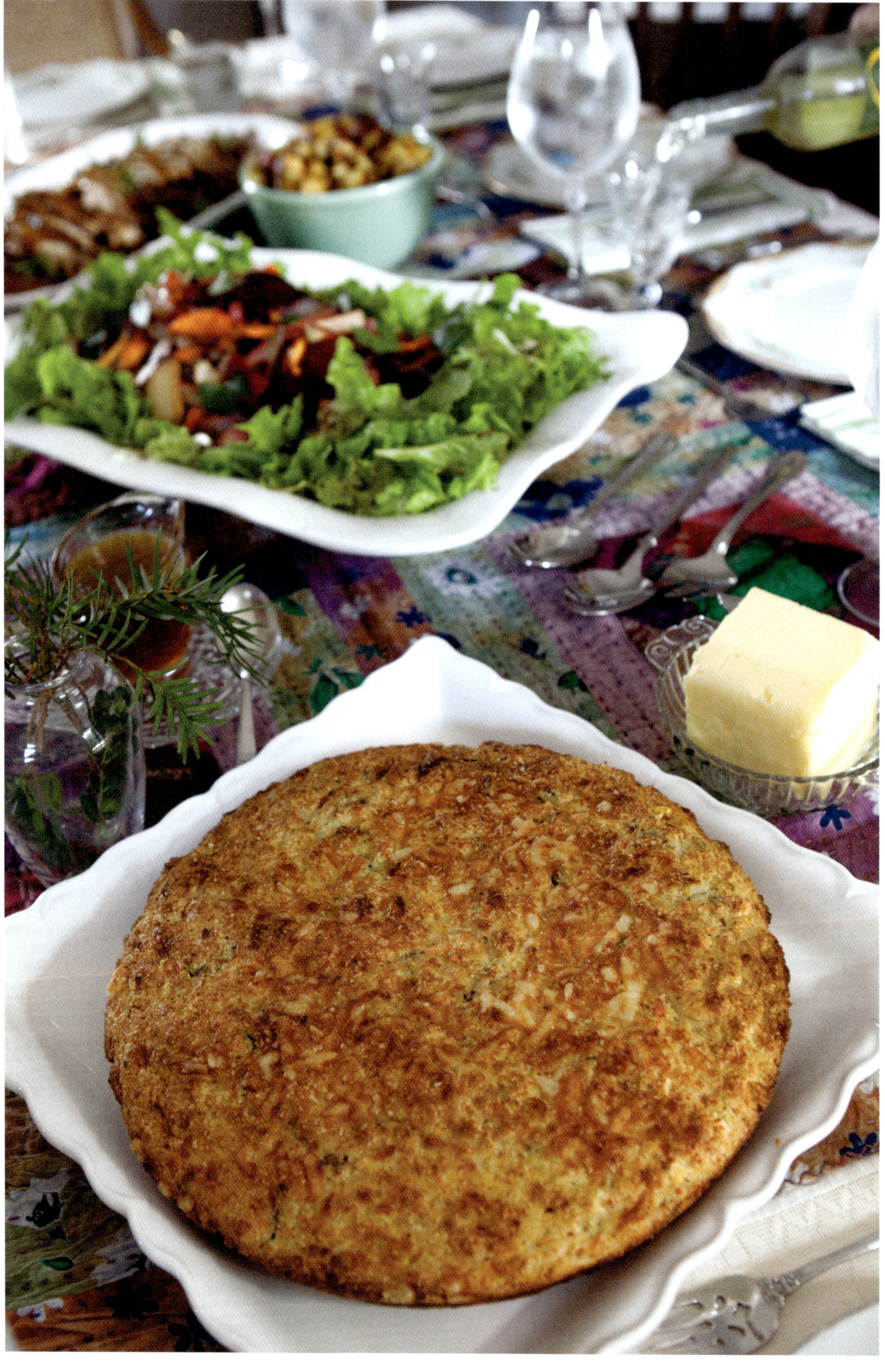

Optional Prep:

You can use all the vegetables without sautéing, but for more sweetness, chop and sauté the onions in 2 tablespoons of butter or olive oil; add hot peppers near the end. After these vegetables are cooked and the heat is turned off, if using frozen corn, add the kernels to the skillet so they can warm.

Preheat the oven to 375 degrees Fahrenheit. Spray your skillet(s) with a nonstick spray. Put the butter in the skillet and the skillet in the oven during preheating. Either remove the skillet once the butter is melted or allow the butter to brown.

In a very large bowl, combine these ingredients: cornmeal, baking powder, baking soda, salt and black pepper, if using. Whisk together briefly.

Add buttermilk, cottage cheese, sour cream, eggs, cheeses (except for 2 tablespoons of the Asiago or Parmesan, to be used for topping), onions, peppers, corn kernels and sorghum. Stir everything together.

Carefully remove the hot skillet from the oven and pour all but about 1 tablespoon of the melted butter onto your batter. (Sizzle!) Set your skillet in a safe place or return it to the oven.

Stir thoroughly. The batter will be thick.

Carefully pour the batter into the skillet. (More sizzle!)

Sprinkle with the reserved grated cheese.

Bake for about 40 minutes, until thoroughly, deeply golden brown. Better to err on the side of overdone than underdone in this case. The temperature in the center of the cornbread should read 185 degrees or a bit higher.

If you are brave and know your skillet, slip the cornbread right side up onto a platter or simply serve it from the skillet. Top with Chef Lee's Sorghum-Lime Drizzle.

Browned Butter: A Cook's Flavorful Friend

New to browning butter? It requires nothing but butter, heat and attention, and it offers a welcome nutty flavor boost.

Here's how to do it. Melt butter over medium heat. Continue cooking the butter until bits of milk protein at the bottom of the pan begin to turn golden brown. Lift the pan off the heat immediately. If your butter threatens to go past gold to dark brown, remove it completely from heat by pouring it into a heat-safe dish.

If you are browning butter in a black skillet in the oven before making cornbread, take the skillet out as soon as you see the first signs of gold; the skillet will retain enough heat to brown the butter a bit more on its own.

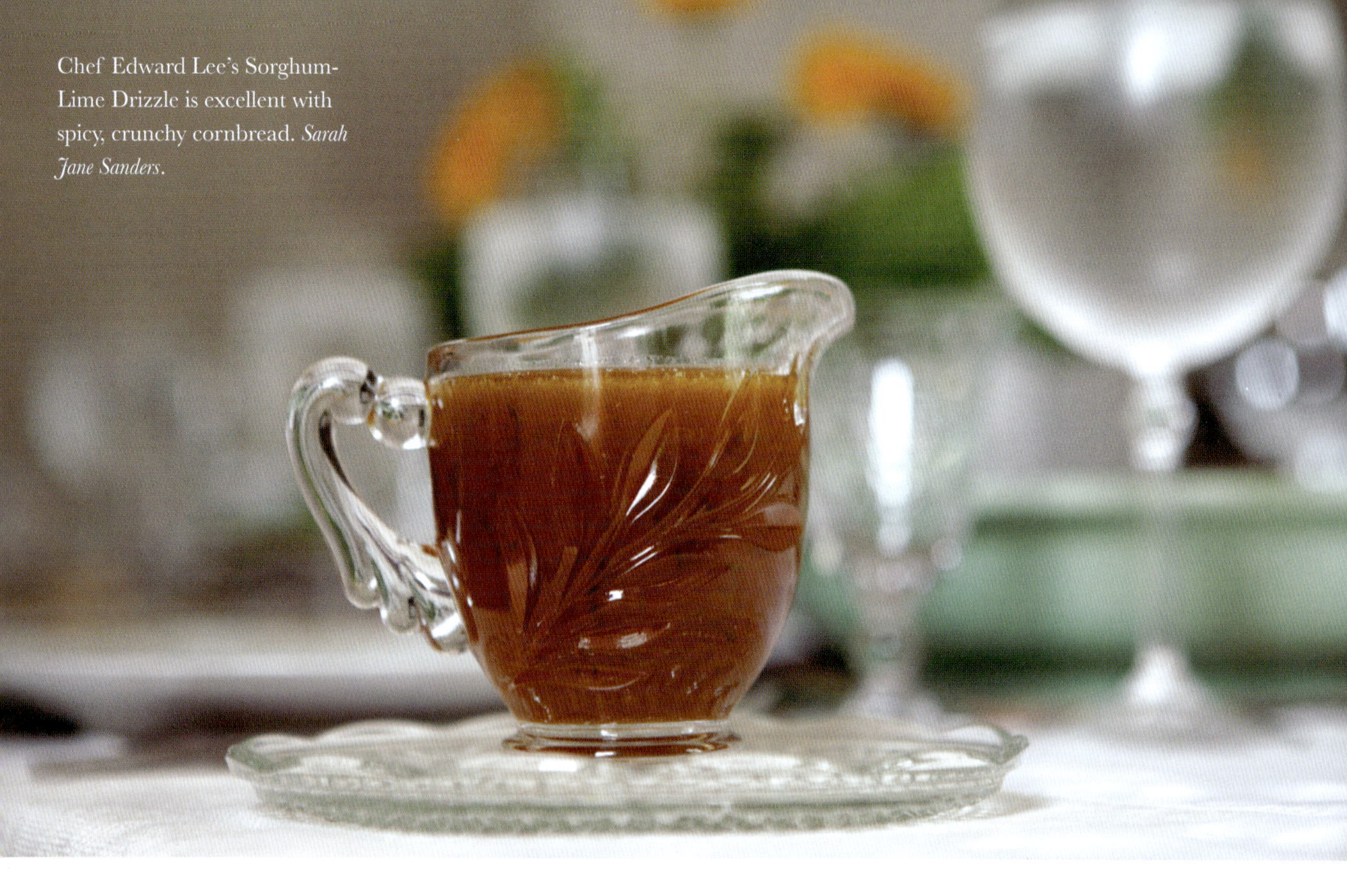

Chef Edward Lee's Sorghum-Lime Drizzle is excellent with spicy, crunchy cornbread. *Sarah Jane Sanders.*

Chef Edward Lee's Sorghum-Lime Drizzle

Louisville chef Edward Lee's 2013 book, Smoke & Pickles, *celebrates locally grown ingredients while using them in intriguing new ways, many influenced by Chef Lee's Korean heritage. Chef Lee treasures sorghum and champions Kentucky's small cadre of skilled sorghum-makers.*

Chef Lee uses this drizzle to sweeten and brighten curried corn griddlecakes. We like it as an optional counterpoint to Rich and Spicy Kentucky Cornbread or any spicy, crunchy food. It does not mind having a tiny sprinkle of added salt.

Yield: About ⅔ cup drizzle

2 tablespoons unsalted butter
½ cup sorghum
grated zest and juice of one lime

Melt the butter. Whisk in remaining ingredients. Keep warm until served.

Double Gingerbread with Whipped Half-Sour Cream and Kentucky Pecans

This tastes—and feels—like contentment itself.

Yield: Serves 8

⅓ cup white sugar
½ cup butter
1 egg
1 cup Kentucky sorghum
2-inch piece fresh ginger, finely grated
2½ cups all-purpose Kentucky flour, or Bloomfield Gluten Free All-Purpose Baking Mix
1½ teaspoons baking soda

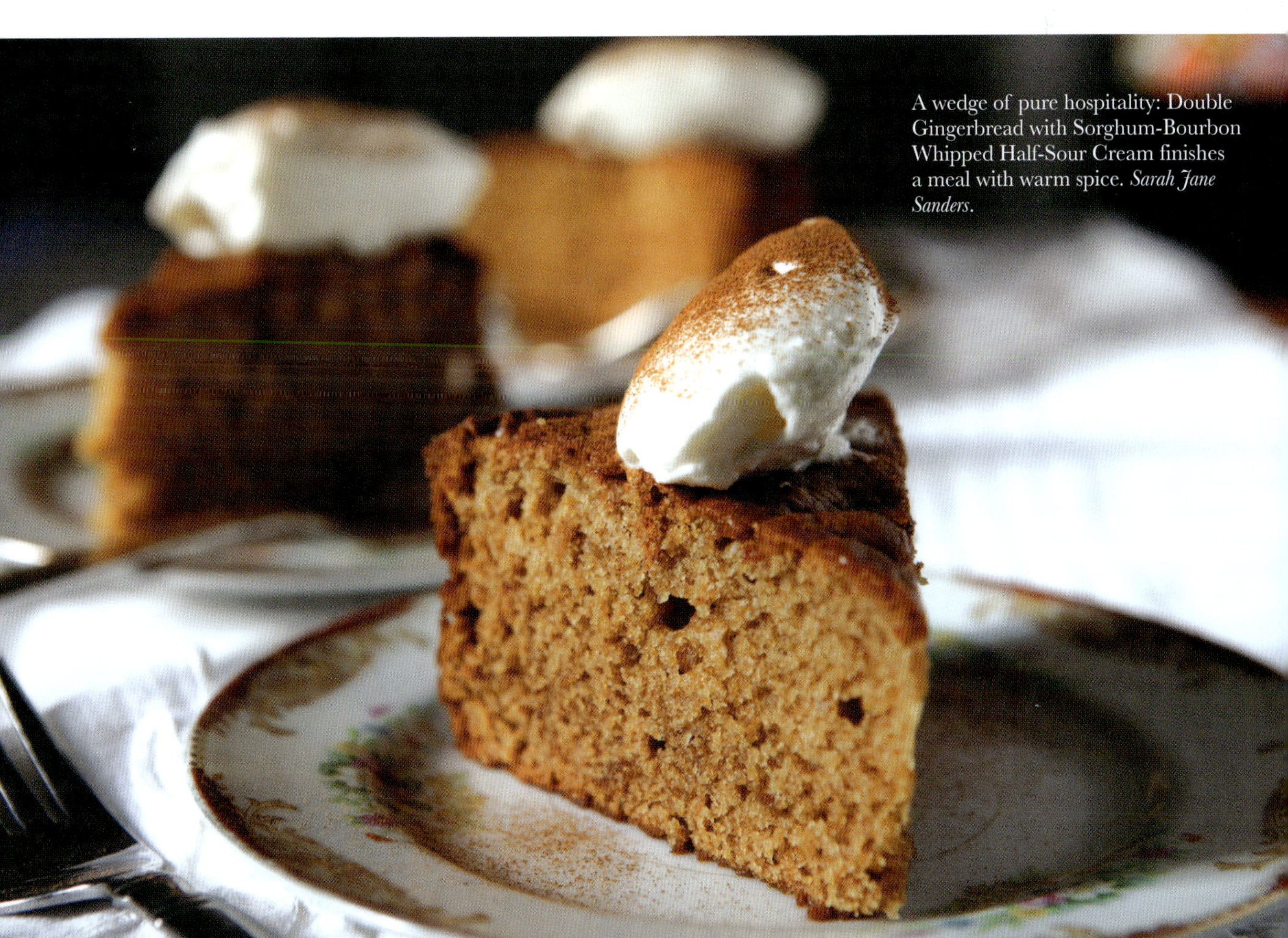

A wedge of pure hospitality: Double Gingerbread with Sorghum-Bourbon Whipped Half-Sour Cream finishes a meal with warm spice. *Sarah Jane Sanders.*

½ teaspoon salt
1 teaspoon ground cinnamon
1 teaspoon ground ginger
½ teaspoon ground cloves
1 cup hot water
Whipped Half-Sour Cream, to garnish
toasted Kentucky pecans, finely chopped

Preheat oven to 350 degrees Fahrenheit. Spray a 9-inch square pan with nonstick baking spray or coat it with butter and flour.

In a large bowl, cream together the sugar and butter. Add the egg, sorghum and fresh ginger. Beat well.

In a bowl, sift together the flour, baking soda, salt, cinnamon, ginger and cloves. Blend gently and quickly into the creamed mixture. Stir in the hot water. Pour into the prepared pan.

Bake 1 hour in the preheated oven, until the center reaches 180 degrees Fahrenheit or a toothpick stuck into the center comes out clean. Slice into small squares and serve warm or at room temperature with a dollop of Whipped Half-Sour Cream (recipe follows) and a sprinkling of toasted pecans.

Make the bourbon version of Whipped Half-Sour Cream (page 43 for a delicious, cooling counterpart that lets the spices shine.

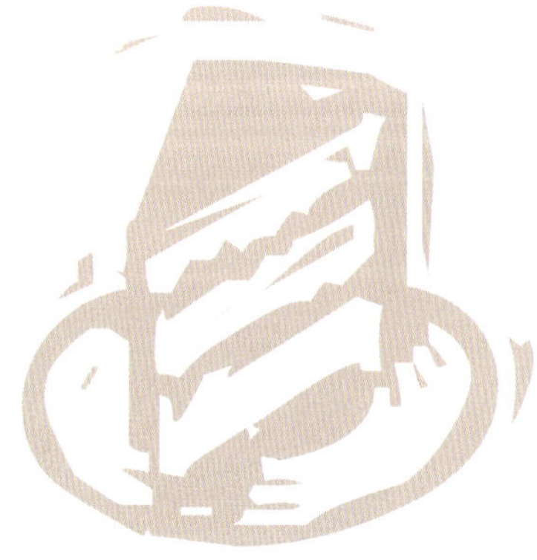

Whipped Half-Sour Cream

People have been known to eat this by itself for dessert. People have been known to eat this instead of dinner. People have been known to eat this in the kitchen instead of sharing with guests.

This easily made dessert topping adds delight and richness to each baked dessert in Classic Kentucky Meals. *The optional add-ins in the ingredient list help tailor the cream to complement particular desserts, but the basic recipe always adds plenty of goodness.*

Yield: Amply enriches 8 dessert servings, with extra for the cook

1 cup heavy cream
1 cup sour cream
3 tablespoons sorghum
2 tablespoons sugar
1 teaspoon good vanilla extract
¼ teaspoon salt

Optional Add-ins:
For Double Gingerbread (page 41), add 2 tablespoons Kentucky bourbon and ⅛ teaspoon ground allspice to the cream.

For Strawberry-Rhubarb Skillet Pudding Cake (page 72), add 2 tablespoons Kentucky strawberry wine, such as Broad Run Vineyards' scrumptious version made from 100 percent Kentucky berries.

For State Fruit Crisp (page 173), add the grated zest of ½ lemon and ⅛ teaspoon ground allspice.

Beat creams together in a stand mixer until softly mounded.

Turn mixer to the lowest speed. Gradually add sorghum, sugar, vanilla, salt and any add ins. Taste and correct seasonings. Try to save enough for others to have with their desserts.

Hood's Heritage Hogs, Mt. Olivet (Robertson County), Kentucky

Hood's Heritage Hogs may be a new farm in Kentucky, but the animals Travis Hood and his family raise—even-tempered, pasture-loving, chef-pleasing Red Wattle hogs—come with some history. Beginning in the 1970s, two different breeders in east Texas each found a small passel—yes, that is one collective noun for a group of hogs—of large, mostly red hogs and began breeding them intentionally. The hogs boast lean, delicious meat and also sport some hoggy bling: a decorative fleshy caruncle—a wattle—dangling beneath each ear. Hood's farm motto? "If it ain't got wattles—it's just a pig."

Some of Travis Hood's customers are beginning to say, "If it ain't Red Wattle, it's just not as delicious." Standing in line at Travis's booth at the Lexington Farmers' Market, customers say to one another, "Have you tried it yet? It tastes like pork *ought* to taste." That taste is richer than commercial pork, without tasting barnyard-ier.

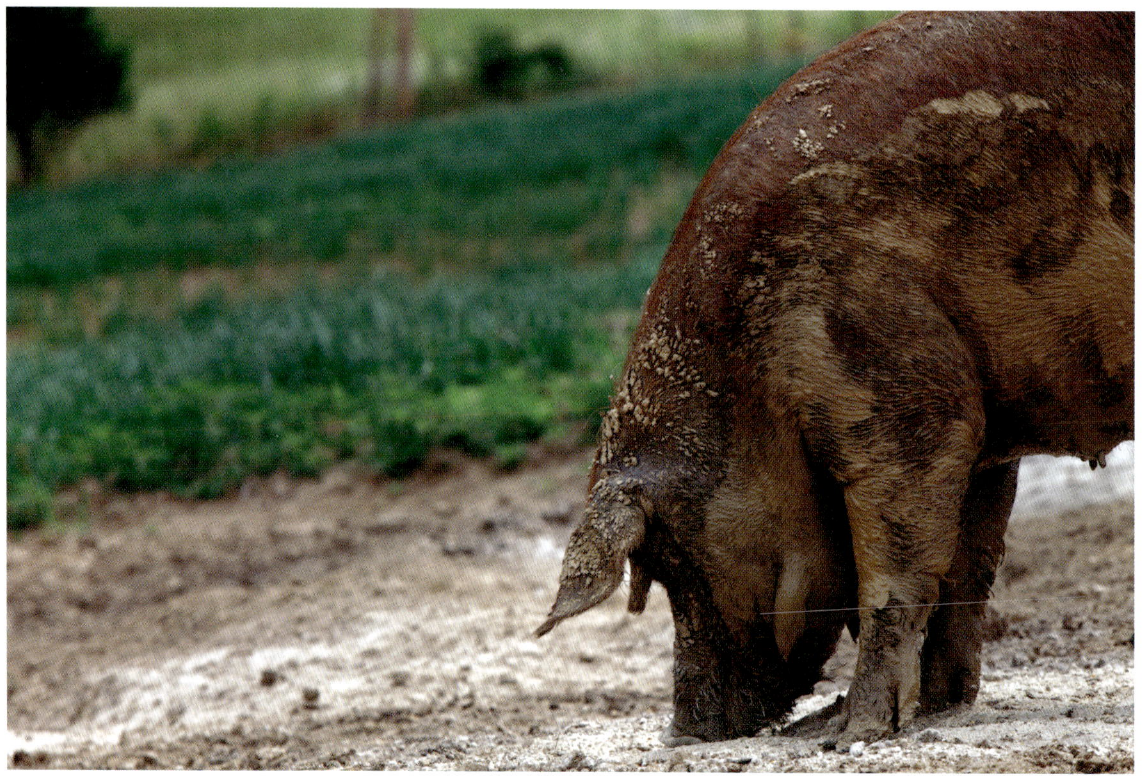

Meet Lucy, the queen of Red Wattle sows—pig mamas—at Hood's Heritage Hogs in Robertson County. *Sarah Jane Sanders.*

Red Wattles grow lean, so their fat does not dominate cuts other than bacon. But pork fans prize the fat of Red Wattles for its mild, sweet flavor and its habit of melting into the meat during cooking, adding moisture and richness. Travis tells customers the Red Wattle fat is healthy, too, with a one-to-one ratio of Omega 3 to Omega 6 fatty acids and 63 percent of the fat unsaturated.

Travis Hood and his family moved their sixty-one Red Wattle hogs to the fields and woods of Robertson County, Kentucky, from Indiana in mid-2013, drawn by several Kentucky advantages. First, the farmscape of hills and woods in Robertson County suits Red Wattle production. The hills boost hoggy exercise. Travis separates food and water by some distance, so as the hogs hike back and forth, their fat and muscle marble together in a way eaters find particularly delicious. Second, in fall, the woods serve up acorns and hickory nuts for hog feed, sweetening their meat compared to corn and soy, which produce "flavors you don't want," Travis said. For feed that must be purchased, though, Hinton's Mill in nearby Mays Lick

Travis Hood, of Hood's Heritage Hogs, encourages a new Red Wattle mom. *Sarah Jane Sanders*.

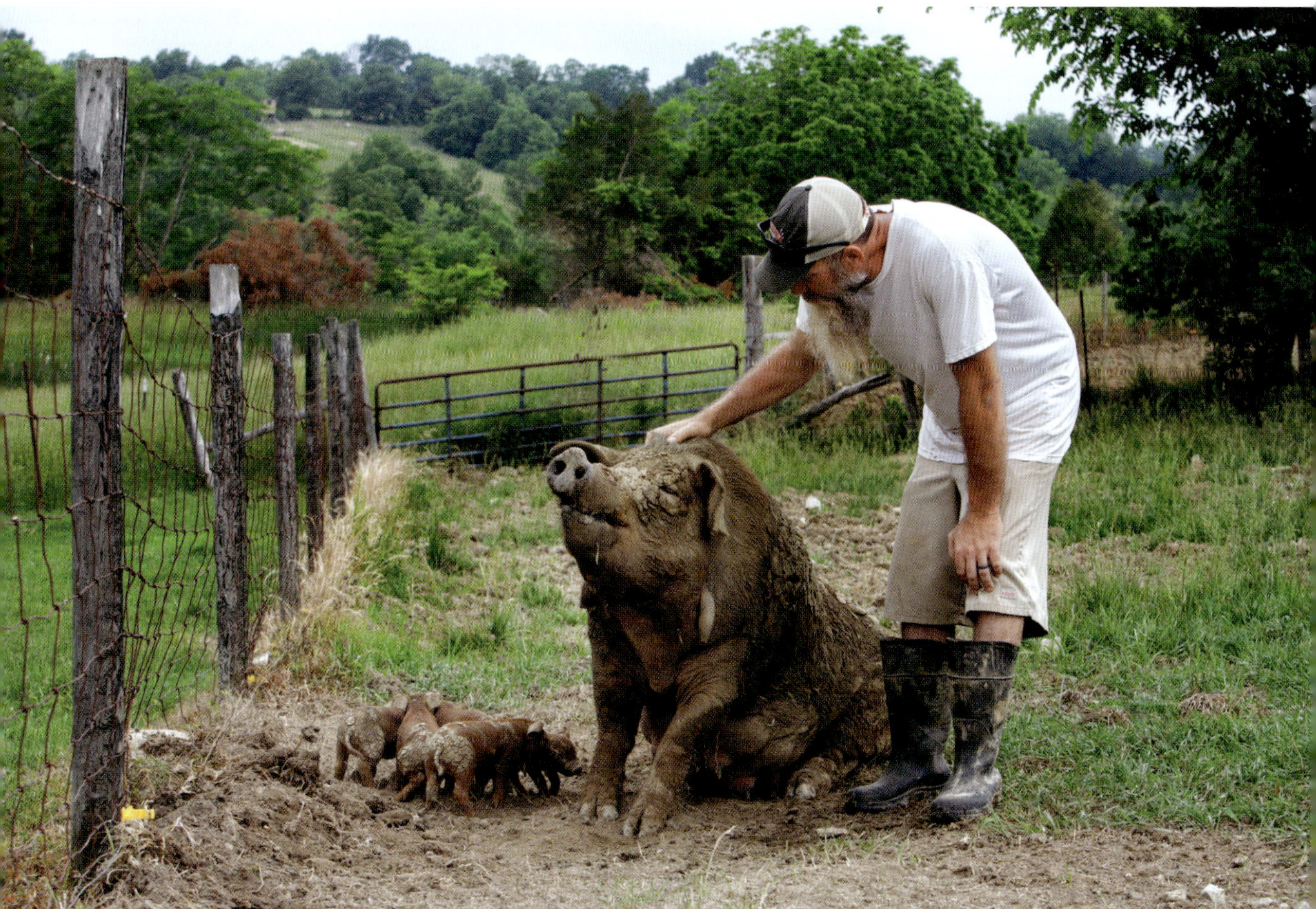

Heritage breeds of animals and plants can be especially well suited for small producers. They often offer dramatically better flavor than commercial breeds and help preserve crucial genetic diversity that will keep our food system resilient and strong. Slow Food USA includes Red Wattle hogs in its Ark of Taste, a catalogue of about two hundred "delicious and distinctive foods facing extinction." The American Livestock Breeds Conservancy includes Red Wattle hogs on its "Threatened" list.

offers prices that are around 50 percent lower in cost than similar feed in Indiana. Finally, Travis says the distance from his Robertson County farm to markets and processing is workable.

In January 2014, Hood's Heritage Hogs processed and offered for sale nine Red Wattles finished on nine acres of "mast," those Kentucky acorns and hickory nuts. Recently some of the expanding passel has gotten Bleugrass Chevre whey for supper, putting a byproduct of local goat cheese production to good use. Other Hood's Heritage Red Wattles thrive on more conventional diets, including corn that has not been genetically engineered.

Growers value Red Wattles because they are good-natured, hardy and grow large rapidly, and because the sows have good mothering skills. The animals reach massive sizes: up to four feet high and eight feet long at the extreme, with weights of up to 1,200 pounds. Travis reported that he has produced hams in the range of 40 pounds each, about double the standard size.

Despite the four-hour trip one way, Travis takes his hogs back to Colfax, Indiana, to This Old Farm, a trusted processor. After raising his hogs carefully and humanely, Travis trusts This Old Farm with the hard, painful and necessary work of slaughtering, butchering, curing and packaging his hogs. This Old Farm cures chemical-free bacon from Red Wattle bellies, jowls and shoulders, using sea salt, celery juice concentrate and turbinado sugar. This bacon may account for a significant portion of the lines that form at the Hood's Heritage booths at farmers' markets.

Chefs and home cooks alike welcome this new source of heritage pork for its flavor and nutrient profile. Those who want more pasture-based foods in their diets appreciate the extent to which Hood's Heritage Hogs depend on pasture and forage. When pigs turn grass and acorns into world-class meat, that's hog heaven, right there. Especially since superb heritage grits and cornmeal from Sunflower Sundries, just fifteen miles away, make the perfect accompaniment for any Red Wattle entrée.

Oberholtzer's Kentucky Sorghum, Liberty (Casey County), Kentucky

Oberholtzer's Kentucky Sorghum, perhaps the largest sorghum operation in the state, has been sweetening Kentucky biscuits and delighting palates around the country for nearly forty years. Sorghum fans treasure the consistency of this sorghum and the family's ability to deliver ten to twelve thousand gallons of sorghum annually that is unfailingly light in both color and sweetness.

Neighbors join the Oberholtzers, a multigenerational Mennonite family, in growing about sixty acres of cane and contributing some of the labor for cultivating, harvesting, milling and cooking the sorghum each year. According to Mr. Alan Oberholtzer, 99 percent of the cane used for their sorghum grows in Casey County.

Finding Oberholtzer's Kentucky Sorghum for sale has become easier in recent years. When the Alan Oberholtzer family moved to Kentucky in March 1976 and began farming, news of their sorghum's goodness spread by word of mouth, first in their county and region of the state and gradually more widely. Now the iconic warm gold-and-brown Oberholtzer's label shows up on shelves at many online outlets, including amazon.com. Sorghum is heavy, though, and jars can break during shipment, so the luckiest people live near a good, local source of Oberholtzer's.

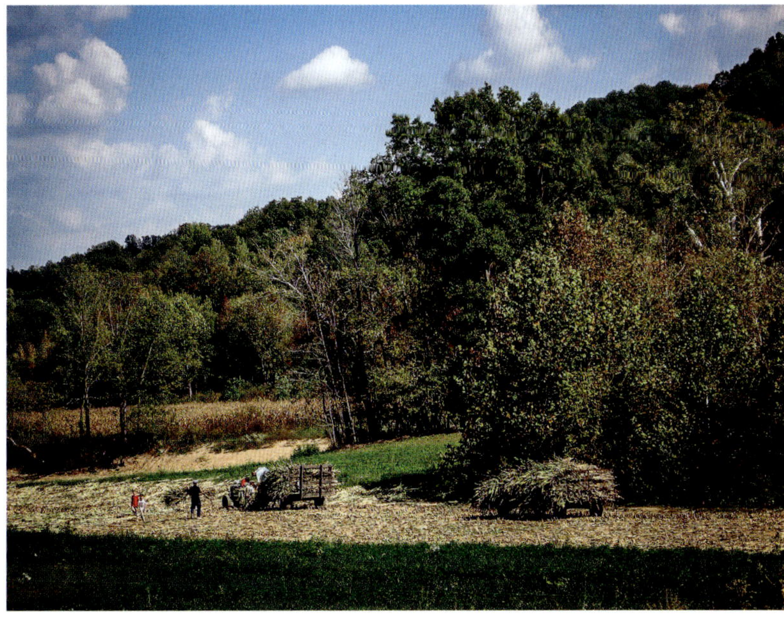

Neighbors work together to cut and haul sorghum cane for Oberholtzer's Kentucky Sorghum. *Rona Roberts.*

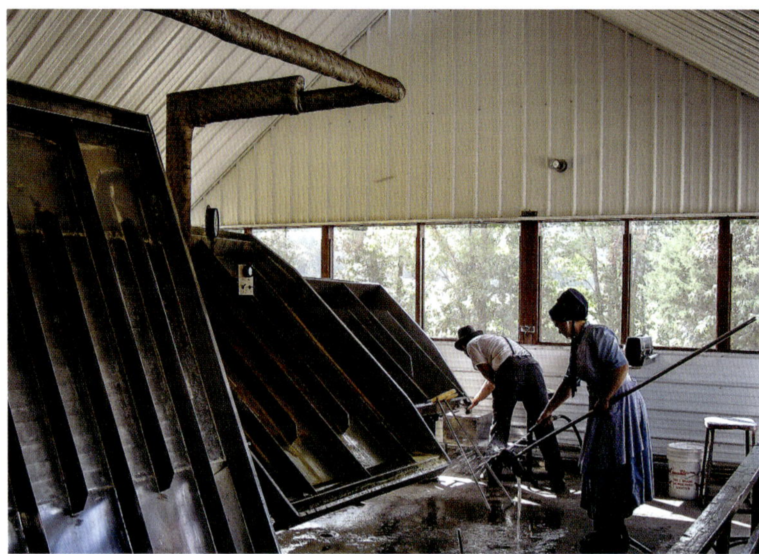

Members of a Casey County Mennonite community of friends and family work together to clean up after a day of making sorghum at Oberholtzer's Kentucky Sorghum. *Rona Roberts.*

Like all pure sorghum, Oberholtzer's Kentucky Sorghum keeps well without refrigeration. The Oberholtzers are among the first to make enough sorghum so grocery stores and online retailers can keep it in stock all through the year.

Until a few years ago, sorghum lovers typically bought enough newly made sorghum in the fall to carry them through a full twelve months because few sorghum makers produced enough syrup to sell year-round. Many people in Sorghum Nation knew the gas station, corner country store or feed store where they could buy the right number of quarts for the upcoming year, with extra to keep for cooking the following year. Buying a year's supply at once worked well, provided the sorghum lovers got to the source before the supply ran out, usually around the end of December. In fact, many families developed systems in which one member shopped for enough sorghum to sustain an extended family and sometimes neighbors for the next year.

As cooking magazines and newspapers feature sorghum recipes more frequently, some customer-oriented small groceries, like Lexington-based Critchfield Meats and Good Foods Co-op, now offer sorghum year-round. Having sorghum available to casual users as well as dedicated aficionados makes a difference in chefs and home cooks coming to depend on its flavors. The Oberholtzers handle a challenging situation well. They make a fine quality food by hand and also manage its distribution so it reaches a fairly wide range of stores and plates. Their beautifully grown and cooked sorghum tastes good every time, for every use.

Meet Sorghum, in All Its Glory and Sweetness

Sweet sorghum syrup results when farmers grow a specific cane plant (*Sorghum bicolor* (L.) Moench), press the juice from its stalks in late summer and then cook that juice until much of the liquid evaporates, leaving a pure, sweet amber syrup. Often in Kentucky, we call sweet sorghum syrup "sorghum molasses" or just "molasses."

Actually, we call it wonderful and delicious, or maybe our mouths are so full of that magical mixture of sorghum, butter and biscuit that we just say "mmmmmmmmmm!" On biscuits or spoon bread, in baked beans and dried apple stack cakes, topping oatmeal or sweetening our tea, sorghum tastes like Kentucky, and Kentuckians eat it every chance we get.

The problem of its proper name bothers outsiders more than it bothers Kentuckians. But we're a welcoming people, so let's clear up the name confusion. True molasses comes from the plants that make white and brown sugar—either *Sacharum officinarum*, better known as sugar cane, or *Beta vulgaris*, the sugar beet. Molasses, a dark sweet syrup, is a byproduct of manufacturing granular sugar.

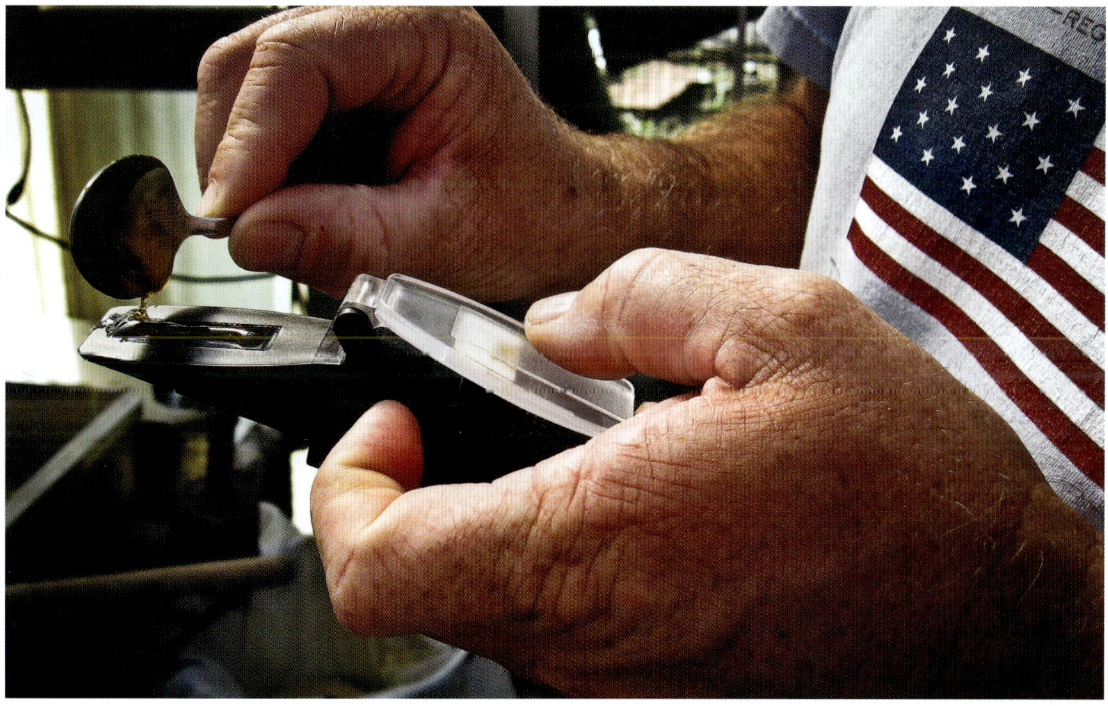

Randal Rock of Country Rock Sorghum in Woodford County prepares to test the sweetness of the sorghum he is cooking. *Rona Roberts*.

In addition to the confusion about the word *molasses*, the term *sorghum* refers both to a grain and to our main focus here, sweet sorghum syrup. Both the syrup and grain have many names around the world, and the plant itself, a member of the grass family, can be used to produce fiber, fuel, food for human beings and feed for animals. In this book, as in the growing number of cooking magazines and cookbooks nationally that embrace sweet sorghum syrup as an ingredient, we simply call it "sorghum."

Sorghum came from Africa. Its path to the United States, and its first plantings in this country, remain murky. Benjamin Franklin refers to "whisk seed"—or broom corn, a sweet sorghum cousin—in a letter to his sister Jane Mecom in 1757. Dr. Michael Bomford, an expert in sustainable agriculture, including sorghum, believes sorghum could have arrived on these shores even before that early date. He documents the assertion others have made that we owe the wonders of sorghum to the shameful barbarity of the slave trade:

> *Sorghum has been grown as a major crop in Africa for thousands of years, and was brought here by slaves (and slave traders) who wouldn't have received the credit granted Franklin. Several slave ships stocked up on sorghum in Africa, to provide rations for the journey across the Atlantic (Judith Carney.* In the Shadow of Slavery: Africa's Botanical Legacy in the Atlantic World. *University of California Press, 2011). Maurice Mathews, a politically active English settler in Barbados in the 1670s–90s, reported "Guiney Corne [sorghum] growes very well here..." and naturalist Mark Catesby, writing in Carolina in 1743, says that sorghum "was first introduced from Africa by the negroes" [...] "who make bread of it and boil it in like manner of firmety." (Peter Wood.* Black Majority: Negroes in Colonial South Carolina from 1670 through the Stono Rebellion. *Knopf, 1974).*

Sweet sorghum syrup comes from a tall, slender cane plant topped by a seed head. Sorghum cane looks a lot like corn when seen from a distance.

Most sweet sorghum histories point to the mid-nineteenth century as the time when interest in sweet sorghum cultivation and production rose sharply in the United States. It is likely that the Northern states needed an alternative to sugar produced in Southern states during and just after the Civil War. During the Prohibition years in the early twentieth century, interest in sweet sorghum as a basis for moonshine may have propelled production to its historical high of fifty million gallons in 1920, the first officially dry year.

Whether innocent gingerbread or devilish White Lightning fueled the passion, sweet sorghum and Kentucky developed a profound love affair. Sweet sorghum

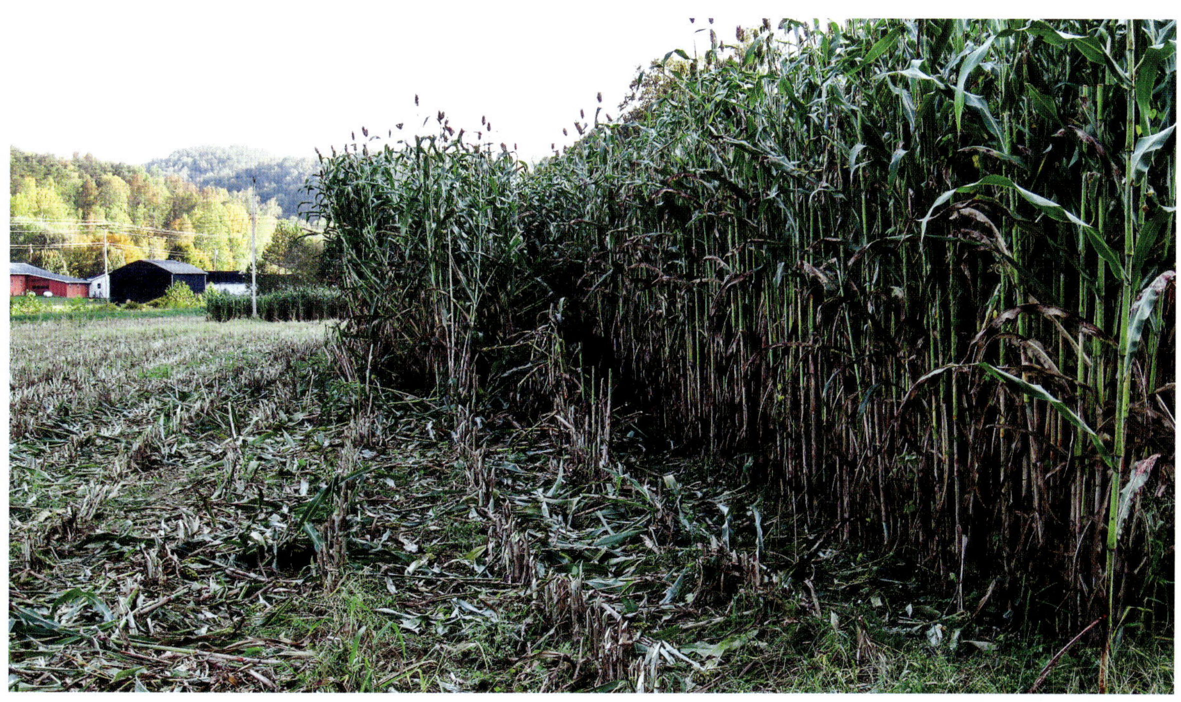

A half-cut field of sorghum cane at Holbrook Brothers Sorghum in Morgan County looks a little like corn. *Rona Roberts.*

grows well in Kentucky's soil and climate, requiring few off-farm inputs like fertilizers or pesticides. Unlike sugar cane, which requires a lot of water and takes up many soil nutrients, sorghum cane thrives even in the face of drought and feeds lightly on the soil.

Sorghum production in Kentucky tickles both our independent streak and our love of community. The members of a farm family could do all the work of producing their own year-round sweetening themselves—plant, harvest, mill and cook—with a relatively modest sorghum mill and cooking pan. Many families, though, chose to carry out the work of harvesting, milling and cooking as community events, memorable gatherings of neighbors and loved ones that included great meals, gossip for the grown-ups and playmates for the children. Many Kentuckians today recall sorghum cooking on their grandparents' or neighbors' land as highpoints of their childhood.

Sorghum production fell to 2,400 gallons in the entire United States in 1975 and is slowly recovering. Now the Oberholtzer family alone produces nearly triple that amount each year (see page 47). In addition, at Townsend's Sorghum Mill in Jeffersonville (Montgomery County), fifth-generation sorghum maker Danny

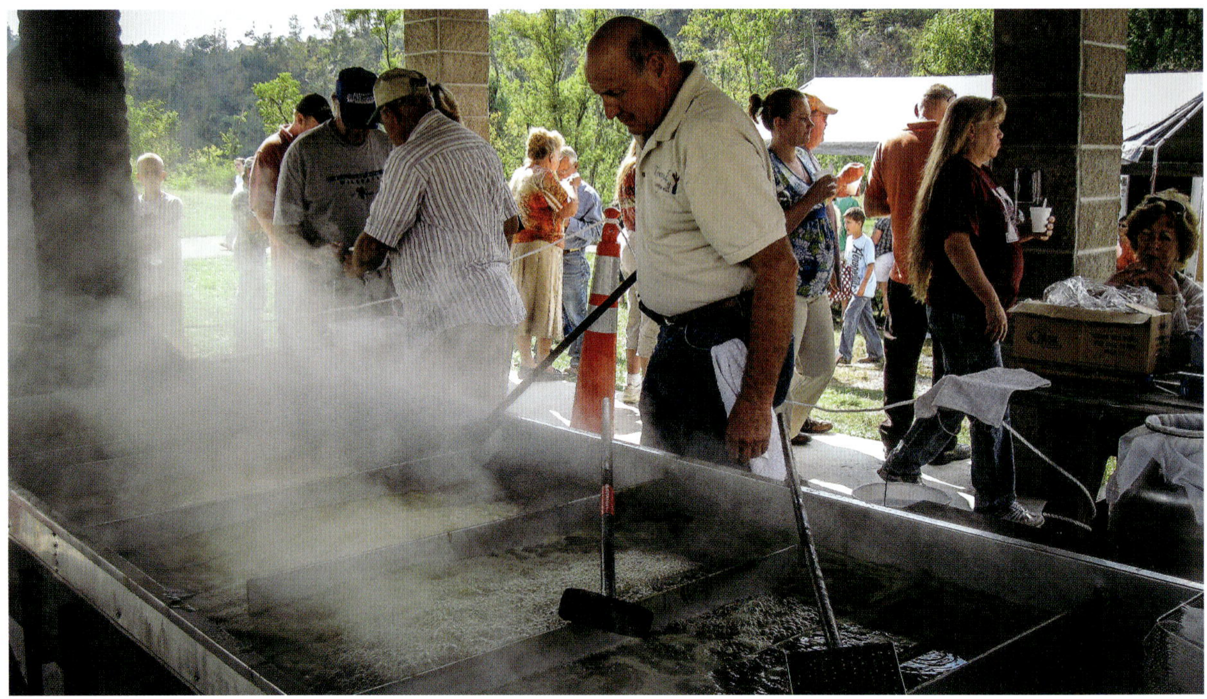

Danny Townsend, of Townsend Sorghum Mill in Montgomery County, cooks sorghum at the Morgan County Sorghum Festival. *Rona Roberts.*

Townsend annually produces thousands of gallons of such high quality that Townsend's has won three grand championships at the National Sweet Sorghum Producers and Processors Association's annual sorghum competition.

Many Kentucky communities embrace beloved local sorghum makers who produce a few hundred gallons each year. Holbrook Brothers in Morgan County—the location of a large sorghum festival each September—grows multiple varieties of cane and makes enough sorghum to sell locally. Country Rock Sorghum, a relatively new Woodford County producer, makes enough sorghum for sale throughout the year in central Kentucky. New sorghum makers like Jacob and Carolyn Gahn, who produce sorghum-sweetened Sweet Grass Granola in Crab Orchard (Lincoln County), and Gary Barr of Barr Farms in Rhodelia (Meade County) have begun growing and making sorghum recently to learn more about cultivating and producing this Kentucky food.

Sorghum's small, promising comeback as a natural sweetener in daily use owes something to the local food movement but much more to growers who like it and understand its virtues in Kentucky's climate and cuisine. Nationally, chefs and food media trendsetters have helped make sorghum more familiar to a wide audience.

As Dan Barber asserts in *The Third Plate*, chefs and visionary producers together help define and refine a cuisine. Barber suggests that firmly settled cuisine influences what growers produce. As Kentuckians embrace sorghum again for many parts of our still unfolding cuisine, we encourage and support a slowly increasing cadre of growers eager to meet our sorghum needs.

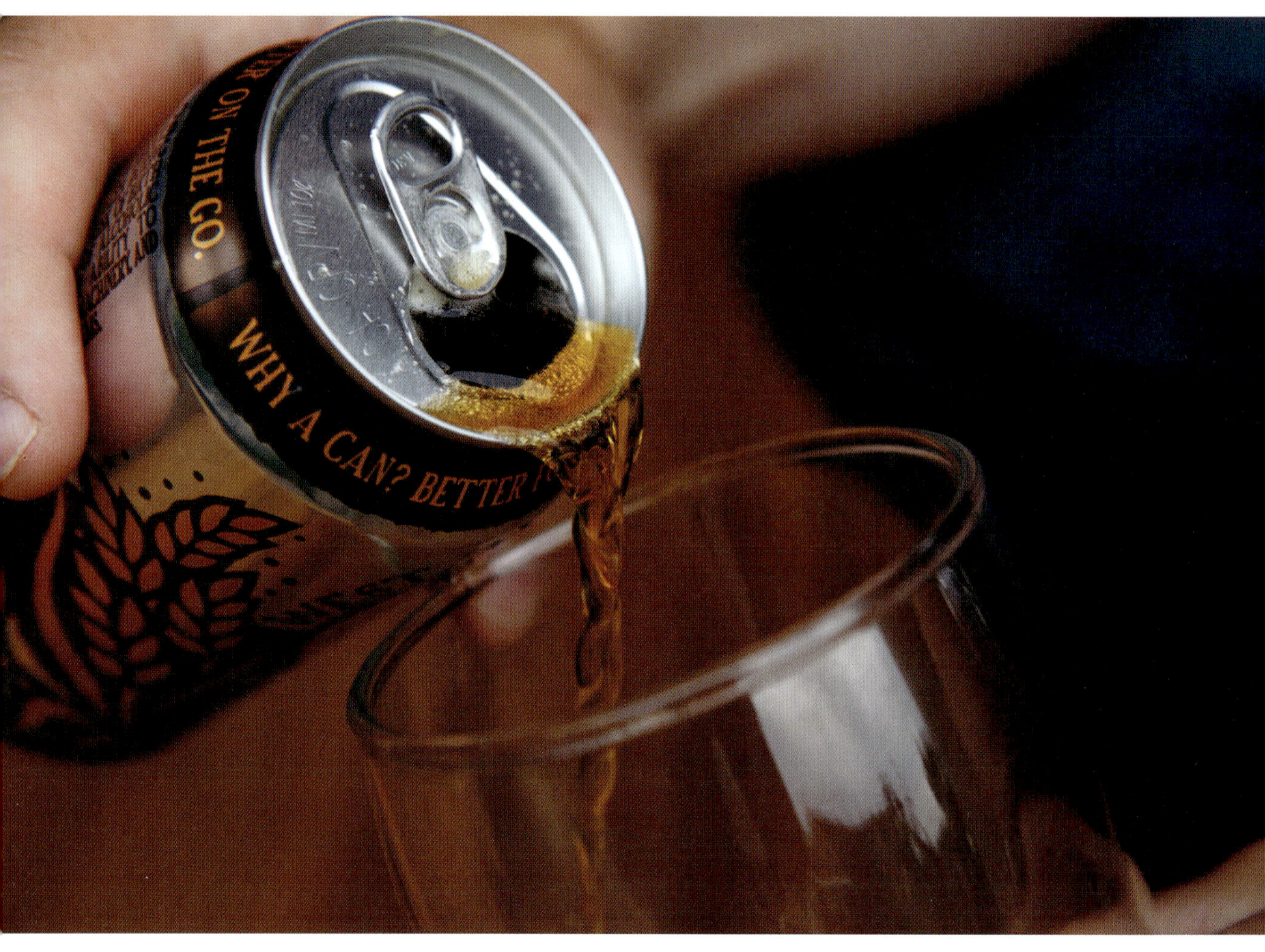

Kentucky craft beers, such as the Amber Ale from West Sixth in Lexington, pair well with many Kentucky foods and have a growing fan base. *Sarah Jane Sanders*.

Meal 2

LOVING ON A CHICKEN AND ITS FRIENDS

Savory roast chicken: how we adore you! You elevate any meal. Side dishes love sidling up to you, basking in your glory—and your flavor-rich juices. On roast chicken days, people wander in the front door like iron filings to a magnet, drawn to that divine smell. Roast Kentucky chicken—we love you right down to the bones!

Everyday Menu
Ruth's "Basted" Chicken
Wilted Dark Green Salad
"Fried" Corn Off the Cob
Seasonal Berries and Fruits

For special occasions or holidays, add seasonal vegetables, pop a few crunchy-tender Kentucky Angel Biscuits in the oven and finish with a swoon-worthy classic Kentucky dessert: Strawberry-Rhubarb Skillet Pudding Cake, with a bit of quick, fresh, homemade whipped cream for emphasis.

Dressed-Up Menu Additions
Asparagus Apotheosis
Country Green Beans: Smoky, Porky
Lemon-Mustard Vinaigrette
City Green Beans: Crispy, Crunchy
Kentucky Angel Biscuits
Strawberry-Rhubarb Skillet Pudding Cake with Wheat-Free Options

Perfect Pairings

- *Cocktail:* Back Porch Swing
- *Wine*: Wight-Meyer Vignoles or Prodigy Traminette for pleasantly fruity acidity
- *Beer*: West Sixth Brewing's Amber Ale for its malty freshness, which bubbles the palate clean for better tastes all through the meal
- *Tea*: Elmwood Fine Tea's Iced Tea Blend for iced tea that stays clear, never cloudy
- *Coffee*: CaffeMarco's Gold Bag blend coffee with the meal-ending dessert, for its clean, strong, non-bitter vibrancy
- *Soundtrack for cooking*: [Some songs on all playlists have adult language and themes.] "Good Day" (Nappy Roots), "Walk Softly on This Heart of Mine" (Kentucky Headhunters), "Country Boy" (Ricky Skaggs), "Can't You Hear Me Callin'" (Bill Monroe & His Blue Grass Band), "Down by the Waterside" (Appalatin), "I've Always Wanted to Sing in Renfro Valley (the Osborne Brothers), "I'm Gonna Sing 'Til the Spirit Moves in My Heart" (American Spiritual Ensemble), "Wake Up, Little Susie" (the Everly Brothers), "Buzzin' Around with the Bee" (Lionel Hampton), "The Storms Are on the Ocean" (the Carter Family), "Two Step" (Laura Bell Bundy), "Uncle Pen" (Ricky Skaggs)
- *Soundtrack for eating*: "Have You Ever Loved a Woman?" (Kentucky Headhunters), "Wordless Chorus" (My Morning Jacket), "Vibraphone Blues" (Lionel Hampton), "Circles Around You" (Sam Bush), "Blue Kentucky Girl" (Loretta Lynn), "Willow Weep for Me" (Lou Rawls, Les McCann), "Only You" (the Hilltoppers), "That's How I Learned to Sing the Blues" (Henry Hipkens), "Sway" (Rosemary Clooney), "Burnin' Coal" (Les McCann)

Back Porch Swing

This take on an early American cocktail, the whiskey smash, showcases Kentucky's renewed production of delicious maple syrup and swings on a graceful frame, back and forth between subtle spiced caramel and mint.

Yield: 1 cocktail

For the Black Pepper–Maple Syrup

1 tablespoon coarsely ground black pepper
¼ cup Kentucky maple syrup
¼ cup water

For the Cocktail

¼ lemon, cut in small pieces, plus slice or wedge for garnish
4 4-inch sprigs fresh Kentucky spearmint or pennyroyal
1 ounce black pepper–maple simple syrup
1 to 2 ounces Kentucky bourbon

Two hours before making the cocktail, combine black pepper, maple syrup and water in a saucepan and gently heat mixture until it just begins to boil. Remove from heat. Cover. Let cool completely. Strain through a fine mesh strainer. Discard the black pepper.

Put lemon and 3 sprigs of spearmint or pennyroyal in a heavy glass or cocktail shaker. With a muddler or the handle of a heavy wooden spoon, push and press the sprigs and lemon to release juices and oils.

Add the black pepper–maple syrup, bourbon (amount adjusted to your preference) and ice. Shake vigorously for 30 seconds.

Strain into a rocks glass filled with crushed ice.

Garnish with lemon and final sprig of spearmint.

Store extra syrup in the refrigerator.

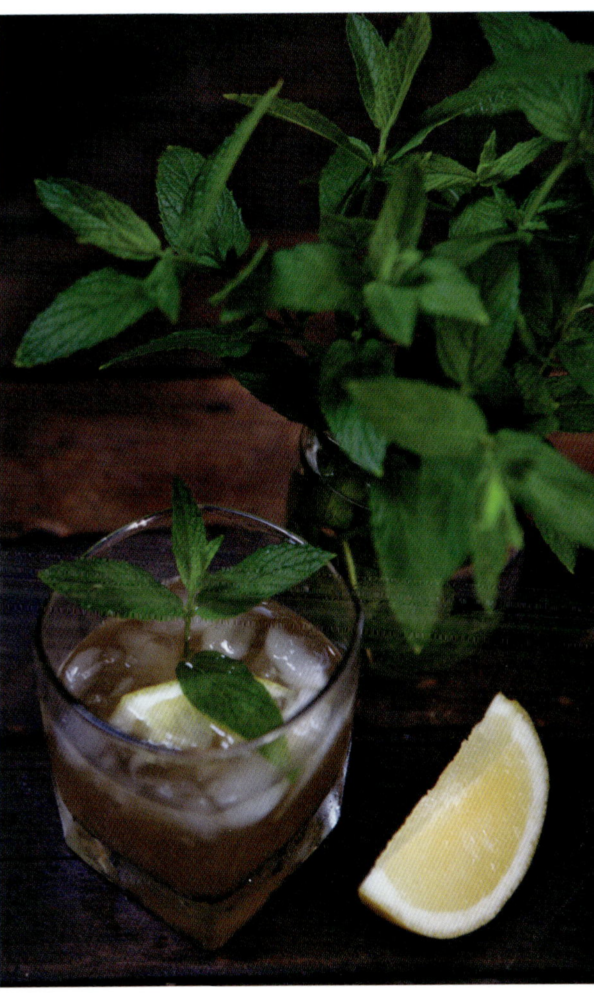

The Back Porch Swing is a graceful, delicious combination of favorite Kentucky tastes in a cocktail glass. *Sarah Jane Sanders.*

EVERYDAY MENU

Ruth's "Basted" Chicken

In order to have Sunday dinner ready when the family got home from church, Mother put a chicken and side dishes in a moderate oven, and away we went. Long services meant falling-apart chicken. The chicken boasts a buttery rub of salt, pepper and paprika that browns lightly on the fork-tender bird. The bird cooks so gently it does not spatter the oven and tastes so good you will want to smack anyone but your mama.

Yield: Serves 6

1 whole chicken, around 3 pounds
⅓ cup fresh butter or olive oil
½ cup (or more) all-purpose flour or finely ground white rice flour
2 teaspoons fine sea salt or table salt
1 teaspoon finely ground fresh black pepper
2 teaspoons sweet paprika

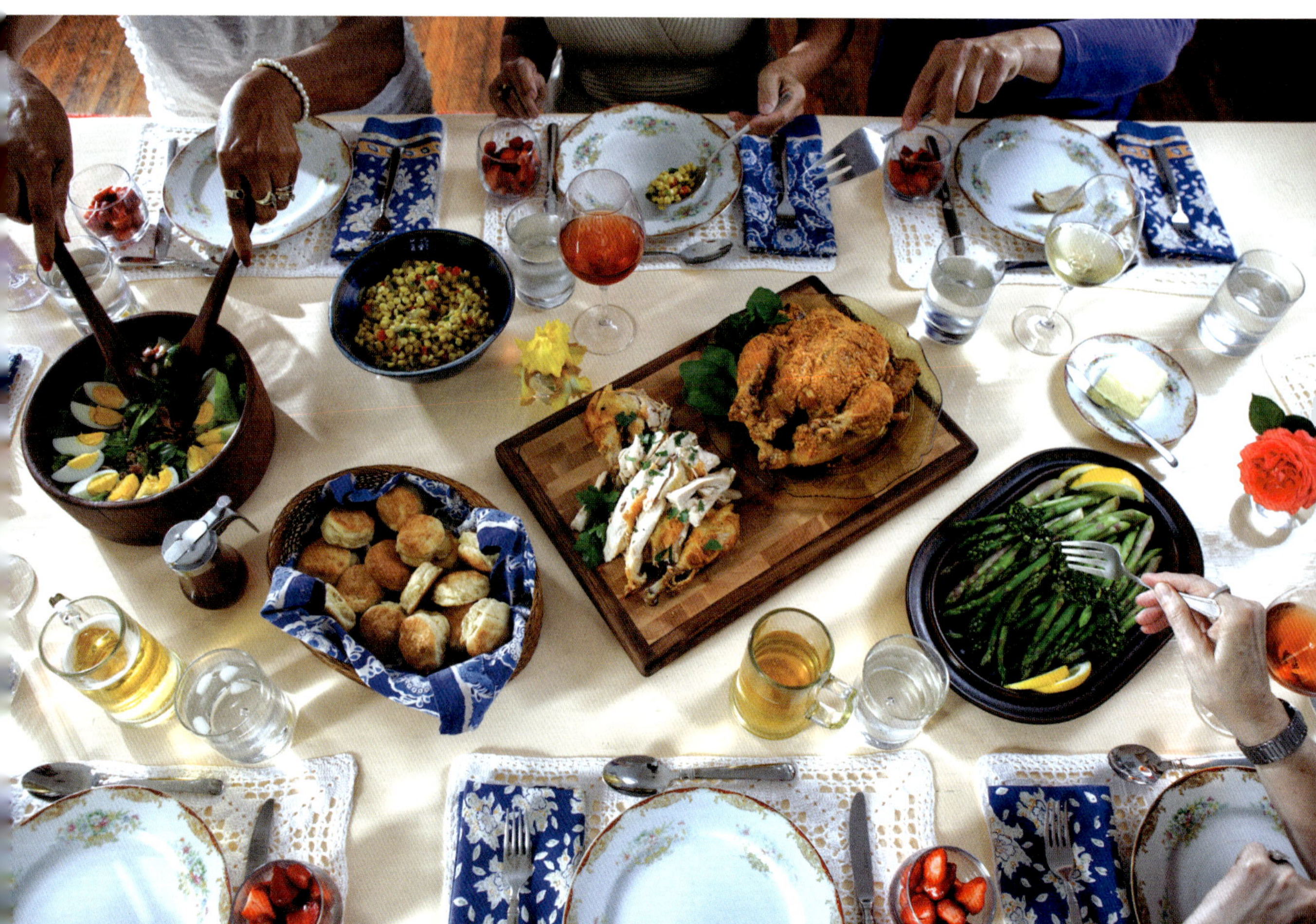

Preheat the oven to 375 degrees Fahrenheit.

Melt the butter in a small saucepan. Brown it lightly if you like (see page 39). Remove from heat and let cool for two minutes.

Stir enough flour into the butter to make a spreadable paste.

Add salt, black pepper and paprika. Mix well.

Put the chicken in an ovenproof baking dish, breast side up. Smear the seasoned flour paste, or "baste," on all its surfaces.

Bake for 75 to 90 minutes, until lightly golden all over. Wiggle the leg joints; they should feel loose. Even better, use an instant-read thermometer to check the temperature in the meatiest inside part of the thigh; it should be at 165 degrees.

Move to a platter; let rest a few minutes before serving.

Homemade Chicken Broth: Too Easy and Too Good Not to Make

Save every chicken bone from this chicken and any other chicken you eat. When you finish eating the chicken, put all the bones in a large pot, cover them with cool water to about double their height, add 1 tablespoon of cider vinegar or distilled white vinegar to help extract useful minerals from the bones and cook on low for twelve to eighteen hours. Use a crockpot or the simmer setting on your stove. Don't bother with adding vegetable scraps unless you have them handy. Don't add salt; this gives much more flexibility later for seasoning different dishes to taste. Just bones, water and vinegar will do the job. Drink, freeze or use in dishes like Braised Shoulder (page 27). If you prefer, freeze bones across several meals to make a larger batch of broth.

Opposite: Friends make the roast chicken meal taste even more wonderful. *Sarah Jane Sanders*.

Wilted Dark Green Salad

In spring, make this salad with tender lettuces. Make it any time of year with all-season greens like chard, curly kale, black kale, arugula or Russian kale. Collards can also work.

Before using mature greens that have tough middle stems, remove those stems by folding the leaves in half and tearing or cutting the stems out. *(See "How to Wash and Prep Greens," page 100.)* *Then cut the stemless leaves into fine slivers.*

Yield: Serves 2 as a meal; serves 4 as a side dish

½ pound good Kentucky bacon, like Hood's Heritage traditional or Australian style
2 large bunches kale, chard or leaf lettuce
2 large or 4 small green onions, both white and green parts, whites slivered and greens chopped into ⅛-inch pieces
2 tablespoons cider vinegar or other mild, unsweetened vinegar
salt and freshly ground black pepper to taste
4 hard-boiled, cooled and peeled eggs, either sliced in round circles or cut into four long quarters

Cook the bacon slowly in a heavy-bottomed skillet until browned and crisp, with most of the fat rendered out into the skillet. Remove the bacon to a cutting board. Chop into small pieces. Set the skillet and bacon fat aside; you will use them again.

Wash the greens. Spin dry. Tear into bite-sized pieces in a large, heat-proof salad bowl.

Top with chopped green onions.

Reheat the bacon fat in the skillet until it just starts to smoke. Then pour it all at once over the torn greens. Toss quickly and thoroughly.

Sprinkle the vinegar over the greens and toss a bit more.

Taste, and if necessary, add salt and black pepper.

Top with chopped bacon and hard-boiled eggs.

Serve.

"Fried" Corn Off the Cob

Although Kentuckians have depended on corn for hundreds of years, sweet corn came to the table more recently, courtesy of a spontaneous mutation. The more we ate the sweet version of corn, the less we wanted the other types. Imagine that!

In the twentieth century, plant breeders obliged our sweet corn tooth by breeding ever-sweeter varieties. At the same time, those of us who long for corn flavor enjoy medium-sweet varieties like 'Butter and Sugar' and 'Ambrosia.' We applaud a resurgence of heritage sweet corn types like 'Country Gentleman' and 'Golden Cross.' All those corns work beautifully on the cob, however you cook them.

When you can't get corn on the cob, or its joys have faded, try this savory-sweet skillet corn that a son developed for his beloved, for whom corn is always ambrosia.

Yield: Serves 8

12 ears fresh Kentucky sweet corn, shucked, silks removed and small blemishes cut out, or 6 cups frozen corn kernels
2 tablespoons good butter or bacon grease
2 tablespoons finely chopped onion, shallot or green onion
2 tablespoons finely chopped sweet or hot (or both) peppers, optional
1 teaspoon salt
fresh herbs for color, flavor and garnish

Note: Fresh sweet corn sticks easily during cooking, so be vigilant. On the other hand, if the corn sticks just a little, and that stuckness gets a bit brown (not burnt brown or black), scrape it off your pan with a hard spatula and stir it into the fried corn for extra tasty caramelized corn goodness.

If using fresh corn, stand each ear of corn up on its wide end in a very large bowl. With a sharp knife, starting at the top of the cob, slice four or five rows of corn at a time away from the cob. Once the kernels are removed, scrape each cob lightly with the back of the knife to add the last juicy bits of corn to the bowl.

Heat the butter or bacon grease over medium heat in your largest cast-iron skillet or other heavy-bottomed frying pan. Swirl to cover the bottom of the pan. Heat until fragrant.

Add the chopped onion or shallot. If using the optional peppers, add them now, stir well and cook 3 minutes.

Add the cut corn kernels and salt. Stir, stir, stir. Cook 10 minutes.

Serve in a sweet bowl. Garnish with finely chopped parsley, chives, thyme or other fresh green herbs.

Seasonal Berries and Fruits

How can we put a delightful, lightly sweet finish on weekday meals with what's fresh right now in Kentucky? Beginning with strawberries in May and going all the way through November's late apples from Reed Valley Orchard near Cynthiana, fresh, seasonal Kentucky fruits help finish our meals fantastically. When you have bits of time during the growing season, bag your own or local farms' or orchards' fresh raspberries, blueberries and blackberries and pop them directly into the freezer for winter delights.

Options for finishing a meal with fresh fruit:

- Fill individual bowls with sliced **strawberries**. Pour a few drops of **balsamic vinegar** onto the berries.
- Fill small glasses with washed, drained **blueberries**. Top with 1 tablespoon **plain whole milk Greek yogurt** and a drizzle of pure **Kentucky sorghum**.
- Put ripe red, yellow or black **raspberries** or **blackberries** in custard cups. Add a squeeze of fresh **orange juice** and ½ teaspoon of **Kentucky maple syrup** to

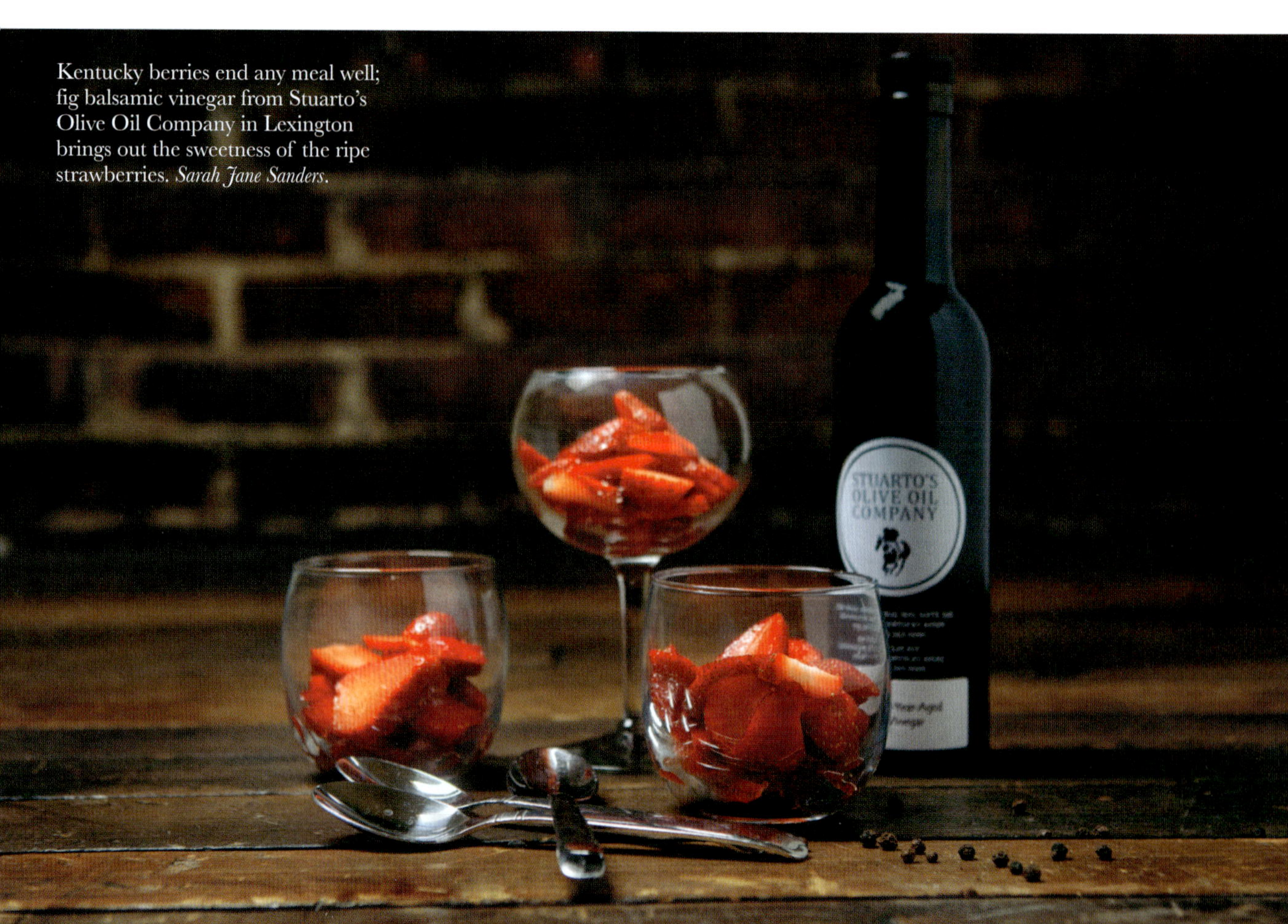

Kentucky berries end any meal well; fig balsamic vinegar from Stuarto's Olive Oil Company in Lexington brings out the sweetness of the ripe strawberries. *Sarah Jane Sanders.*

each. Add a teaspoon of Kentucky **strawberry, raspberry or blackberry jam** or **dessert wine** if you like.

- Slice beautiful **Kentucky apples** thinly onto small saucers—they can be peeled or not, your choice. Fan out the slices from half an apple on each saucer. For two apples on four saucers, make a drizzle. Mix together 1 tablespoon of your favorite Kentucky sweetener—**sorghum, honey or maple syrup**—with 2 teaspoons **lemon**, **lime** or **orange juice** or **white balsamic vinegar**. Stir in ⅛ teaspoon each **vanilla** extract and **salt**. If you want, add a quick grind of black pepper. If you have fresh mint outside your back door, shred a few leaves on top, just because you can.

Options for finishing a meal with frozen fruits in winter:

- Cook a quart of frozen Kentucky **blackberries** or **mixed berries** just until boiling. Remove from heat. Add two tablespoons **sorghum syrup**, 1 tablespoon **lemon juice**, a quick shake of **salt** and ½ teaspoon **vanilla extract**. Stir and serve in individual bowls. Top with a grating of **lemon peel** and 1 teaspoon of **sour cream**, **heavy cream** or **whole milk Greek yogurt**.
- Cook a quart of **frozen Kentucky sour cherries** or **gooseberries** over medium heat until boiling. Reduce heat to medium low. Add a **cinnamon stick** or ½ teaspoon **ground cinnamon**, along with ⅓ cup **mild Kentucky honey**, **maple syrup** or **sugar**. Cook five minutes. Remove from heat. Stir in ½ teaspoon **vanilla extract** and ¼ teaspoon **almond extract**. Stir and serve in individual dessert dishes. Top with a teaspoon **sour cream**, **heavy cream** or **Greek-style whole milk yogurt**.

Finding Sources of Locally Grown Foods

If you don't know where to look for locally grown food for sale in your county or town, check these resources:

- Local Harvest, www.localharvest.org, a national site, supports searching for particular foods in one location or for all growers in a specific geographic area.
- The Kentucky Department of Agriculture maintains a directory of all farmers' markets in the state, organized by county, at http://www.kyagr.com/marketing/farmers-market-directory.aspx.
- The Kentucky Farm Bureau manages a certification program for roadside farm markets and maintains a listing at https://www.kyfb.com/federation/program-links/roadside-farm-markets.

DRESSED-UP MENU

Asparagus Apotheosis

Some vegetables say "fancy" on the table, even when they are easy to grow and utterly familiar. Asparagus, because it has a short season of perfection, tops that list for Kentucky tables. And green beans, whether tender and smoky or crisp and garlicky, please multitudes.

Yield: Serves 8

2 pounds fresh asparagus
2 tablespoons unsalted butter
1 teaspoon fine sea salt or table salt

Asparagus Prep

Snap off and discard the bottom inch or so of two pounds of asparagus from your prized bed or a local farmer's patch. Rinse the spears well, and then lay them down in a flat dish and cover them with cool water as you prepare to cook them. This soak encourages any last bits of earth or sand to leave the tips.

Pour ½ cup water into the bottom of a medium pot that has a close-fitting lid. Put the asparagus spears in a vegetable steamer and into the pot.

Cover the pot and bring the water to a boil over high heat.

After four minutes—careful with that steam—test carefully with a fork by piercing the base of spears; look for a little resistance but no hard spots. Cook longer if needed, checking after each minute.

When the asparagus is done, use tongs to move it to a serving dish.

Carefully remove the steamer basket and empty the hot water. Set the empty pot over medium heat. Add the butter. Melt, swirl and keep a close eye on it. As soon as the milk solids begin to brown, turn off the heat. Put the asparagus back in the pot, sprinkle with salt, and shake to coat all spears with salty, browned butter.

Serve immediately.

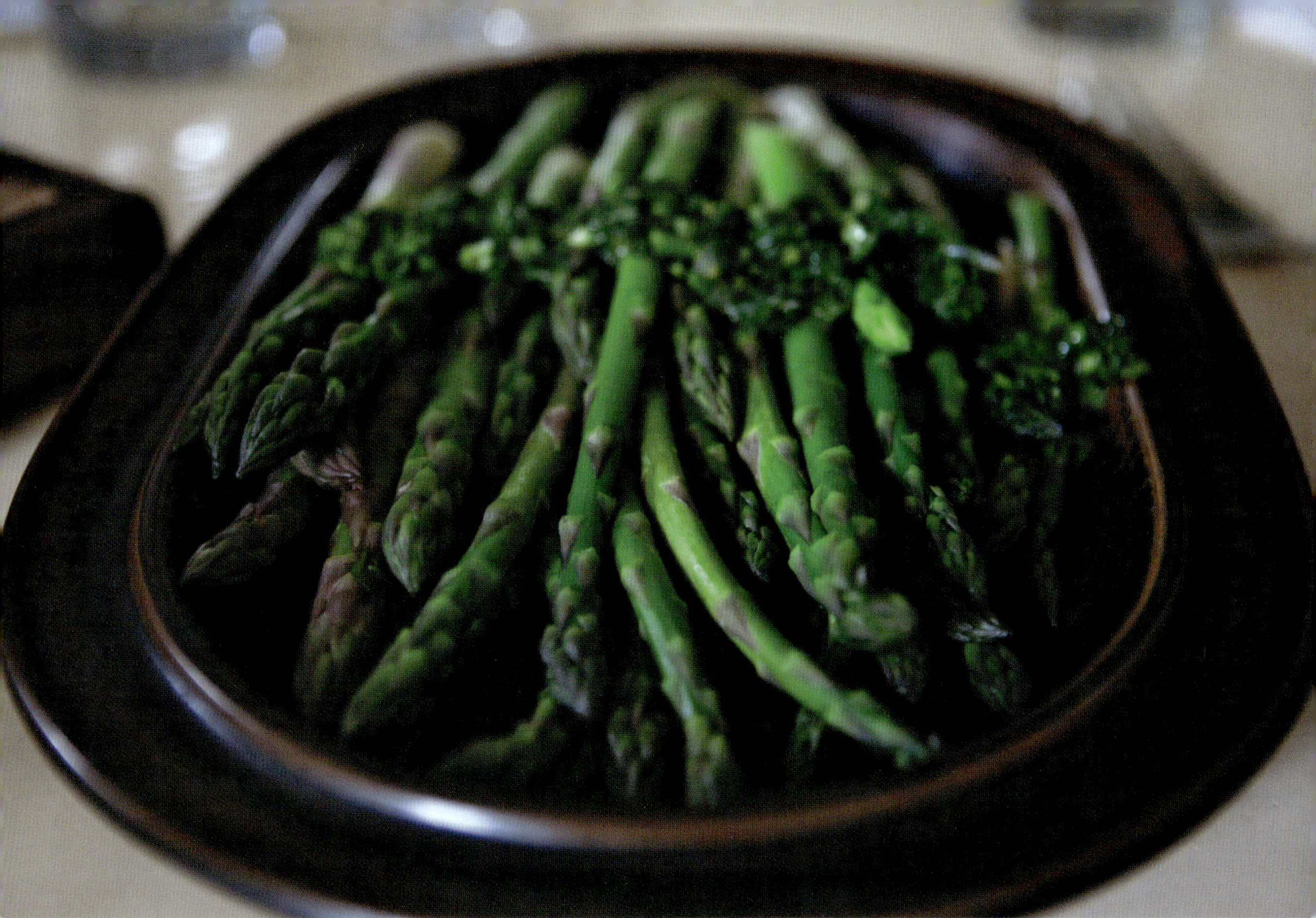

Asparagus may be Kentucky's favorite green vegetable, especially in spring. *Sarah Jane Sanders.*

One Amazing and Simple Variation

Squeeze half a lemon into the browned butter before you add the asparagus. For extra pizazz, use a sharp, fine grater to add tiny bits of lemon zest to the top of the asparagus before serving.

One More Good Option

Cool the steamed spears quickly in iced water. Drain thoroughly. Top with Lemon-Mustard Vinaigrette (page 67).

Green Beans, Country or City

Green beans? We love them city style, we love them country style and we love them any time.

Country Green Beans: Smoky, Porky

That smoky pork flavoring we adore requires a long cooking time, which may explain some Kentuckians' notorious habit of cooking perfectly good green beans so long that they turn into tasty gray mush—that, and the fact that in traditional working farm families, the beans held up fairly well to hours of cooking while the cook spent the morning outside, working in the garden, doing the wash or baling hay.

With the resurgence of heritage green beans that produce lots of actual beans and have tender hulls—called "horticultural," "greasy" or "cornfield" beans—we can have our beans well-cooked, well-seasoned and nicely textured. In addition, cooking the smoked pork on its own before adding the beans works to preserve precious beany freshness with judicious medium cooking instead of long cooking.

These beany types of green beans appear in farmers' markets in late summer. They can appear in your garden, too, courtesy of decades of work by Bill Best of the Sustainable Mountain Agriculture Center, Inc., in Berea, Kentucky. Visit the seed catalogue at www.heirlooms.org to choose from more than one hundred types of green beans that will work well with medium cooking.

Yield: 8 servings

1 country ham hock or up to ½ pound bacon ends
2 pounds prepared fresh horticultural green beans: strung, snapped and rinsed thoroughly in cool water
salt, to taste

In a large, covered pot over low heat, cook smoked pork in a gallon of water for 1 to 2 hours, or until falling-apart tender.

Turn off the heat. Remove the pork to a bowl or cutting board. (It will return shortly.) Add the prepared green beans to the water. Cook over medium heat until at a low boil; turn the heat down to get a steady simmer.

Meanwhile, once the pork cools enough to handle, tear or cut it into very small pieces and return it to the pot with the green beans.

Cook 30 minutes. Carefully fish a bean or two from the pot and taste for tenderness. The hulls will likely be quite tender. The beans themselves should have creamy insides. If they feel or taste like raw starch, cook for five minutes more, retest and continue until the bean texture is utterly pleasing. Add a bit of salt if needed.

If more than a couple of tablespoons of liquid remain in the pot with the beans when they are done, turn the heat to high and stay right with the beans until the liquids reduce just to cover the bottom of the pan. This infuses the pot liquor flavor into the beans. Another good option is to leave the pot liquor in the pan or serving bowl to savor as a special treat with cornbread.

Taste for salt; add if needed. Serve immediately.

The No-Pork Option: Cook the green beans in seasoned chicken broth, preferably your own (see page 59). Add 1 tablespoon butter or olive oil at the end of the cooking time. Taste for salt; add if needed.

Lemon-Mustard Vinaigrette

Top steamed, cooled green beans or asparagus with this tangy vinaigrette. Use it also as the dressing for vegetable salads (page 130) and slaws. No fresh lemons? Use a light vinegar instead.

1 teaspoon prepared mustard (optional)
1 teaspoon each salt and freshly ground pepper, or to taste
6 tablespoons good olive oil
2 tablespoons freshly squeezed lemon juice
1 tablespoon fresh tender herbs, chopped fine, for garnish (optional)

In a small bowl or glass measuring cup, stir together the mustard, salt and pepper. Whisk or stir in the olive oil. Whisk or stir briskly as you add the lemon juice. Pour the vinaigrette over the vegetables; top with herbs. Use immediately.

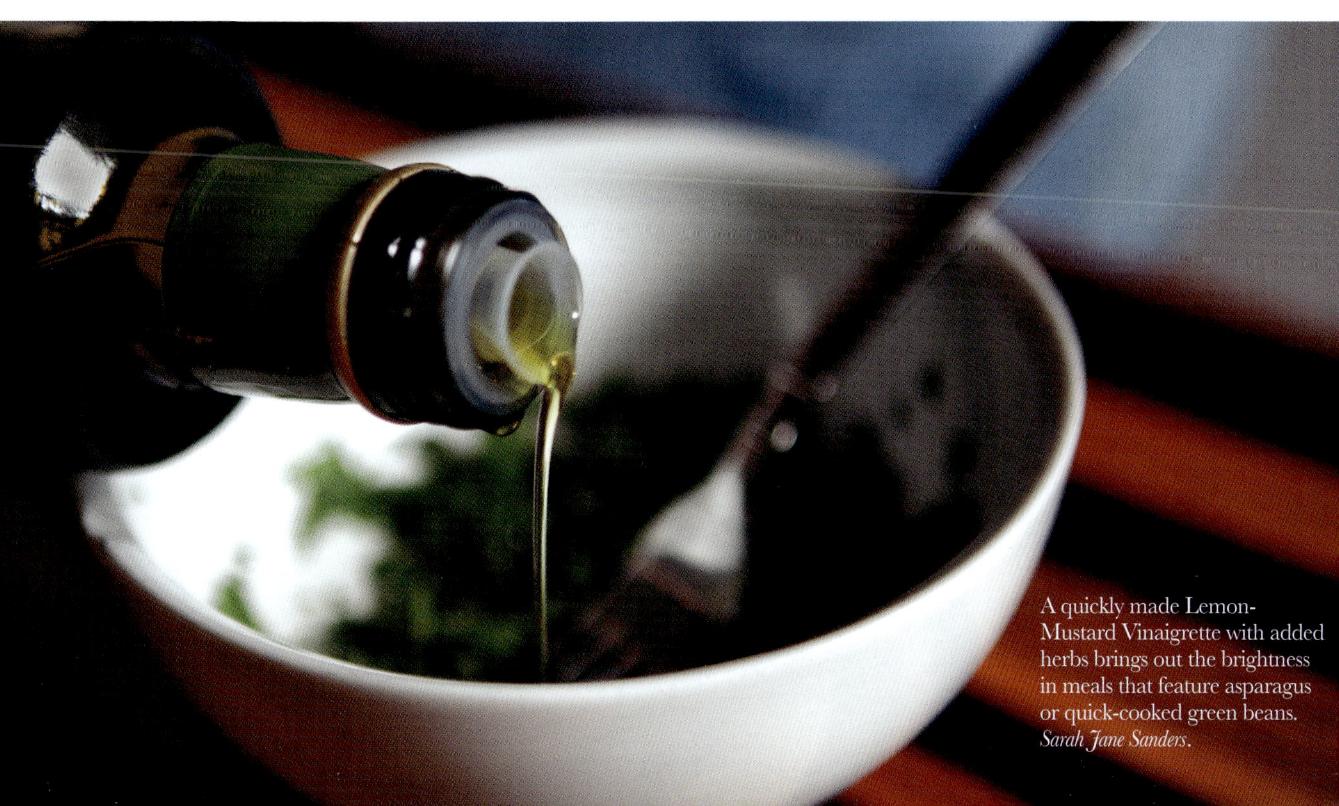

A quickly made Lemon-Mustard Vinaigrette with added herbs brings out the brightness in meals that feature asparagus or quick-cooked green beans. *Sarah Jane Sanders.*

City Green Beans: Crispy, Crunchy

Slender, almost beanless "haricot vert" or filet-type green beans, such as French 'Fins de Bagnols' or 'Maxibel,' grow perfectly in Kentucky gardens. They go from bush to plate almost as quickly as corn on the cob, and in fact, when utterly fresh, they bring some of corn's same vegetal sweetness from Kentucky's earth onto your plates.

Yield: 8 servings

1 tablespoon fine sea salt or table salt, and more to taste
2 pounds prepared fresh filet-style green beans, whole with tips if very young, tips broken off if they are a little tough or broken into pieces if your family likes them better that way
1 tablespoon butter or olive oil

Add salt to two gallons of water in a very large covered pot. Bring it to boil.

Watch the steam! Add the cleaned beans to the pot.

Cook three minutes. Use tongs to fish out one or two of the larger beans; cool slightly. Taste for doneness, or pierce with a fork. These should be crisp and a bit yielding to the teeth or fork but not totally tender.

Continue cooking if needed; test at one-minute intervals. Fresher, smaller beans cook much more quickly than older, larger ones.

When the beans are done, carefully pour the contents of the pot through a colander or strainer

Eggstra Credit: Keep on Topping!

Bacon!

Bacon is not an herb, but it may as well be given how much Kentuckians like to use it. Cook three slices until crisp and crumble on top of either asparagus or crispy green beans.

Eggs!

Crumble a fresh, peeled hard-boiled Kentucky egg on top of the vegetables and herbs. Or serve either green vegetable warm with a topping of freshly poached eggs, a pat of butter, salt and pepper. Call that dinner, right there. Or supper. Or lunch. Or brunch. Or midnight snack.

set in a clean sink. Shake the colander to remove as much water as possible from the beans.

Put the butter or olive oil in the still warm pot, return the green beans and shake or stir until they are well coated. Taste for seasoning, and add a sprinkle more salt if needed.

Serve immediately.

Option: For a crisp, cool salad, drain the cooked green beans, and then plunge them into ice water to cool them quickly. Drain thoroughly. Serve with Lemon-Mustard Vinaigrette (page 67). Keep going if you like: add any three finely chopped, tender fresh herbs, about 1 tablespoon each.

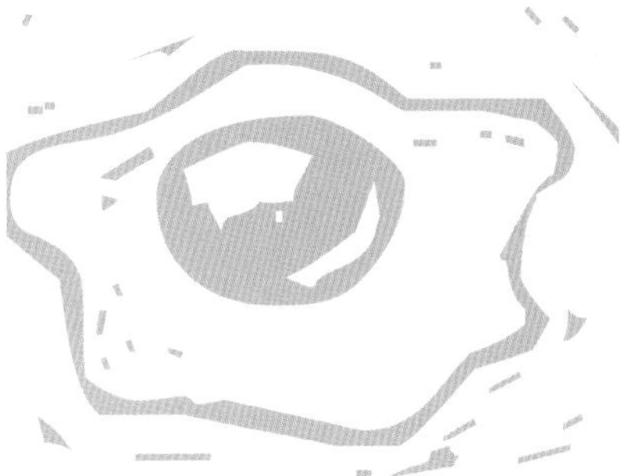

Kentucky Angel Biscuits

In 1965, Floyd County postmaster Irene Hughes asked her fellow postmasters across Kentucky to solicit recipes from their communities' finest cooks for a fundraising cookbook to help her church pay for a new roof. What's Cooking in Kentucky, *in continuous print since 1965, reveals the best recipes of real twentieth-century Kentucky cooks. The biscuit section alone inspires thoughts of a grand biscuit-tasting event.*

From Payneville, Kentucky, Ruby Yates submitted a recipe for "Mother's Angel Flake Biscuits." These unusual and delicious pastries added a new option to many Kentucky kitchens: refrigerated dough that keeps well for more than a week and makes it easy to produce tender, homemade biscuits in about five minutes, plus twelve minutes in the oven. Having the dough on hand means any weeknight meal can suddenly turn special.

The recipe below makes several changes from the original, including a touch of cornmeal for crunch, but we credit Ruby Yates, Irene Hughes and What's Cooking in Kentucky *as the inspiration for this fine food.*

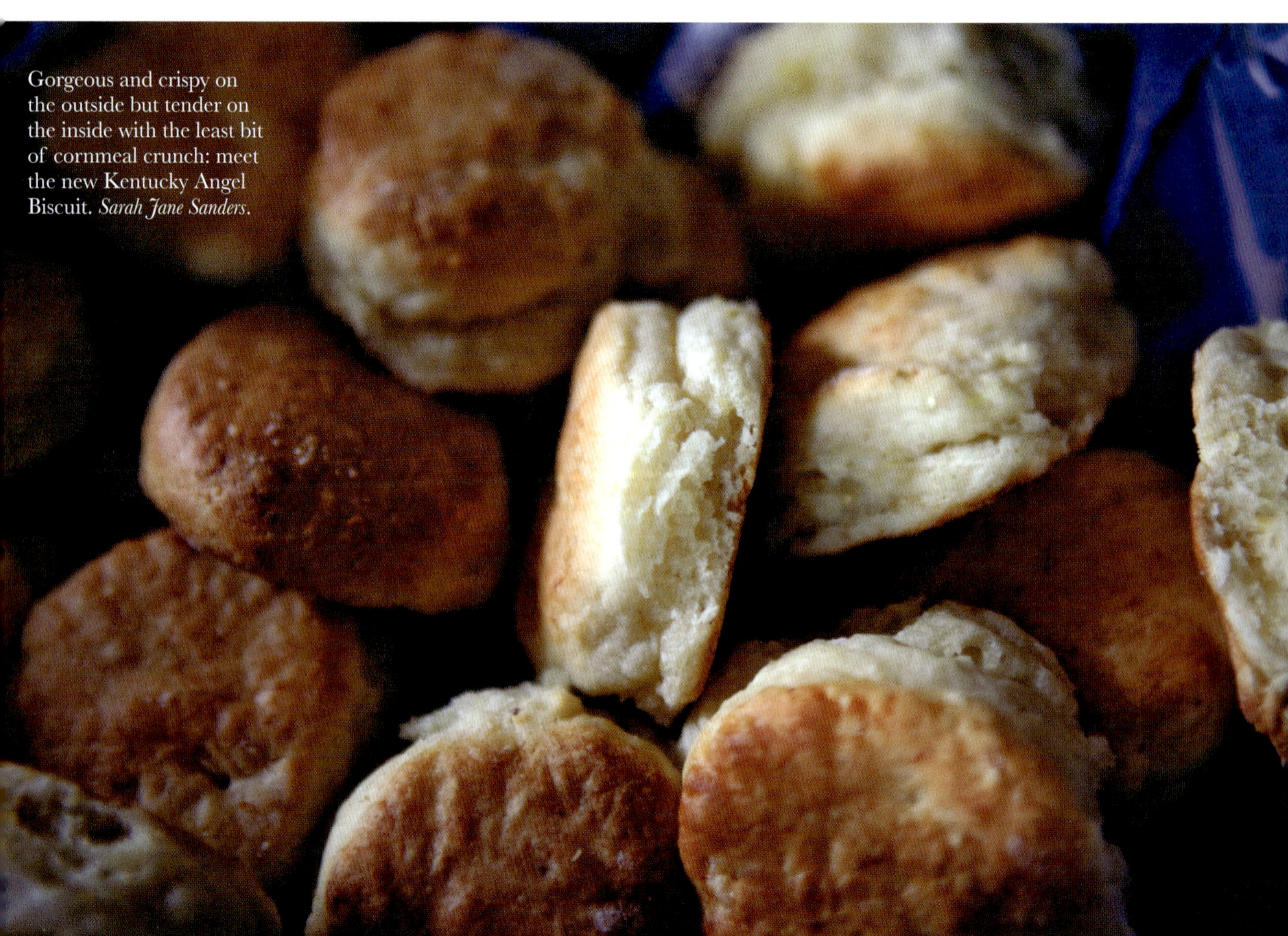

Gorgeous and crispy on the outside but tender on the inside with the least bit of cornmeal crunch: meet the new Kentucky Angel Biscuit. *Sarah Jane Sanders.*

Yield: At least 160 small biscuits, but make only what you need for each meal.

5 cups unbleached all-purpose flour, shaken or stirred to lighten it before measuring
¼ cup cornmeal, any kind
1 package or 2 ¼ teaspoons yeast
1 tablespoon baking powder
1 teaspoon baking soda
1 teaspoon fine sea salt or table salt
1 tablespoon light sorghum, honey or maple syrup
¾ cup butter or lard, melted and cooled to room temperature
2 cups buttermilk (or a bit more if your buttermilk is extra thick)

Put flour, cornmeal, yeast, baking powder, baking soda and salt in a large bowl. Stir together.

Add sweetener, butter or lard and buttermilk. Stir together until thoroughly mixed; then stir 20 more strokes.

Cover and refrigerate.

When ready to bake, preheat oven to 400 degrees Fahrenheit.

Roll dough out on a floured cloth or board. Cut with a biscuit cutter, without twisting.

Place biscuits touching if you like soft sides; separate by an inch if you like them browned all over.

Bake 12 minutes, or until golden on top.

Don't forget the sorghum and butter when you serve these!

Strawberry-Rhubarb Skillet Pudding Cake with Wheat-Free Options

Whether you use fresh strawberries and rhubarb in spring or frozen versions in any other season, this combination of a fruit and a vegetable stalk combine to make a new flavor, not like either ingredient on its own. Many evangelists for the blend are converts who formerly objected to rhubarb on (slimy) principle but finally trusted the innocent strawberry enough to take a tiny bite, just to shut up hectoring loved ones who insisted on sharing this perfect blend of tart, sweet, floral and fruit flavors.

This recipe works well in a seasoned black skillet, ceramic-lined heavy pot or a 9- by 13-inch glass baking dish. Add a bit of Whipped Half-Sour Cream (page 43), as a counterpoint to the sweet-tart fruit.

Yield: Serves 10–12 generously

For the Pudding Cake:
½ cup sugar, plus 4 tablespoons, divided
¼ cup water
1 tablespoon freshly squeezed lemon juice
3 cups (15 ounces) cleaned fresh or frozen rhubarb stalks, chopped in pieces about ½-inch wide or less
2 cups (10 ounces) cleaned fresh or frozen strawberries, green tops removed, chopped in halves or thirds
2 tablespoons all-purpose flour or gluten-free all-purpose baking mix (Bloomfield, King Arthur or other brand), plus ¾ cup
2 large eggs
¼ cup whole milk
½ cup butter, melted and cooled (or brown the butter if you like [see page 39])
½ teaspoon pure vanilla extract
⅛ teaspoon almond extract (optional)
2 tablespoons cornmeal, any color or grind
1 teaspoon baking powder
½ teaspoon fine sea salt or table salt
⅛ teaspoon freshly grated nutmeg (optional)

For the Optional Crunchy Topping:
⅓ cup all-purpose flour or gluten-free all-purpose baking mix
1 tablespoon sugar
⅛ teaspoon salt
1 heaping tablespoon butter, either cold or at room temperature
½ cup sliced almonds, the almond-shaped thin flakes (optional)

Put a rack in the middle of the oven and preheat to 350 degrees Fahrenheit.

Prepare the crunchy topping, if you are using it. In a small bowl, stir together flour, sugar and salt. Rub or cut in the butter until the mixture looks pebbly. If you are using nuts, add them last and blend lightly. Got extra time? Find that lemon rind and grate up to a teaspoon into the topping mixture. Stir lightly and set aside.

Prepare the fruit base.

Pour the ½ cup sugar, water and lemon juice into a 9-inch skillet or heavy cooking pan. (Extra credit: caramelize the sugar.) Bring to a boil over medium-high heat. Lower the heat to medium. Add the rhubarb. Cover and cook five minutes.

Meanwhile, put the strawberries in a large bowl. Add 2 tablespoons flour or gluten-free baking mix and 2 tablespoons sugar. Stir together well. When the rhubarb has cooked five minutes, turn off the heat and distribute the strawberry mixture all over the hot rhubarb. Let this rest. (If you are using a 9- by 13-inch glass baking dish, spray it with nonstick spray or butter it well, and pour this rhubarb-strawberry mixture into it.)

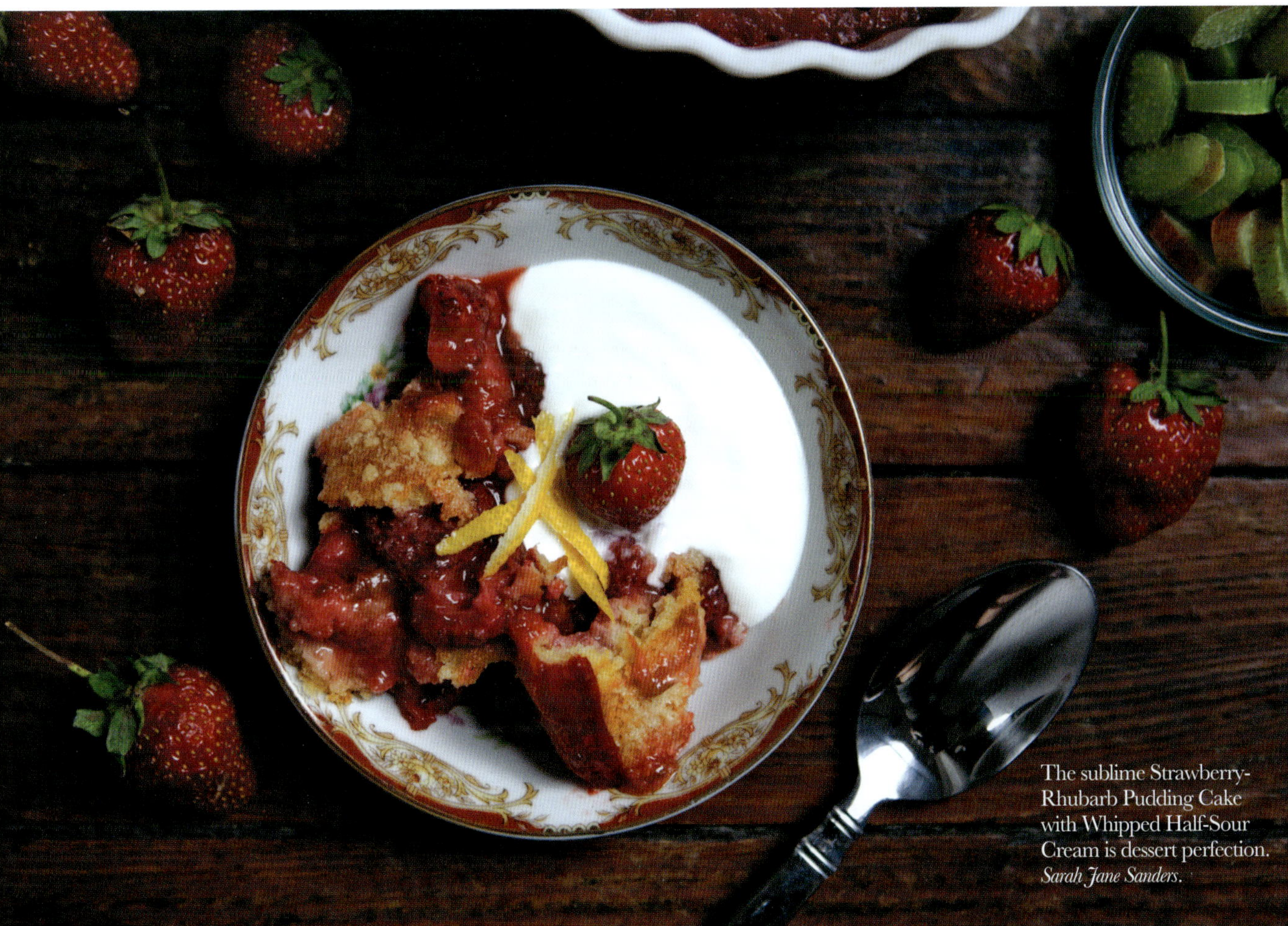

The sublime Strawberry-Rhubarb Pudding Cake with Whipped Half-Sour Cream is dessert perfection. *Sarah Jane Sanders.*

Prepare the batter.

In a medium bowl, whisk the two eggs until light. Add milk, melted butter and vanilla and almond extracts.

In a separate small bowl, mix together the remaining ¾ cup flour, cornmeal, remaining 2 tablespoons sugar, baking powder, salt and nutmeg, if using. Add the dry ingredients to the wet ingredients and stir until they combine into a thin batter.

Put the pudding cake together.

Pour the batter evenly over the rhubarb-strawberry mixture. If you are using the crunchy topping, sprinkle or drop it over the batter; it does not have to be evenly or perfectly distributed.

Bake for 25 minutes, or until light brown. If you use a thermometer, the temperature in the center of the pudding cake should be 185 to 190 degrees. Remove from oven.

Serve immediately, or let cool to room temperature. It is splendid with plain or strawberry wine–infused Whipped Half-Sour Cream (page 43).

Elmwood Stock Farm, Georgetown (Scott County), Kentucky

The colors of the late September peppers drew me to Elmwood Stock Farm's booth at the Lexington Farmers' Market more than fifteen years ago. Good farming practices, kind and generous farmers, and the quality of Elmwood food now make this distinctive 550-acre organic farm operation central to my household's food supply and our understanding of positive agriculture's possibilities and challenge.

Two generations of Bell and Stone families now farm the famed Maury loam of this glorious Bluegrass land. They follow four earlier generations of Scott and Bourbon County farmers who practiced good stewardship, including crop rotation, pasture improvement, composting and thrift.

Kay Bell, mother of Ann Bell Stone and John Bell, both of whom farm full time at Elmwood, said, "Cecil and I tried to get them to do anything but farming. We grew

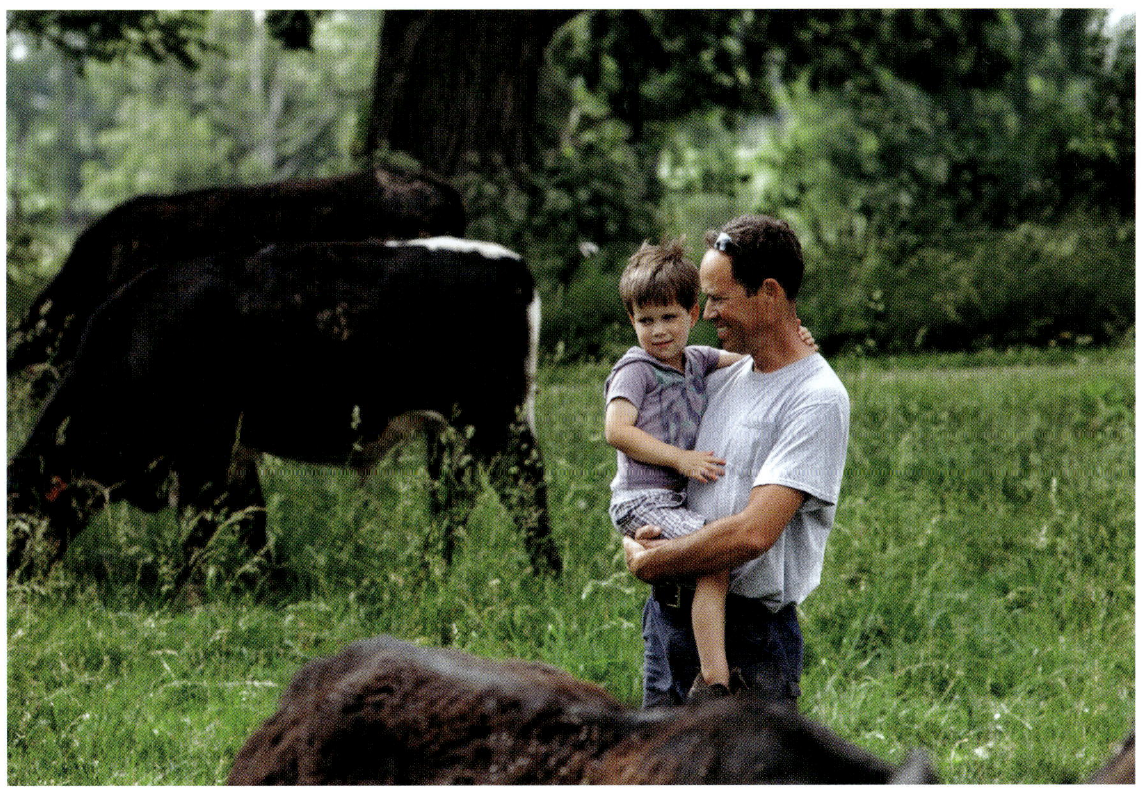

John Bell, of Elmwood Stock Farm in Scott County, carries his son to visit their certified organic, pastured Black Angus cows. *Sarah Jane Sanders.*

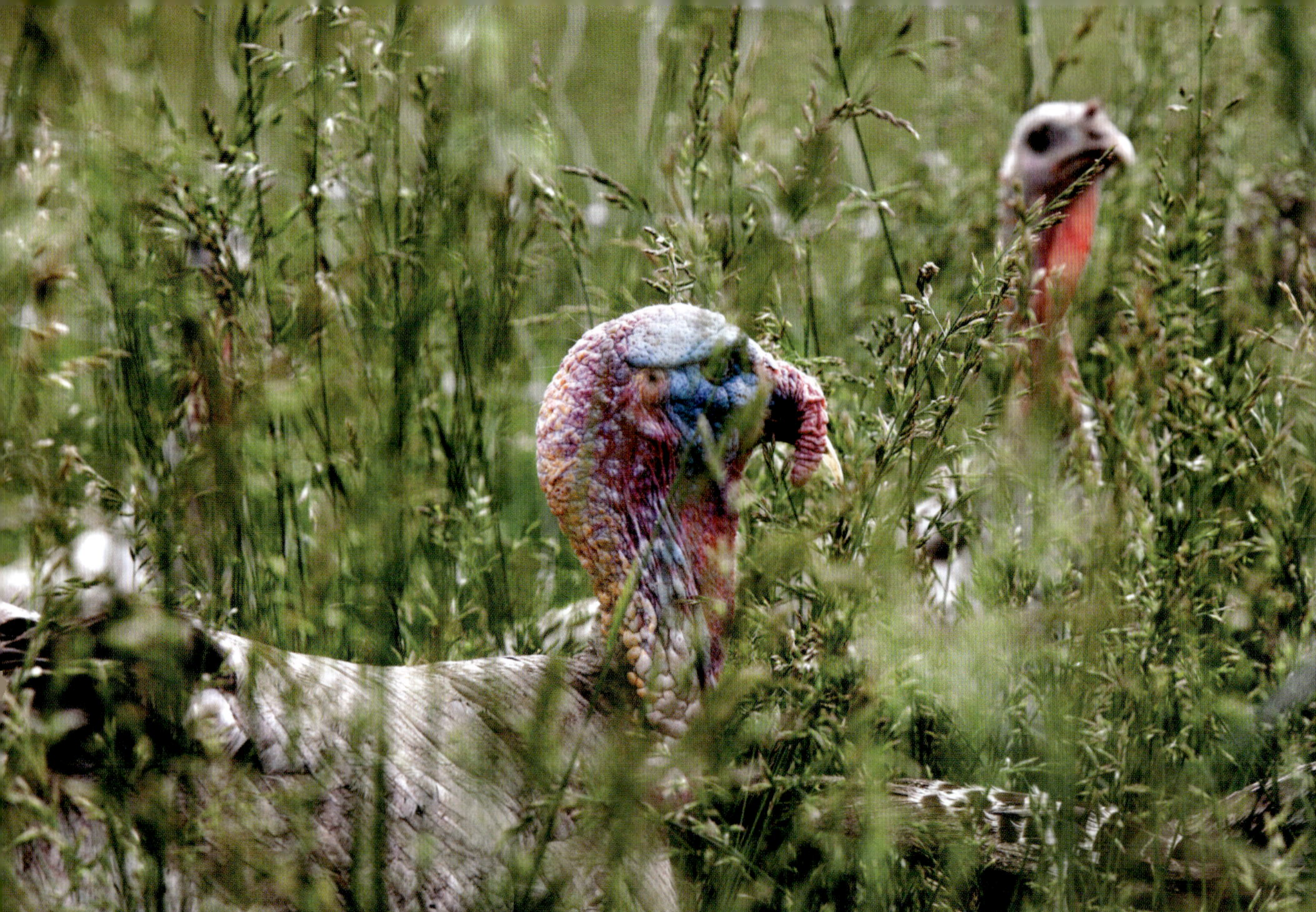

Elmwood Stock Farm organic turkeys enjoy the spring pasture. *Sarah Jane Sanders.*

Black Angus cattle and tobacco, and we couldn't see how that would support another family. They had other ideas, and we think it's great."

One winter, John and Ann, along with organic farmer Mac Stone (now Ann's husband), went to Minnesota to an Acres USA conference on production-scale organic agriculture. Afterward, they agreed to begin work toward organic production of beef, lamb, chickens, eggs, turkeys, vegetables and fruits. Now the farm provides most of the support for the three families who live on it.

Elmwood feeds several hundred central Kentucky families through year-round CSA subscriptions (more than four hundred during the main growing season) and year-round participation in local farmers' markets. Many Elmwood products sell to area restaurants and institutional buyers as well. Ann writes a thoughtful, interesting newsletter, complete with excellent recipes, for inclusion in every CSA share.

The care the Bell and Stone family members invest in their land shines through in the flavors of their food. Soil fertility and health derive from a carefully planned seven-year crop rotation. The Maury loam's carefully tended health delivers sweetness to the organic strawberries, richness to the pastured organic eggs and ultimate umami to the certified organic Black Angus beef.

Elmwood Stock Farm produces 234 varieties of 72 different crops each year, from organic beef soup bones through pantry staples like organic sweet purple, red, yellow and white potatoes, as well as special delights like delicate organic strawberries and red raspberries. While organic berries and sweet corn have built-in customer appeal, Elmwood's growers use their gentle leadership style to educate customers to try new foods like Bordeaux spinach, Delicata squash, Green Zebra tomatoes, Bourbon Red turkeys or watermelon radish.

It is hard to see weakness in this venerable farm. It seems as solid as limestone bedrock. More than thirty mouth-dropping blue ash, bur oak, kingnut and chinkapin oaks, each more than 250 years old, grace the fields. Yet Elmwood Stock Farm faces frightful pressures that go beyond any farm's expected vulnerability to weather, labor and markets. One edge of the farm shares a Georgetown city boundary, complete with a tightly packed subdivision. Another subdivision may soon abut a different portion of Elmwood's boundaries. Worst

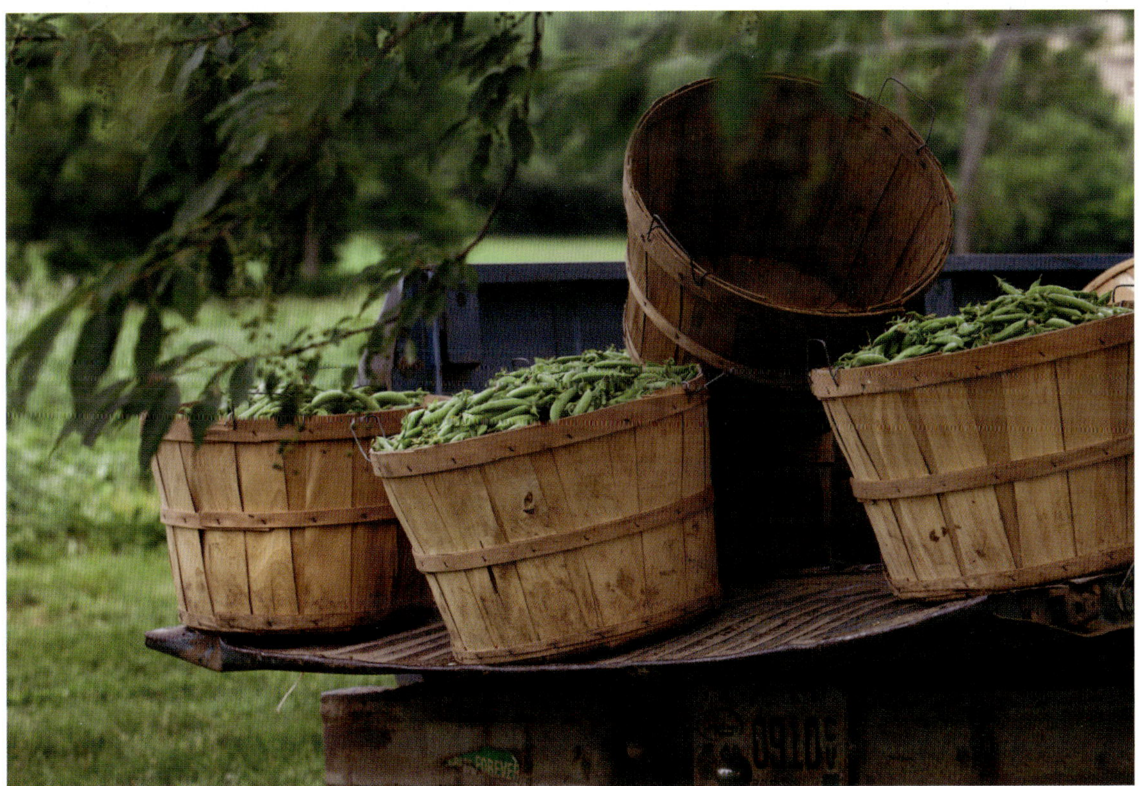

Customers are waiting for the spring pea harvest at Elmwood Stock Farm. *Sarah Jane Sanders.*

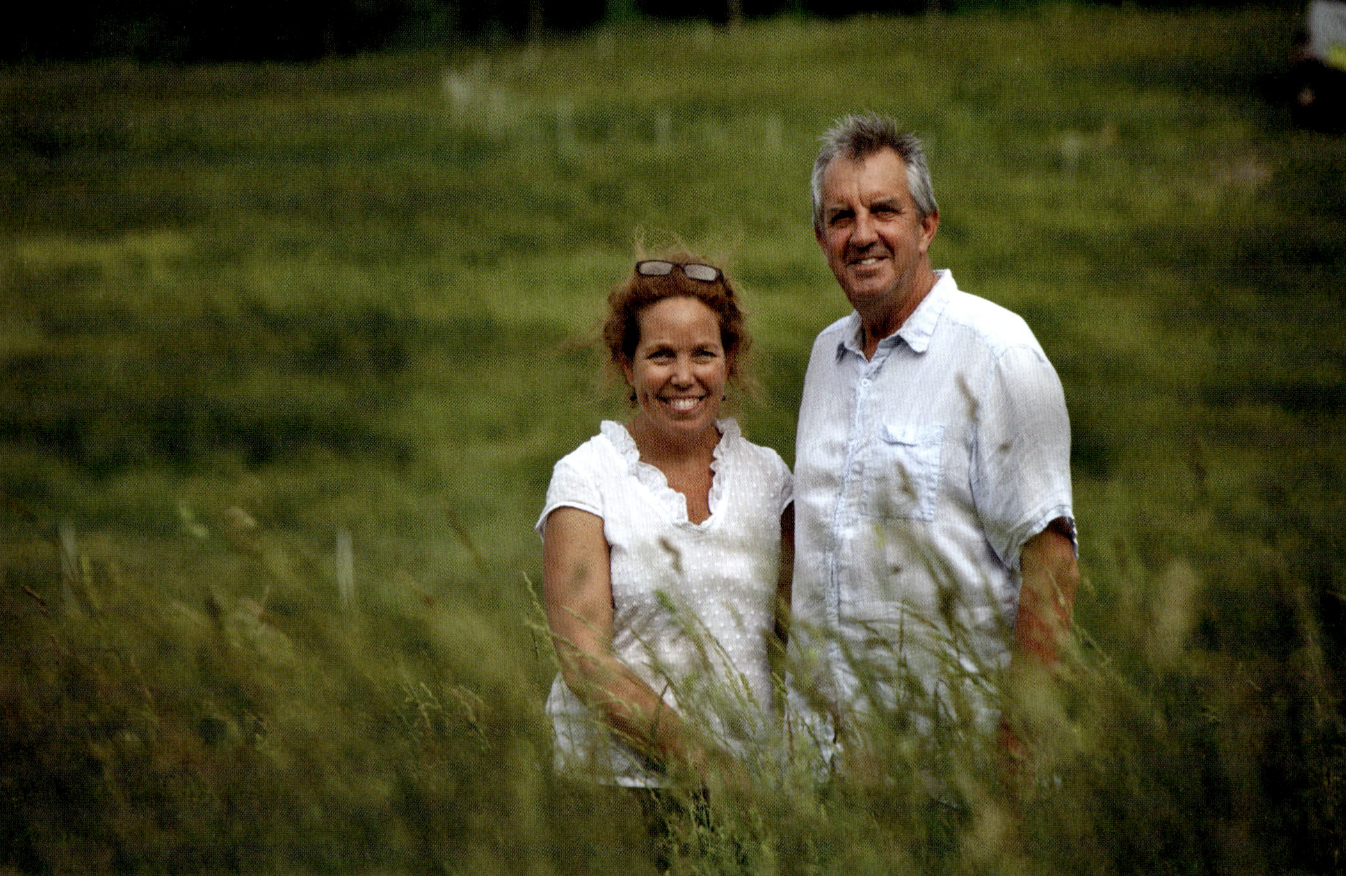

Ann Bell Stone (left) and Mac Stone from Elmwood Stock Farm, along with Ann's parents, Kay and Cecil Bell, and Ann's brother and sister-in-law, John and Melissa Bell, carry on farming as a family's chosen work for six generations. *Sarah Jane Sanders.*

of all, a proposed four-lane connector road that would bisect the farm has already received approval—despite Elmwood objections—from local and state planning bodies.

Building organic soil—helping nature repair the damage from past overuse, toxins and other interrupters of soil health—takes patience, persistence and time. Neither Kentucky law nor Scott County ordinances recognize and protect the value of organic stewardship as a public good, nor do they recognize how the civic and public engagement of Elmwood Stock Farm leaders stands as an important demonstration for growers and eaters everywhere about what organic production makes possible.

Carrying on a long history of advocacy for sustainable agriculture and good farming practices within many organizations, Mac currently chairs the National Organic Standards Board. In addition, he and Ann champion sustainable agriculture through groups like Southern Sustainable Agriculture Working Group (SSAWG) and Organic Association of Kentucky. Both have served in leadership roles on the board of the Lexington Farmers' Market.

Elmwood Stock Farm began growing and marketing organic food before most customers understood either the value of organics or the astonishing amount of work and record keeping certified organic production requires. The Bell and Stone families' farming, leadership, advocacy and service demonstrate the flowering of Kentucky agriculture's potential, rooted in five previous generations' dedication to Kentucky land. The farm's vulnerability to development and road construction demonstrate the fragility of organic farming and the need for policy support to protect the good that organic farming offers all of us.

Henkle's Herbs & Heirlooms, Nicholasville (Jessamine County), Kentucky

Mark and Velvet Henkle farm in an unusual setting: lush, large, open suburban backyards less than five minutes from the heart of Nicholasville, Kentucky. These larger-than-garden/smaller-than-commodity plots, plus a heated greenhouse and unheated high tunnel (hoop house), sustain at least eighty tomato varieties that cover the tomato rainbow. At least twenty-five varieties of peppers grow there too, both hot and sweet, along with at least ten special types of herbs.

Mark and Velvet Henkle met in Nicholasville at the end of eighth grade when Velvet, "kicking and screaming," according to Mark, moved from Lexington to Nicholasville with her family. They married about ten years later, in 1998. Velvet started her own business, Velvet Touch Catering, in 2002. Initially, Mark and Velvet grew herbs for Velvet's business, unaware that the "growing bug" had bitten them and that soon one catering company might not be able to absorb all the leaves, stems and flavors their rich Bluegrass soil could yield.

From May through November 2005, Mark interned with legendary tomato producer and seed saver Bill Best. Bill Best as a tomato coach and mentor? That's like landing Wynton Marsalis for trumpet lessons. Mark and Velvet have produced a new tomato variety, 'Velvet Touch,' which is offered for sale at heirlooms.org, the seed catalogue for Bill Best's Sustainable Mountain Agriculture Center. The tomato is described as "a cream colored tommy toe that appeared as a mutant in the garden of Mark and Velvet Henkle."

Henkle plants grow without pesticides. Based on need, Mark releases beneficial insects like lacewings, lady beetles and others suggested by Blair Leano-Helvey, a University of Kentucky entomology graduate who runs Entomology Solutions in Louisville. "We use beneficial insects everywhere, outdoors and in the hoop house and greenhouse. We released some in the greenhouse to control fungus gnats and mites. We've used lacewings in the high tunnel and have released beneficial nematodes to deal with flea beetles and

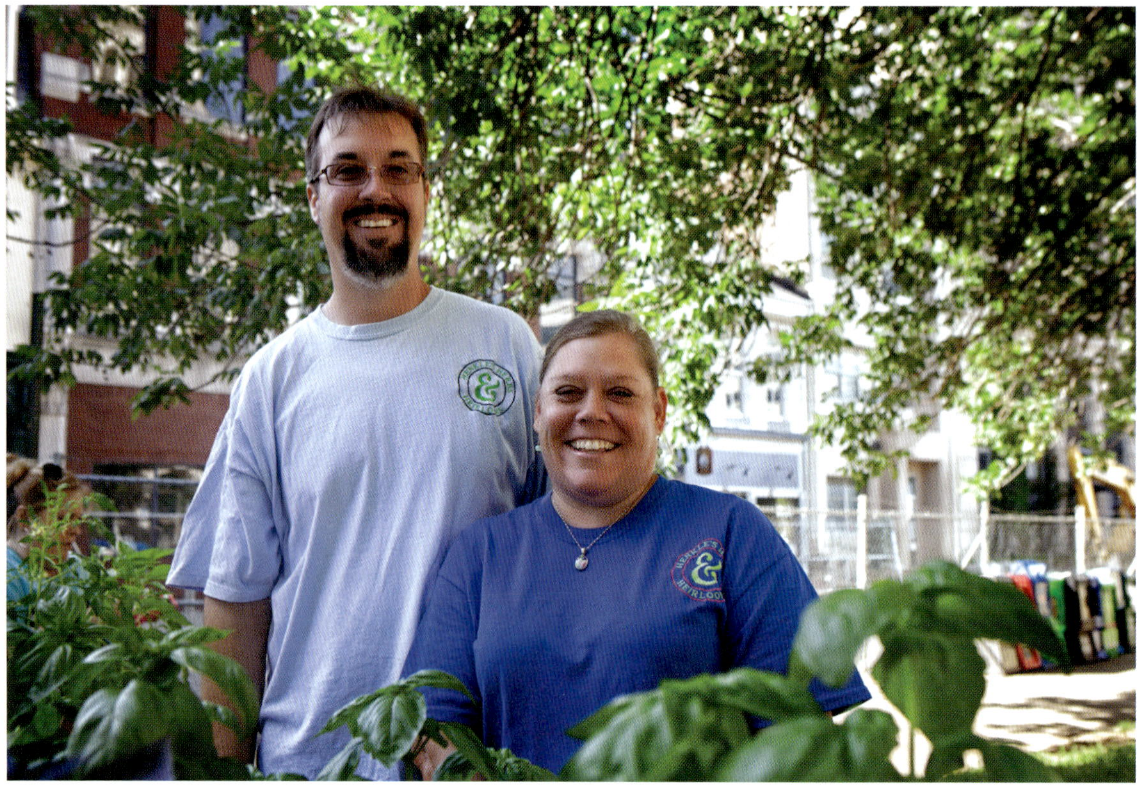

Mark and Velvet Henkle bring smarts and persistence to the work of growing tomatoes, peppers and herbs year-round at Henkle's Herbs & Heirlooms in Nicholasville. *Sarah Jane Sanders*.

potato beetles," he said. The Henkles grow all their own plants from seeds, according to Mark, "so customers will know we are doing it right and maintaining integrity" and also to keep from having diseases hitchhike in, as happened in the devastating 2009 late tomato blight that obliterated many tomato crops on the East Coast.

Like all good farmers, Mark and Velvet use inventive tactics to boost and stabilize production in their relatively small space. Big recent capacity boosts come from two structures they have built: the 2012 hoop house—an unheated, plastic-covered greenhouse—and the 2014 greenhouse heated with a wood-burning furnace.

University of Kentucky horticulture professor Emery M. Emmert invented hoop houses, also known as "high tunnels," in the late 1940s. These protective, unheated structures help growers protect plants from wind and weather extremes and increase yield. Many hoop house growers can produce fresh greens through most winter months and bring tender crops like tomatoes and strawberries to market a bit earlier than field-grown crops. Because they are producing outside the usual growing cycles, hoop house farmers often need young transplants at atypical times of year; many have found they need a heated structure as well that allows them to germinate seedlings for off-season planting.

Mark and Velvet will use their new, heated greenhouse throughout a full winter for the first time in 2015. They plan to germinate seeds timed to produce early transplants. With good fortune in addition to their good farming, they intend to produce the early tomatoes that delight many of their customers.

Mark and Velvet built both their hoop house and heated greenhouse with typical farmer thriftiness and ingenuity—with used parts, personal and family labor, a variety of small grants and dogged persistence across time. The Natural Resources Conservation Service, part of the U.S. Department of Agriculture, helped fund the hoop house. The Agricultural Development Fund of the Governor's Office of Agricultural Policy helped with the costs of the wood-fired boiler that heats the greenhouse, and the Jessamine County Community Agricultural Investment Fund reimbursed many greenhouse construction and boiler costs.

Mark and Velvet sell the products from their intensive backyard farming operation to customers at the Saturday and Sunday editions of the Lexington Farmers' Market during the growing season. Direct marketing to customers makes up most of their sales; some restaurants also buy significant amounts of tomatoes from them. Soon, if all goes well, all customers will enjoy more Henkle's Herbs & Heirlooms foods for more months of the year, thanks to Mark and Velvet's steady work to make good use of available backyard growing space for food production.

Corn: The Plant That Made Kentucky Possible

Talk about timeless. The corn we love to eat so many different ways today from the cob, as chips, in cornbread or spoon bread, out of popcorn bowls and even pickled—sustained people living near and traveling through what is now Kentucky from about AD 1000 until 1750. Then European immigrants took up the seed basket and planted corn—*Zea mays*, known to many as maize—to feed themselves and their livestock. Today, we continue to rely on corn-based foods that Native Americans and early European settlers would recognize and enjoy while simultaneously adding new forms of corn to Kentucky's palate. Mexican immigrants to Kentucky bring their own cultural history with corn, extending back at least several millennia; so we now find excellent handmade tortillas, tamales and other Mexican foods made with corn in most Kentucky towns.

Corn suited the earliest Kentuckians because it grows well in our soil, tastes good, feeds livestock, dries and stores easily, keeps a long time, travels well and yields fiber useful for bedding, baskets and footwear. Since this is a cookbook, we will concentrate on corn in Kentucky food and drink.

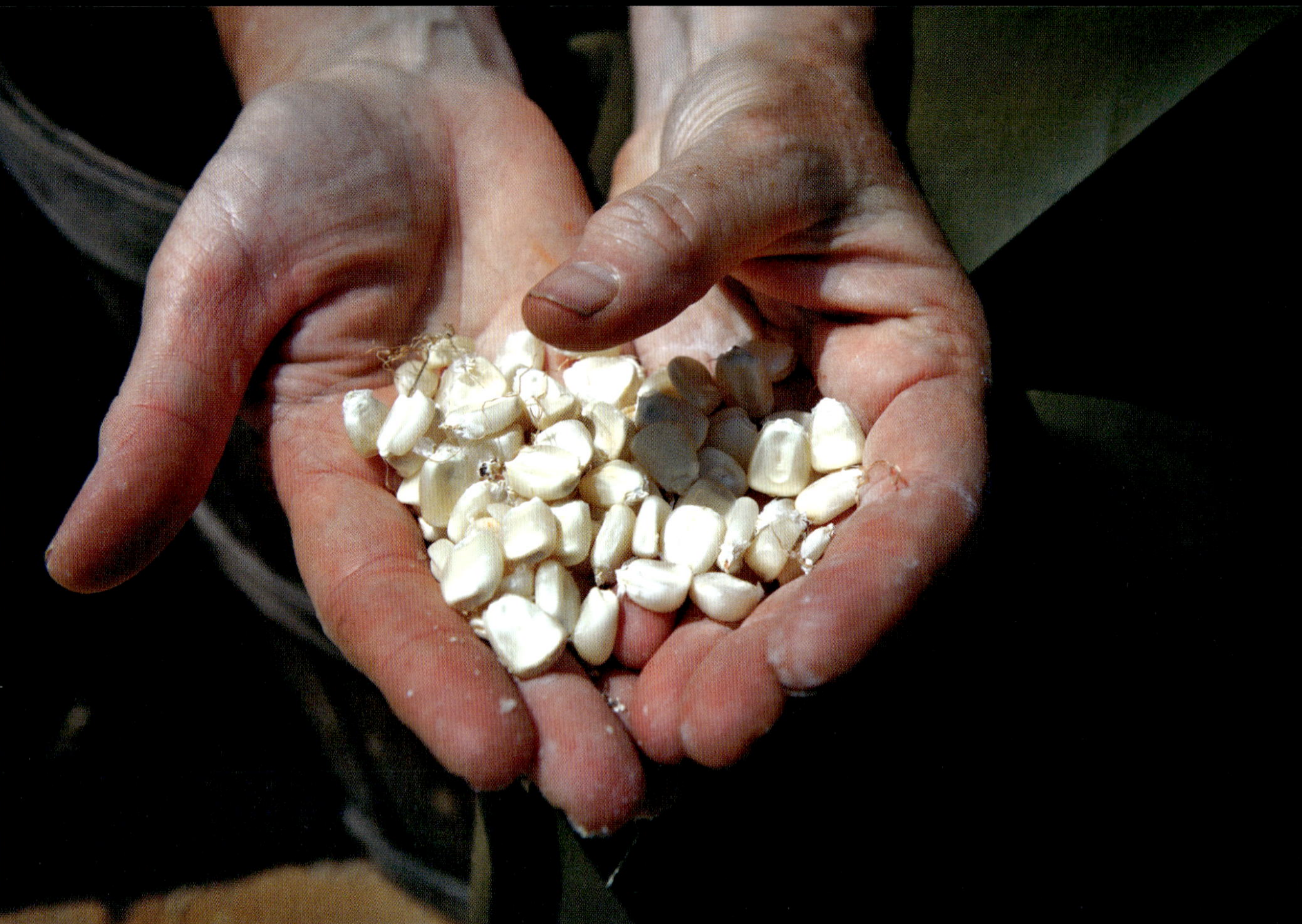

Jennifer Gleason of Sunflower Sundries in Mays Lick holds shelled organic Hickory King Corn. *Sarah Jane Sanders.*

In *The Kentucky Encyclopedia*, researchers Marty Godbey and Jeanette S. Duke devote much of the "Foodways" entry to corn's importance in Kentucky meals past and present. Kentuckians needed food they could grow and process themselves; corn obliges by growing well on freshly cleared land and by completing the full circle from edible seed to many more seeds in one growing season. A family can grow, harvest, store, process and cook corn without needing major equipment or outside help, although the arrival of water-powered mills in the late 1700s and mechanical corn shellers, first patented in 1839, surely made it easier to nourish a family with corn.

Early Kentuckians depended on corn. According to *The Kentucky Encyclopedia*, "It was a basic ingredient in breads, porridges, cakes, and even whiskey…Fresh corn was roasted on the ear, or removed from the cob and stewed in a skillet, but the most prevalent form was meal, finely ground from kernels of dried corn placed in a wooden mortar and pounded with a wooden pestle…Depending on how it was cooked, cornmeal mixed with water became ash cake, corn pone, mush, griddle cakes, cornbread, or johnny cake." The *Encyclopedia* also notes, "Kentucky's famous corn pudding, spoonbread, and chess pie came from custardy additions to corn."

While Kentuckians enjoy grits—especially those embellished with cheese and garlic—and adore fresh summer corn eaten from the cob or "fried" in a black skillet, cornbread holds pride of place as the preferred year-round vehicle for delivering corn to Kentucky tables. This is true in spite of a "progressive" campaign in the early 1900s to replace cornbread with wheat-based biscuits in Appalachia. According to American studies scholar Elizabeth Englehardt, well-educated women who had migrated to Appalachia lacked understanding of the great benefits of cornbread to self-reliant people, and championed biscuits as healthier and cleaner.

As a homegrown, hand-harvested crop that can be combined with a few other homegrown ingredients to produce tasty, nutritious food quickly and with minimal equipment, cornbread suited Kentucky's resilient farming families much better than expensive wheat-based bread. We do love biscuits now, too—not to mention yeast rolls—but cornbread retains its status as a mainstay of delicious, home-based everyday meals in Kentucky.

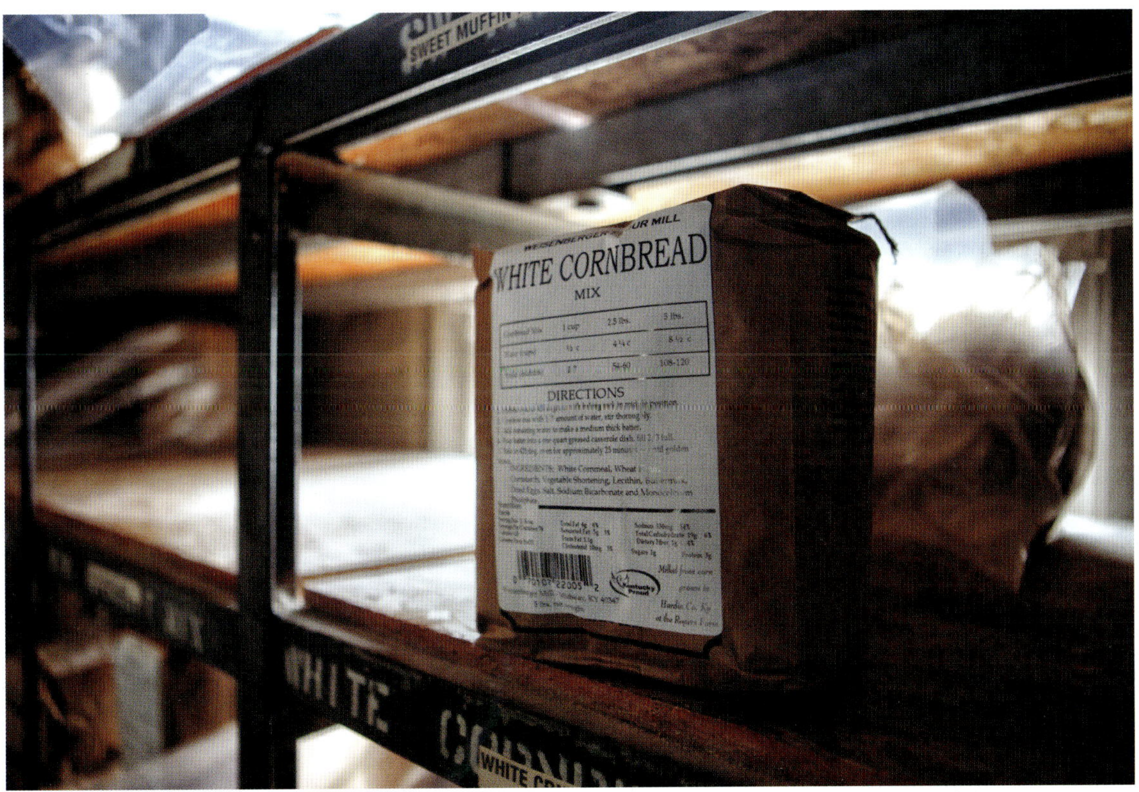

Customers in a hurry love the white cornbread mix from the historic Weisenberger Mill near Midway. *Sarah Jane Sanders.*

In fact, some Kentucky families still grow a favorite heirloom corn and keep or share a small mill, ensuring their supply of the best flavors for their cornbread. Most favorites for cornmeal in Kentucky are "dent" corns, which require a long growing season and feature a sweet flavor, a soft starch and easy milling. Gloria and Don Williams in Menifee County grow Tennessee Red Cob, a white dent corn, and also like Boone County White corn, another dent variety. They own a small stone mill and grind their dried corn to their own exact preferences. Gloria and Don like the sweetness of the dent corns and treasure the utter freshness that comes from "just in time" grinding of their own dried corn seed.

Dent corns, according to heirloom grain authorities at Anson Mills in South Carolina, usually have a small dent in the top of each kernel, in contrast to flint corns, which have a rounded top, harder starch, longer keeping qualities and, in some cases, a shorter growing season. Both popcorn and sweet corn belong to the flint category, with some exceptions.

'Hickory King' corn, a dent heirloom developed before 1875, boasts many fans in Kentucky. Sunflower Sundries, longtime artisanal producer of organic soaps, jams and mustards in Mays Lick, Kentucky, added heirloom 'Hickory King' cornmeal and grits to its products in 2012. Recently, a collective of growers living near Mays Lick organized to grow enough 'Hickory King' corn to launch Hickory King Collective corn chips, which Sunflower Sundries sells online and in Kentucky and Ohio.

Humans like to drink corn, too, once it has been made into whiskey. Bourbon uses at least 51 percent corn as its base, and unaged corn whiskey, like moonshine, typically requires an even higher percentage of corn. The Kentucky Distillers Association reports that in 2013, the nine thousand people working in Kentucky's bourbon industry almost matched the nearly ten thousand corn growers in the commonwealth. Although not all Kentucky bourbon distillers use Kentucky corn for their products, an estimated ten to fifteen million bushels of Kentucky corn become mash and then bourbon.

Corn dishes take up more and more of the Bluegrass table, as many Kentuckians embrace corn-based Mexican dishes that seem both familiar and exotic at the same time. Corn and beans show up as "soup beans and cornbread" and as tacos. Hominy, still produced by hand in some parts of the state, appears in *pozole*, a maize stew.

At the same time, food pioneers keep inventing new uses for corn. *Gilt Taste*, the now-defunct online curator of fashionable food and style, showcased "Corn Butter," a single-ingredient dish made by juicing fresh sweet corn kernels and then cooking them gently until natural cornstarch thickened the mixture into a rich spread.

A new approach to corn cultivation may eventually change how producers grow Kentucky corn. At present, corn must be planted from seed each year, and each corn plant dies within that year, requiring planting from seed again the following year. Some researchers, like Wes Jackson, founder of the Kansas-based Land Institute, believe a perennial corn can be developed that will thrive across multiple years without requiring replanting. Perennial corn would work with nature to avoid many of the ways annual corn cultivation depletes the land. As a perennial plant, corn could make a circle back toward its distant origin as a grass that appeared and grew on its own. Perennial corn will require human cultivation, but perhaps it will lessen the earth's workload by growing deep roots and staying in place. In any case, we count on corn growing in Kentucky and sustaining us as far into the future as we can imagine.

Meal 3
PUTTING THE KENTUCKY IN BURGERS, MUSHROOMS AND DOGS

Grilled meats make lots of Kentuckians verrrrrry happy. Even though some fearless Type G grillers fire up the coals year-round and wear their shorts outdoors in ten-degree weather to do the smoky deed, it's easier for many of us to haul out a black skillet and get griddling. Increasingly, chefs say skillet cooking is ideal for ground meats, thanks to the ways fats are saved for the savoring. So it's your choice: fire up the charcoal or turn on the burner, indoors or out. Either way, use fine Kentucky ingredients, and this meal will give you Happy Mouth Syndrome.

Everyday Menu

Grilled or Griddled Kentucky Burgers, Main-Dish Mushrooms and Bacon-Wrapped, Cheese-Stuffed Sausages
Dark and Bright Kale Salad
Really Amazing Baked Beans
Fresh Kentucky Potato Salad

For special occasions or holidays, or once every summer, make a burger-and-dog meal memorably homemade and memorably great. Kentucky meats or mushrooms, homemade mustard, pickles, ice cream and the sorghum–peanut butter lusciousness of Thoroughbred Cream Cheese bars reward modest effort with stunning tastes.

Dressed-Up Menu Additions

Basic Country Mustard
Aunt Bea's Homemade Immediate Pickles
Buttermilk-Maple Ice Cream
Thoroughbred Cream Cheese Bars

Perfect Pairings

- *Cocktail:* The Redbird State
- *Signature Nonalcoholic Drink:* Sour Cherry Lemonade
- *Wine*: Harkness Edwards Night Heron for depth that stands up well to the beef, or Chrisman Mill's First Vineyard Reserve
- *Beer*: West Sixth IPA for the hoppy connections with the greens, garlic and onions in the side dishes
- *Tea*: Rooibee Red Tea, Unsweetened, for its clean, light taste
- *Coffee*: Righteous Roast Coffee's Single Origin Mexican for its clarity with the sweet dessert
- *Soundtrack for cooking*: [Some songs on all playlists have adult language and themes.] "Botch-A-Me" (Rosemary Clooney), "One Big Holiday" (My Morning Jacket), "My Old Kentucky Home" (Johnny Cash), "Girls' Night Out" (the Judds), "Gone Camping" (Reel World String Band), "Oh, Susannah!" (University of St. Mary's Choir), "Knows What Tomorrow May Bring" (Henry Hipkens), "Man of Constant Sorrow" (Ralph Stanley), "Bowling Green" (the Everly Brothers), "Foster/Arr Halloran: Nelly Bly" (Chanticleer)
- *Soundtrack for eating*: "The Little Mohee" (Bradley Kincaid), "I Like Beer" (Tom T. Hall), "I'm No Stranger to the Rain" (Keith Whitley), "Keep on the Sunny Side" (the Carter Family), "The Sporting Bachelors" (various artists), "It Beats for You" (My Morning Jacket), "The Swapping Song" (Burl Ives), "It Don't Mean a Thing If It Ain't Got That Swing" (Lionel Hampton), "Kentucky" (Billy Joe and Norah), "I'll Remember April" (Les McCann), "Jeanie with the Light Brown Hair" (Thomas Hampson), "This Town Can't Get Over You" (Henry Hipkens)

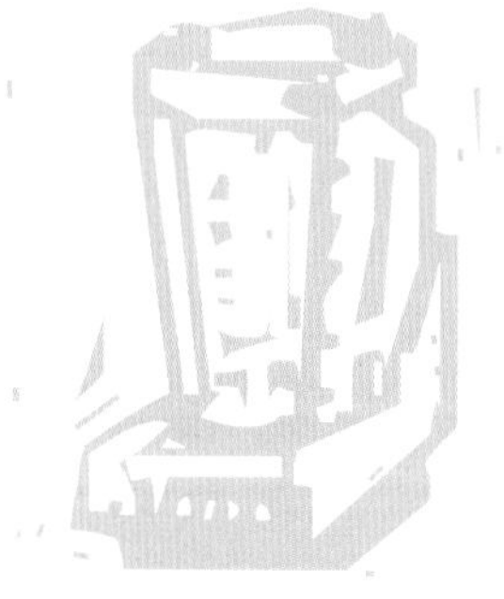

The Redbird State

This exquisite coral cocktail tastes like June in Kentucky, when sour cherries ripen in abundance and the season for drinking delicious rosé wines begins. We used Horseshoe Bend's Rosé of Cabernet Franc 2009 for this spectacular cocktail. Reed Valley Orchard near Paris and other orchards throughout Kentucky have begun increasing their cherry production. Growing your own means you are more likely to have precious cherries when you want them. Montmorency cherry trees thrive in Kentucky without sprays of any kind, and they delight the eye with their lovely fruits.

The cherries must be picked, pitted, cooked a bit, blended, strained and chilled before use here, so plan ahead. The drink, with its whisper of rose as well as rosé, rewards your effort.

Yield: One cocktail

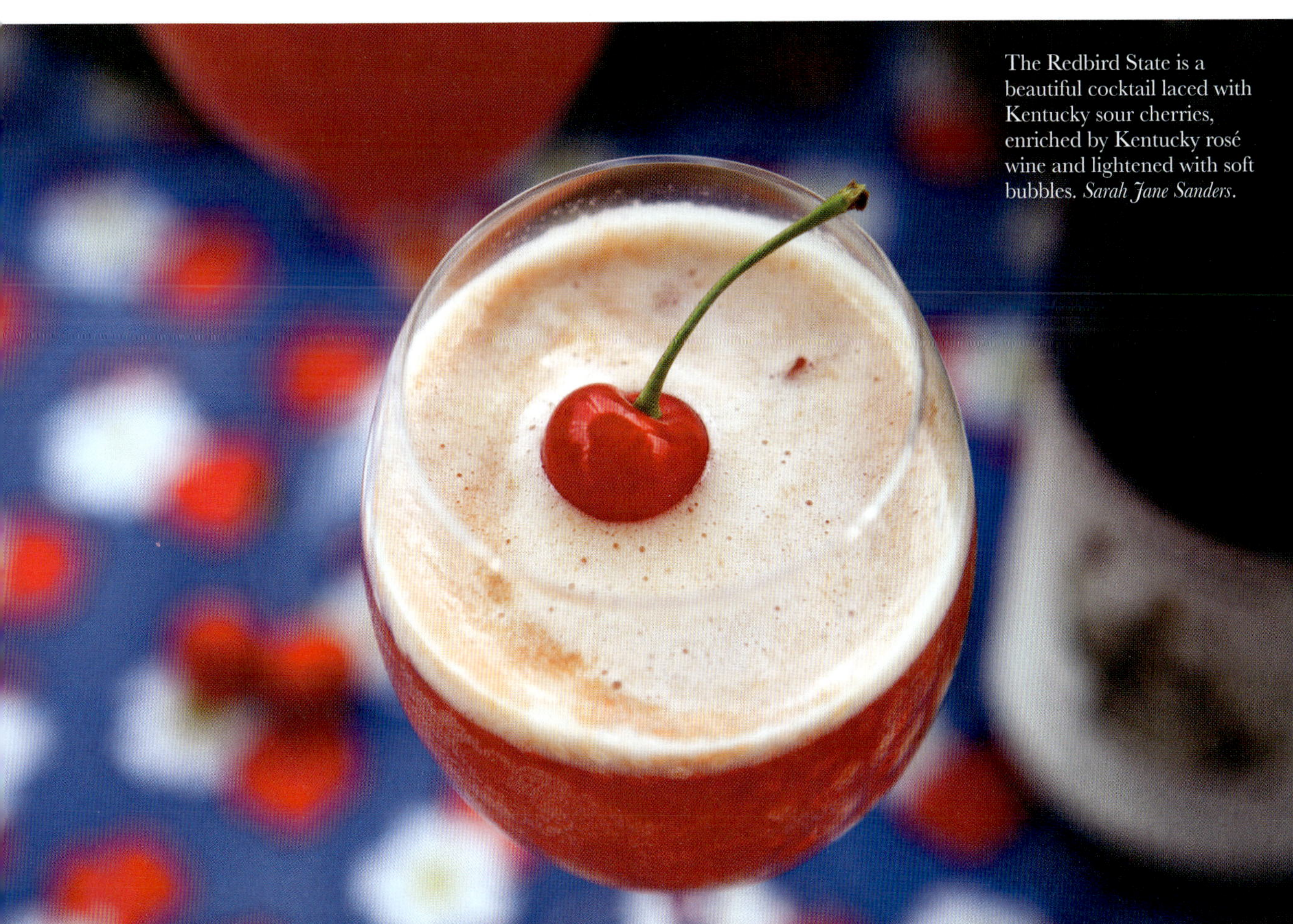

The Redbird State is a beautiful cocktail laced with Kentucky sour cherries, enriched by Kentucky rosé wine and lightened with soft bubbles. *Sarah Jane Sanders.*

Cherry Purée

Yield: about $1\frac{3}{4}$ cups cherry puree, enough for 8 generous cocktails or a full recipe of nonalcoholic Sour Cherry Lemonade (see page 91).

1 pound fresh, tart cherries, pitted
1 cup water
3 tablespoons sugar or a light-flavored Kentucky honey, such as Nickels Pure Raw Kentucky Honey

In a medium saucepan over medium-low heat, cook the cherries, water and sweetener gently for 30 minutes, until the cherries are very soft.

Let the cherries cool to room temperature.

Blend in the blender until as smooth as possible, about five minutes.

Strain the purée through a fine mesh strainer.

Chill mixture in the refrigerator for at least 1 hour.

Refrigerate any leftover purée for up to four days.

3 tablespoons sour cherry purée
1 drop rose water extract
3 ounces dry Kentucky rosé
soda water
ice

Nearly fill an 8-ounce rocks glass with ice cubes.

Pour the sour cherry purée over the ice cubes.

Follow with the drop of rose water extract and the rosé. Stir well.

Fill the glass with soda water, and stir gently.

Garnish with a cherry or unsprayed rose petals.

Simple Syrups

Simple syrups are liquid sweeteners that mix easily in cold drinks; often they are made with equal volumes of sugar and water. In *Classic Kentucky Meals*, we use Kentucky sorghum, maple syrup and honey, as well as sugar, for making simple syrups for drinks.

To make a simple syrup, stir 1 cup sorghum, maple syrup, honey or sugar and 1 cup water together in a glass bowl or jar until the mixture is clear. You can cook it, but it's not necessary.

For a few drinks, including the Sour Cherry Lemonade, granulated sugar works best because it yields a clear syrup and adds no flavors of its own. Store simple syrups in the refrigerator.

Sour Cherry Lemonade

Yield: 8 servings

1½ cups sour cherry purée (page 90), or to taste
2 cups freshly squeezed lemon juice (from 10 to 14 lemons, depending on size)
1 cup simple sugar syrup, or to taste (See "Simple Syrups," page 90)
6 cups club soda (1½ liters, or 4 12-ounce cans)
fresh unpitted cherries or thinly sliced lemon "wheels" for garnish (optional)

Fill a large pitcher or glass gallon jar with ice. Pour in the cherry purée, lemon juice and simple syrup. Stir well. Add the club soda and stir well again. Fill tall glasses with ice and pour the lemonade in. Garnish glasses with unpitted cherries or lemon wheels.

Sour Cherry Lemonade pleases all ages. *Sarah Jane Sanders.*

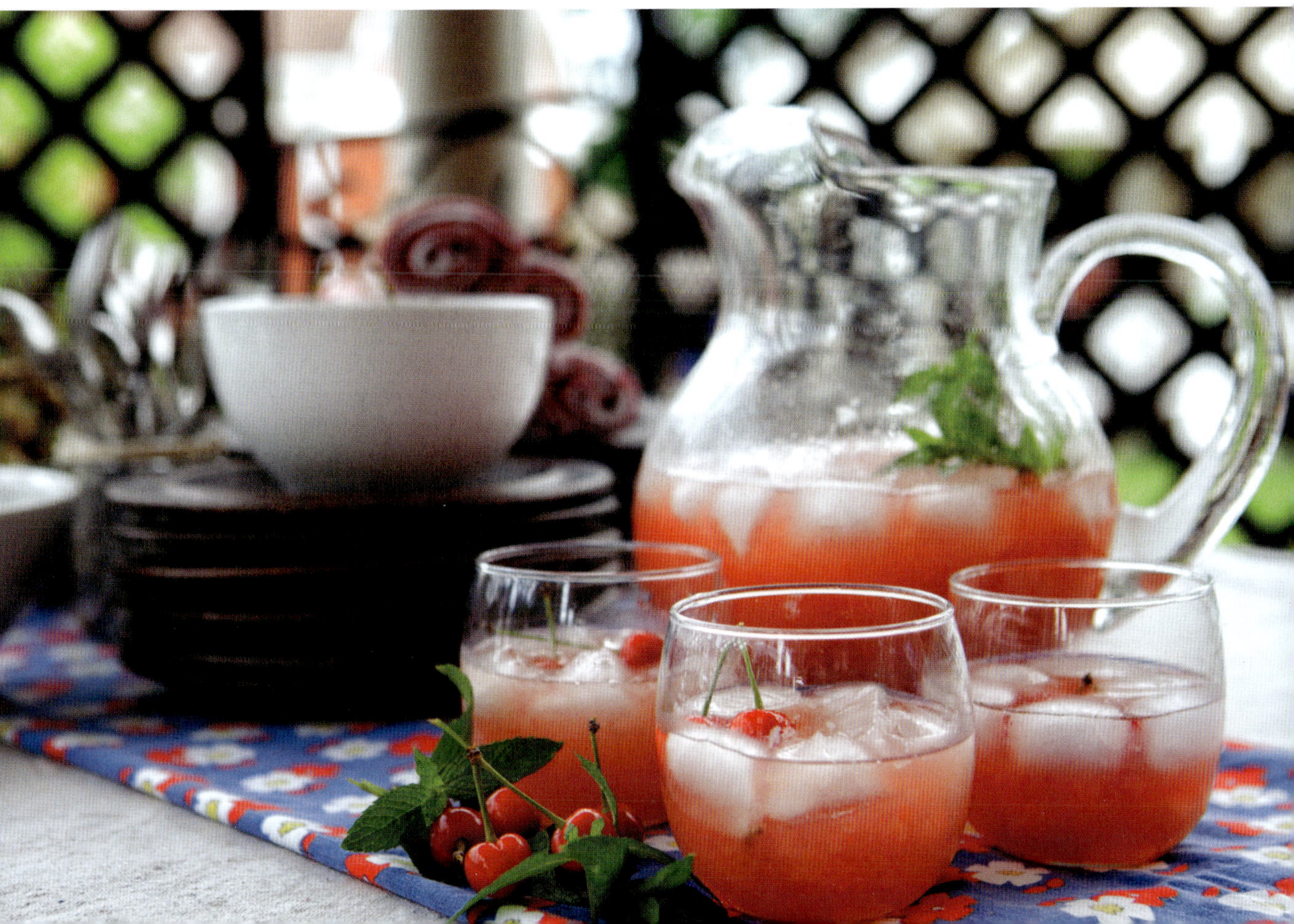

EVERYDAY MENU

Grilled or Griddled Kentucky Burgers, Main-Dish Mushrooms and Bacon-Wrapped, Cheese-Stuffed Sausages

Summer, for omnivores, means grilling hot dogs, brats and hamburgers; eating them on the porch or patio; and sharing with friends. For vegetarians—and, with care, vegans—grilled or sautéed Kentucky, shiitake or oyster mushrooms can turn cookouts into umami feasts. So we suggest always including mushrooms in the grill mix—and ideally no one takes offense at the proximity of meat to meatlessness.

Kentucky-made burgers, dogs or brats, mushrooms—these may be simple foods, but each is beloved for its rich flavors. Recipes are hardly needed for these favorite foods. A few tips may help, though.

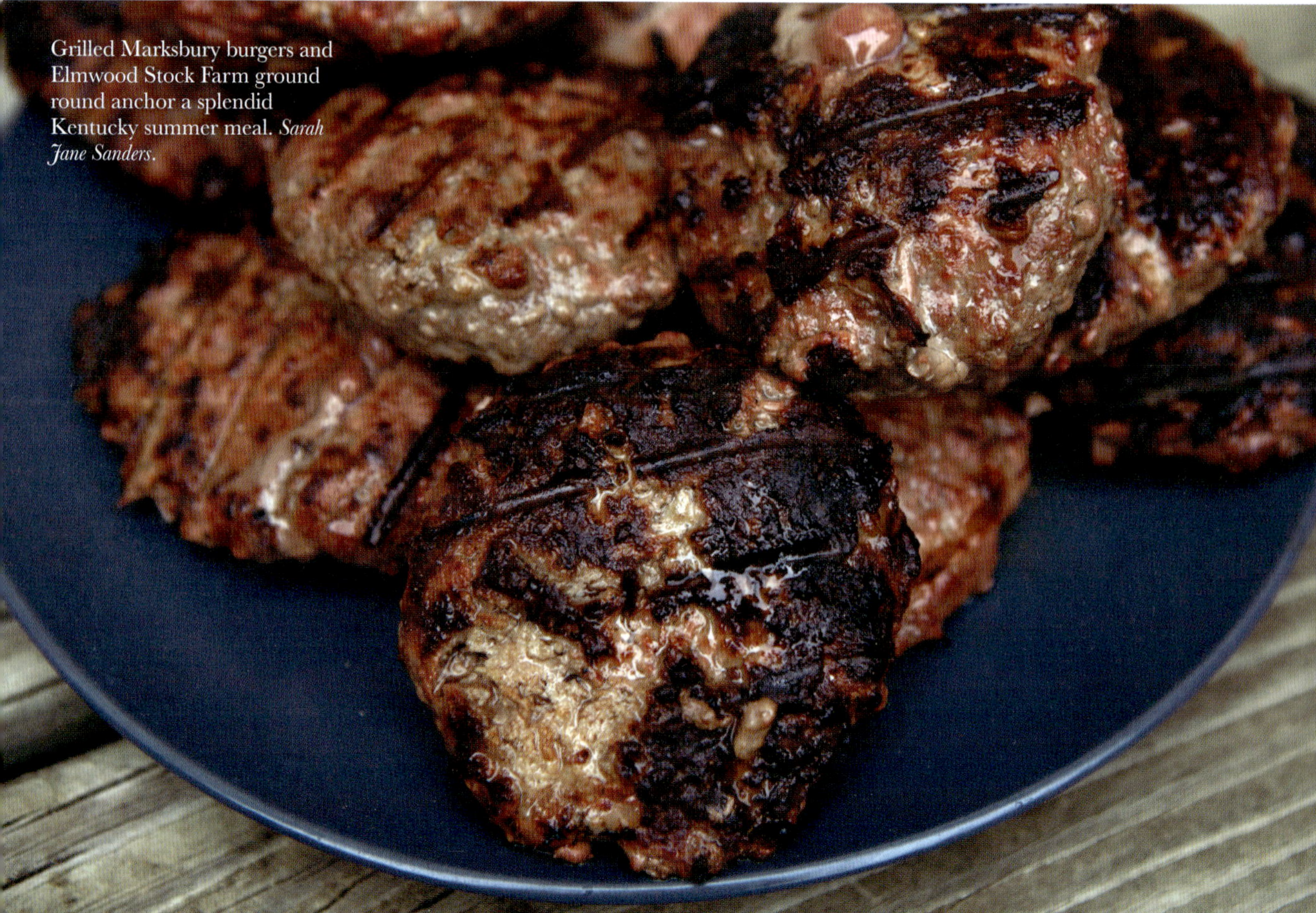

Grilled Marksbury burgers and Elmwood Stock Farm ground round anchor a splendid Kentucky summer meal. *Sarah Jane Sanders.*

Grilled or Griddled Kentucky Burgers

Grill if you like; you know how!

Think inside the house. If it's raining, or it's January or it's fifteen minutes until mealtime, haul out your iron skillet and heat it to medium high. Cook 3–4 minutes; flip, cook 3–4 more minutes for medium rare. Why skillet griddling instead of grilling? Sam Sifton of the *New York Times* checked with burger gurus and concluded, "The point is to allow rendering beef fat to gather around the patties as they cook, like a primitive high-heat confit." In other words, the burgers steep in their own goodness so all their flavor reaches the table. Skillets work well for brats, dogs and bacon-wrapped sausages, too; those cook best at medium-low heat, sloooowly.

Let us not forget cheeseburgers. Some people do not consider a cheeseless burger worth the effort of chewing. Kentucky cheese makers excel at producing richly flavored cheeses that complement the savor of Kentucky burgers. We name some cheese names and sources in "Fine Cookout Ingredients: Local Examples" on page 95. Add all the slices you like to the top of nearly done burgers. Melt. Indulge.

Local Meats Often Come Frozen

Most likely, the meats you buy locally will be frozen. Don't be put off by this. It's a side effect of the small scale of local meat production, and that small scale is your best guarantee of safe, delicious meats. With local meats, flavors will likely surprise you by their depth, even after freezing. Local farm families and local economies will benefit from your local purchases. It's worth the search and the defrosting to be part of all that goodness.

Main-Dish Mushrooms

While a few Kentucky pioneers like Blue Sky Ranch and Sheltowee Farm produce mushrooms commercially, most likely you will need to go grocery shopping for your mushrooms. Grilled or roasted portobellos slipped between buns a couple decades ago, and these days, many grocery stores offer them year-round. Brush with olive oil and grill or sauté quickly over medium heat; sprinkle with salt and pepper. Delicious.

Want to get fancy with your portobello? Warm a skillet gently and add generous olive oil, salt and pepper; add a couple cloves of diced garlic; add the juice of one lime; cook the portobello cap-side down in this brew slowly, slowly, until it sighs and relaxes flat. Turn it over, cook a few more minutes, put it in a bun or not, and savory-salty-sour-earthy flavors will reward the eater with each bite.

Bacon-Wrapped, Cheese-Stuffed Sausages

We had a lot of summer cookouts on the farm when I grew up. My favorite meals included what we called "Pigs in Blankets," though we did not mean the cocktail sausages wrapped in dough that also go by that name. Our pigs were dogs—hot dogs—and our blankets were bacon strips. We split the dogs (pigs) almost through lengthwise; stuffed them with a good, hard cheese; snuggled everything cozily into place with an all-around wrap of uncooked bacon; and then held that bacon in place, mostly, with toothpicks.

We cooked these wonders over a fire or coals, not charcoal, using sticks freshly cut from the nearby woods. The bacon cooked quickly, dripping fat that made flames spurt even more. With smoke, sizzle and a little patience, the cheese melted to liquid, and the hot dog cooked through and became a carrier for smoke and bacon flavors.

Oh, yum. Each bite included crunch, smoke, bacon, melted cheese, Mother's spicy-sweet homemade ketchup—Grandma Carolyn's Ketchup made in Georgetown works just as well—and a maximum-umami hot dog. Heaven! These days, it's local heaven.

Here's how to put together and cook an extraordinary feast of Kentucky sausages stuffed with Kentucky cheese and wrapped in Kentucky bacon blankets. (See "Fine Cookout Ingredients" on page 95 for sources for the key ingredients.)

Yield: Serves 8

8 Kentucky hotdogs, bratwurst, knockwurst or other good sausage
8 ounces good Kentucky cheese
8 slices good Kentucky bacon
16 pitted, halved Medjool dates or a slather of seedless Kentucky blackberry or black raspberry jam (optional)
16 wooden toothpicks

Split each sausage lengthwise, nearly all the way through, but not quite.

Insert slices or rectangular bars of good Kentucky cheese along the length of the sausage. Insert four date halves or a nice ribbon of jam, if using.

Fold the sausage closed. Wrap it with good Kentucky bacon. Use toothpicks to pierce through all layers and hold the bacon in place.

Cooking Options

You can cook these several ways. Here are three options.

Start these on a hot grill. Be prepared for serious flame-up. Squelch it with a lid. Quickly remove the flame-kissed sausages to a baking sheet and slide them into a 325-degree oven. Cook 30 minutes, turning every 10 minutes to brown the bacon evenly. Cook longer if needed for the cheese to be melty and the bacon to be crisped to your taste.

Cook over gentle heat in an iron skillet (or two) on the stovetop. Take your time. You may want to break or shorten the toothpicks, or remove them once the bacon is brown enough to hold its shape around the sausage. Keep cooking gently until the bacon is very brown and the cheese is very melty.

Cook over indirect heat on a grill. As long as flame-ups are no problem, continue cooking until—you guessed it—you have very brown bacon and melting, oozing, delicious warm Kentucky cheese.

Fine Cookout Ingredients: Local Examples

Here are examples of the many yummy local choices we have in Kentucky today for summer cookout foods and for burgers, cheeseburgers and bacon-wrapped, cheese-stuffed sausages in particular.

Meats

- Ground beef and hot dogs from Marksbury Farm Market in Lancaster
- Ground bison from Kentucky Bison in Goshen
- Pork hot dogs and bacon from Stone Cross Farm in Taylorsville
- Pastured organic ground round and ground beef, beef hot dogs, bratwurst, mettwurst and Italian sausage from Elmwood Stock Farm in Georgetown
- Beef bratwurst from Colcord Farm in Paris
- Bratwurst, bacon and ground pastured pork from Hood's Heritage Hogs in Mount Olivet
- Lamb sausage from Two Shakes Ranch in Springfield or Four Hills Farm in Salvisa
- Pastured organic ground turkey from Lazy Eight Stock Farm in Paint Lick
- Veal sausage from On Tapp Dairy in Springfield

Even Your Charcoal May Come from Kentucky

Chances are fair that your charcoal originated in Kentucky.

- Kingsford produces charcoal at a manufacturing site in Burnside, along with other locations.
- Cowboy Charcoal produces a variety of charcoal grilling products at facilities in Monticello and Albany.
- A new company in Lexington recently began selling "Bourbon Barrel Grillin Char," pieces of charred bourbon barrels that can be tossed onto the coals to infuse the smoke with that signature Kentucky scent.
- Louisville's Bourbon Barrel Foods sells its grill wood to home cooks.

Cheeses

- Kentucky Derby, Sassy Redhead, Wensleydale or others from Boone Creek Creamery in Lexington
- Bellemoral Plain, Smoked or with Chives from Cloverdale Creamery in Taylorsville
- Pyrenees Plain or Applewood Smoked from Good Shepherd Cheese in Owingsville
- Cheddar, Smokehouse Cheddar, Aged Cheddar, Monterey Jack or Pepper Jack from Heavenly Homestead Cheese in Windsor
- Asiago, Aged Cheddar, Chipotle Colby, Norwood, Kentucky Bleu or many others from Kenny's Farmhouse Cheeses in Austin

NOTE: Some of the items above are available at grocery stores in Kentucky and southern Indiana. Many are available at Good Foods Co-op in Lexington. Some are available online.

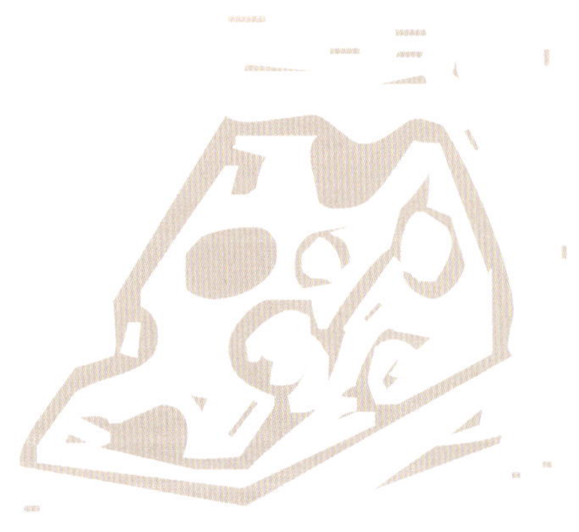

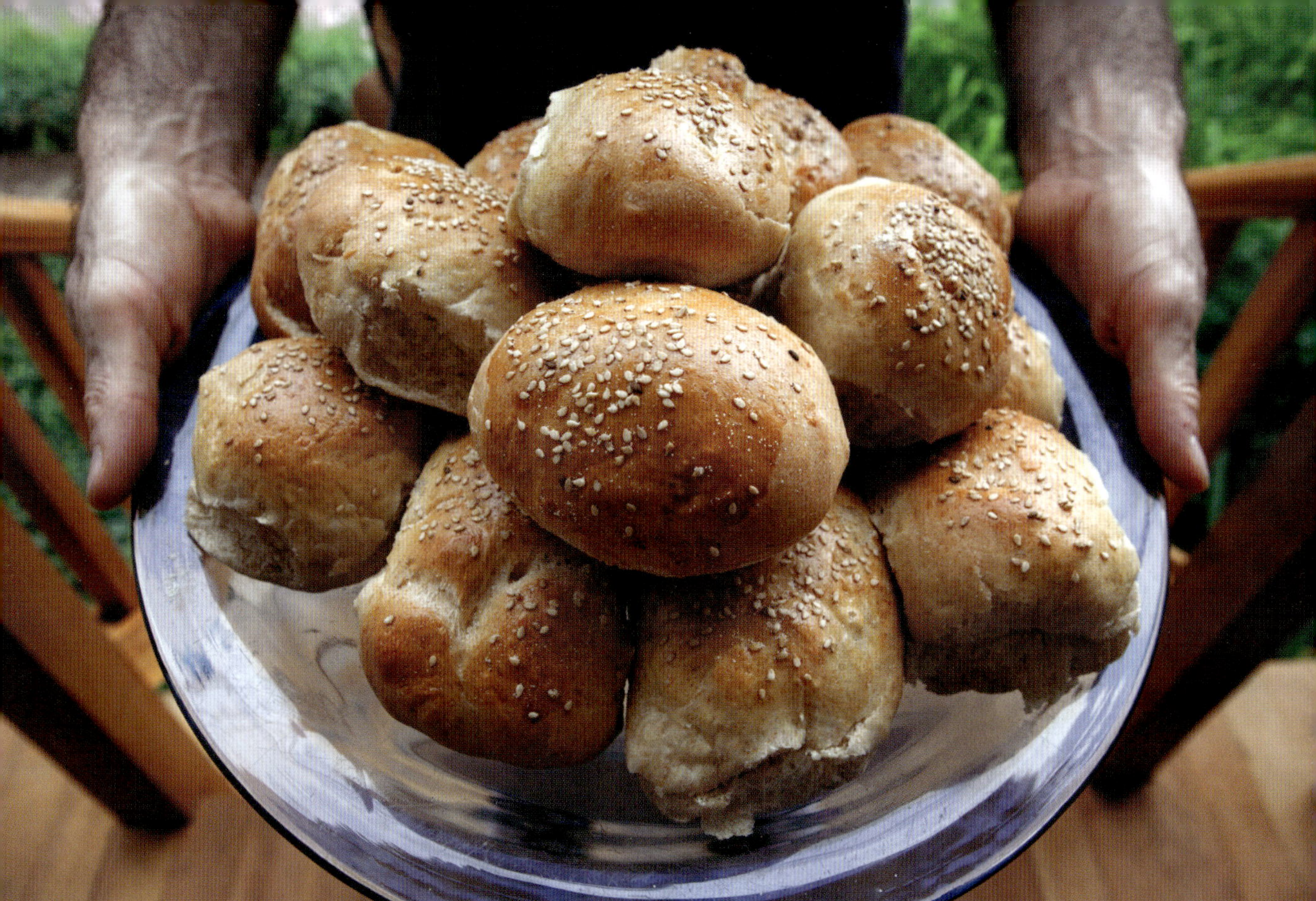

Homemade hamburger buns make every burger better. *Sarah Jane Sanders*.

Buns

For regular, weekday meals, store-bought hamburger and hot dog buns may not excite us, but they do their job. For a bit more flavor, look for these options:

- potato buns
- onion rolls
- whole wheat buns
- English muffins instead of buns (for burgers)

If you live in New England instead of Kentucky, enjoy those top-split hot dog buns. They invite and reward griddling or grilling buns for added flavor.

When you want to dress up a grilled or griddled meal by making your own buns, it's not as hard as you think, even if you need wheat-free buns. Go to http://www.savoringkentucky.com/even-more-homemade for links to bun heaven.

Dark and Bright Kale Salad

Kale? Yes, please. We've had kale in Kentucky forever and ever. Kale salad? Different story. This salad leans ever so gently toward cooking the kale before dressing it. Light cooking may help us absorb some of kale's goodness; we'll let the nutrition investigators make that determination. For cooks, though, the light sauté we give these greens helps make the salad tender and may reduce bitterness. Of the many types and nationalities of kale (curly, Russian, Siberian, etc.), the kale-of-many-names (Lacinato/black/Tuscan/dinosaur) starts out more tender and less bitter than other types and sometimes appeals to people who snub other kinds of kale. We use it for this salad when we can; other kale types also work.

Yield: Serves 8

3 large bunches (a large work bowl full) of Lacinato kale (also known as black, Tuscan and dinosaur kale) or other kale
3 tablespoons olive oil
3 cloves garlic, slivered or diced, or more to taste
½ teaspoon salt
1 lemon, juice extracted and set aside, rind removed with a fine grater and set aside
⅛ teaspoon crushed red pepper flakes
black pepper, to taste
2 tablespoons grated Kenny's Farmhouse Asiago, Heavenly Homestead Parmesan or similar richly flavored cheese
3 tablespoons finely chopped toasted pine nuts, toasted slivered almonds or toasted Kentucky black pecans, hickory nuts or walnuts (optional)

Wash the kale thoroughly (see "How to Wash and Prep Greens," page 100). If your kale is Lacinato, just trim the toughest end of each stalk a bit. Save the stems and ends for the chickens. Stack the kale and slice it into ½-inch-wide "ribbons." Aim for 10 loosely packed cups of stemmed, sliced kale leaves. It's okay if some water droplets hang on.

Heat the olive oil over medium heat. When you can smell it, add the garlic; stir quickly and immediately. Cook 30 seconds or so.

Add the kale ribbons and salt to the skillet. Stir and cook for 2 minutes, until the kale visibly relaxes and turns brighter green.

Remove the kale and garlic from heat and lift with tongs into a medium-sized bowl. Add the lemon juice, red pepper flakes and black pepper. Toss until thoroughly combined. Taste; add salt if needed.

Top with lemon zest, cheese and chopped nuts, if you are using them. Serve warm or at room temperature. The kale is greenest if served immediately.

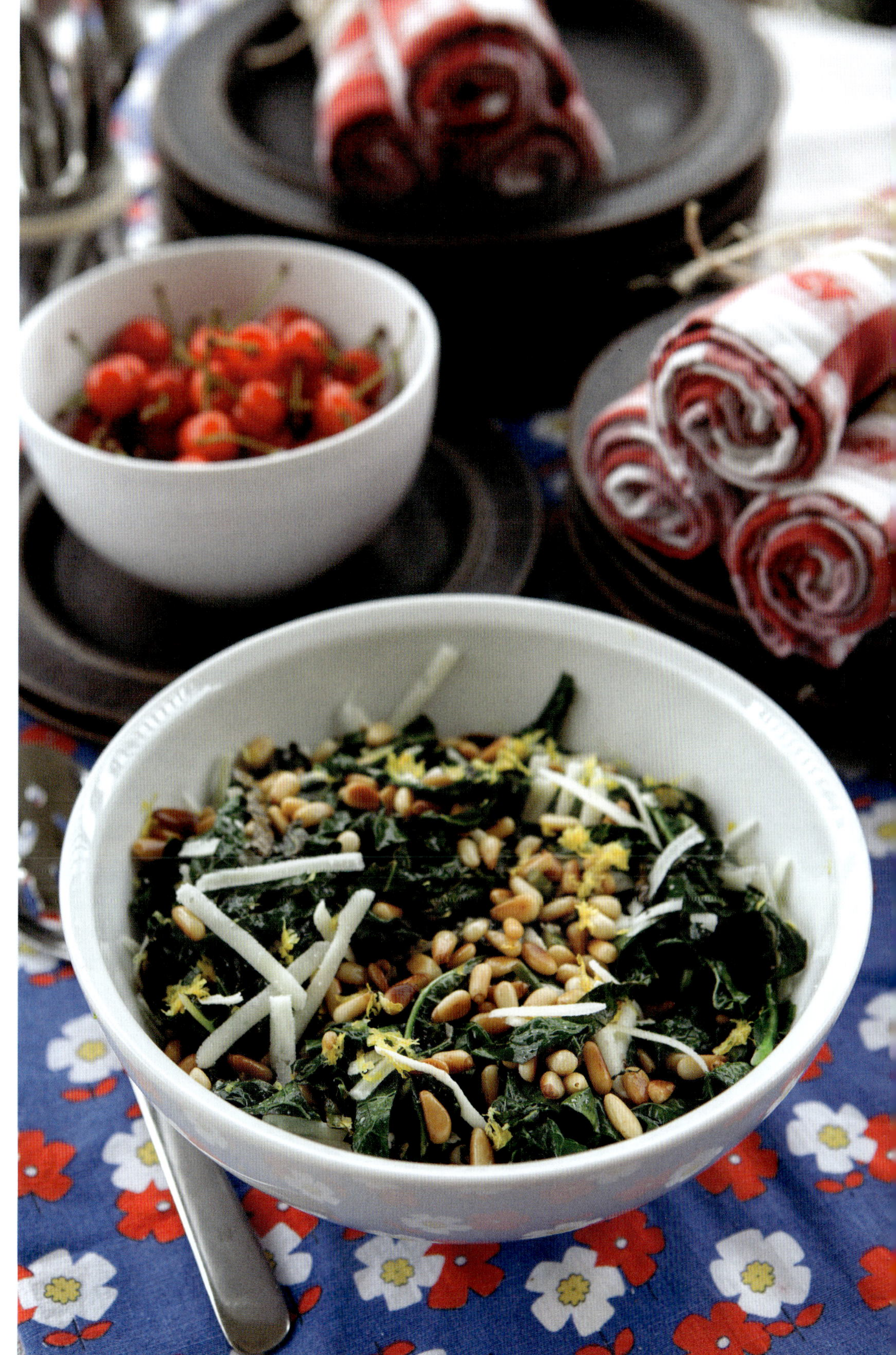

The Dark and Bright Kale Salad makes great nutrition available with excellent taste and crunch. *Sarah Jane Sanders*.

Lemons Like It Quick

Grated lemon zest—one of a cook's best flavor boosters—steadily loses its punch after grating. Lemon juice, similarly, becomes less potent if squeezed well ahead of cooking time. Lemons' most intense flavors come from grating and squeezing just before use.

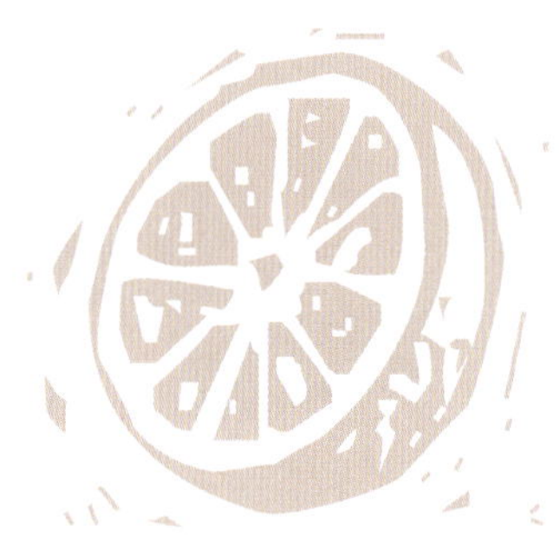

How to Wash and Prep Greens

Yes, it takes time, water and patience to clean greens. Yes, a little handwork in the service of fantastic food can calm, soothe and even redeem your day. Put on an apron, put on some Les McCann to make you both mellow and energetic and get to it. Fill your largest bowl, clean dishpan or cleaned sink with water. Add the greens, swish and let them hang out in the water a few minutes while grit settles to the bottom of the bowl. Lift the greens out onto a clean sink sideboard or into another clean large bowl. Drain the water, rinse away the grit that settled out, and repeat this soak/swish/settle process until no grit whatsoever is left. It sometimes takes as many as eight "waters" before the dishpan of water is completely clean when you lift the greens out.

If the greens have thick, tough ribs, fold each leaf in half, hold by the leaf edge and strip out the rib, or cut it out with a sharp knife. For some preparations you will need to use a salad spinner or towels to make the greens as dry as possible.

Really Amazing Baked Beans

I grew up with great food at home, where my family ate nearly all our meals and grew most of what reached our table. On special occasions after Sunday school and church service, we enjoyed a midday meal at the Elk Spring Valley Baptist Church. Mother often took from-scratch baked beans, nearly black on top from long hours in a slow oven and the home-cured bacon on top. Those lovingly prepared and shared community feasts expanded my understanding of the goodness of homegrown, home-cooked food.

In The Kentucky Barbecue Book, *Wes Berry names the main baked bean crime: "Too many places dump pork and beans out of a can and heat them up." Don't do that. Do this.*

Yield: Serves 8–10

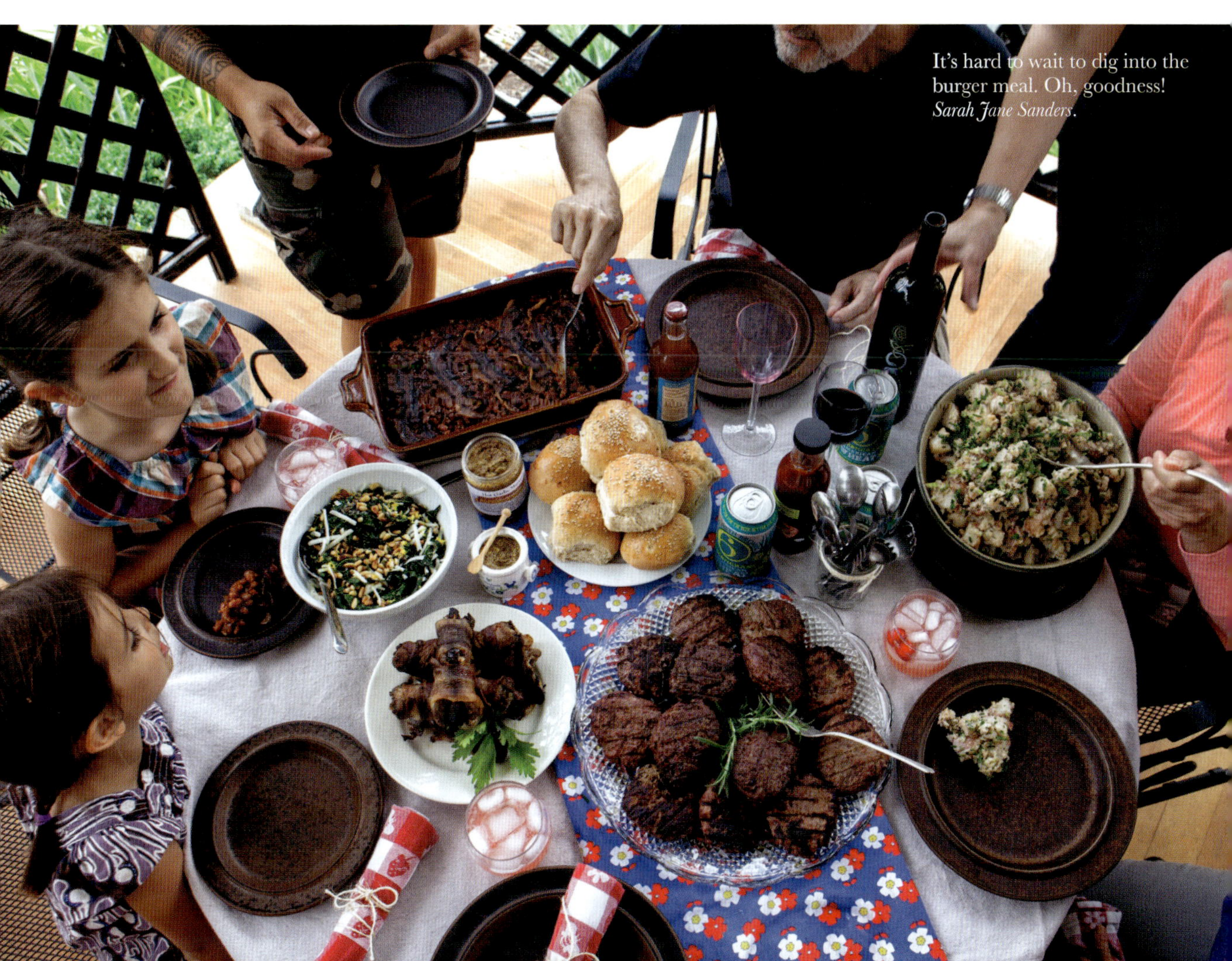

It's hard to wait to dig into the burger meal. Oh, goodness! *Sarah Jane Sanders.*

4½ cups cooked navy or white beans (see "About Cooking Navy Beans from Scratch," page 103), or 3 15-ounce cans
1 cup diced onion
1 large sweet or green pepper, diced
1½ cups ketchup (Grandma Carolyn's Ketchup contributes extra flavor layers)
¼ cup coarse-grain mustard (homemade Basic Country [see page 106] or Sunflower Sundries' Hot Garlic adds good taste)
⅔ cup Kentucky sorghum
⅓ cup firmly packed brown sugar
3 tablespoons white or raw sugar
½ teaspoon ground cinnamon
½ teaspoon ground cumin
1 tablespoon or more Kentucky hot sauce, such as Screamin' Mimi's, or 1 scant teaspoon Sav's Piment
1 teaspoon black pepper
1½ teaspoons salt
8 thick slices Kentucky bacon, such as Hood's Heritage Hogs jowl bacon or Stone Cross Farm bacon

Note: Vegetarians and vegans, leave the bacon off, and these beans will not offend.

Preheat oven to 325 degrees Fahrenheit.

In a large bowl, mix together all ingredients except bacon. Put bean mixture in a heavy, ovenproof casserole dish or glass baking dish.

Lay uncooked bacon strips across the surface, touching or overlapping as needed. Cover as much surface as possible.

Bake beans uncovered and undisturbed for at least 2½ hours or up to 4 hours—as long as needed to get a glossy, nearly black surface on the well-cooked beans.

Cooking notes: Let's try for excellence. The goal here is perfectly soft, perfectly integrated flavors, with beans just barely still intact, and no other chewy bits except the beautiful bacon. All that and the beans should be moist, with a bit of glisten showing where the bacon doesn't cover the surface, and with just a hint of sauce in the spaces among them. Test during cooking: fish one bean out (select from different parts of the baking dish when testing), cool it a bit and then check its texture and flavor.

Yes, you can overcook these beans. They can become too dry. Cooking time and texture will vary some depending on the type of ketchup you use and how juicy the initial unbaked mixture is. If everything is looking too dry around the edges before the bacon turns dark brown, sprinkle the surface with ¼ cup water. Repeat if needed.

About Cooking Navy Beans from Scratch

The first five steps below work also for preparing the beans for Perfect Smoky Pinto Beans (page 156) for cooking from scratch.

For Really Amazing Baked Beans, start with 2 cups—about 1 pound—dry navy beans.

- Spread the beans on a baking sheet. Remove any stones, badly off-color beans or other debris.
- Pour the dry beans into a colander and rinse thoroughly with plain water.
- In a very large bowl or pot, make a brine by stirring together 1 gallon of water (16 cups) and 3 tablespoons salt until the salt dissolves.
- Soak overnight or up to 24 hours. (The brining, with its positive effect on dry beans, comes from *Cook's Illustrated*'s experiments.)
- Drain the brine away. Rinse the beans thoroughly; drain again.
- Put the beans in the cooking pot, completely cover with cool water and add 1 cup more water for a slow cooker or 2 cups more water for stovetop cooking. Add ½ teaspoon baking soda. Stir well.
- Bring to a boil and then reduce heat to a low bubble. Set a cover on the pan slightly ajar to keep foam from boiling over.
- Cook until tender but not mushy. The time required varies by bean age and type, soaking length and type of cooker. Begin testing at 45 minutes by spooning a bean out and checking its texture. Cooking the beans properly can take as long as 6 hours in the slow cooker or 3 hours on the stovetop.
- Stop cooking when the beans are creamy inside, and not yet breaking apart.
- Drain extra liquid by pouring through a colander into a bowl. That liquid can be used for soups, for a quick warm drink or for pet food.
- Extra beans freeze well for later use.

On the other hand, if you need to speed things along, cover the baking dish with foil for the first 90 minutes of cooking. You may need to turn the oven up to 350 or even—gasp—375 degrees for the last half hour of cooking.

Fresh Kentucky Potato Salad

My mother remains my all-time favorite cook. She made whatever was available taste as good as it possibly could. Mother felt the same about her own mother. I have to confess, though, that Mother made two foods that I dreaded as a child, both for the same reason. Her potato salad and meat loaf both contained large pieces of onion, a vegetable with a bite that scared me. To be fair, I never liked anyone else's potato salad, either: too mustardy, too gooey, too pickly, too mealy—always too something or not enough something else.

And then one day, after I had spent perhaps thirty years refusing to acknowledge that potato salad had any reason to exist, I bumped into a Craig Claiborne recipe for a French-style potato salad dressed with something close to a vinaigrette. No mayonnaise in sight. And so began my personal Potato Salad Redemption project. I no longer have that original recipe, but I remember and follow faithfully two of its premises: use small, waxy "new" potatoes, and—unimaginable until I tried it—sprinkle the just-cooked, just-sliced warm potatoes with dry white wine before adding other ingredients and the dressing.

Yield: Serves 8

4 pounds, give or take, waxy potatoes, peeled or not—your choice
2 teaspoons salt, divided
½ cup dry white wine
1 small yellow or white sweet or regular onion, cut into chunks
2 tablespoons coarse-grain or sweet mustard
2 teaspoons light Kentucky sorghum, honey or maple syrup (omit if you use sweet mustard)
2 tablespoons light-colored vinegar (options include distilled white, white balsamic and rice vinegar)
black pepper to taste (crushed red pepper is good in small amounts, too)
½ cup olive oil
1 cup toasted, chopped walnuts (optional, but some crunch is vital)
1 cup finely chopped celery (optional)
¼ cup coarsely chopped parsley
¼ cup finely chopped green onion tops or chives
1 tablespoon each other tender fresh herbs in your garden (chervil, marjoram, dill or tarragon, for example)

Scrub potatoes if leaving skins on; cover with cool water and add about another inch. Add 1 teaspoon salt. Cook over medium heat until just tender.

Drain. Let cool for a few minutes. Chop the potatoes coarsely while they are warm. Put them in a large work bowl and sprinkle immediately with wine. Set the slightly tipsy potatoes aside while you make the dressing.

Put the dressing ingredients in a blender: onion chunks, mustard, sweetener of choice (only if your mustard is not sweet), vinegar, remaining teaspoon salt and pepper. Pulse five or six times to soften and combine. Set the blender to medium speed, and run for one minute. Continue running at medium speed as you drizzle olive oil slowly through whatever little opening your blender offers in its lid. Once all the olive oil is added, turn the blender up to medium high for one minute to make a smooth, moderately thick dressing.

Add the toasted walnuts and celery to the salad, if using. Toss well.

Pour about half the dressing over the potatoes. Stir or lightly toss to coat each potato lightly. Taste and adjust seasonings. Add more dressing as needed to dress each potato piece lightly.

Add the herb seasonings of your choice. Refrigerate leftover dressing for up to a week. It makes a fine sandwich spread.

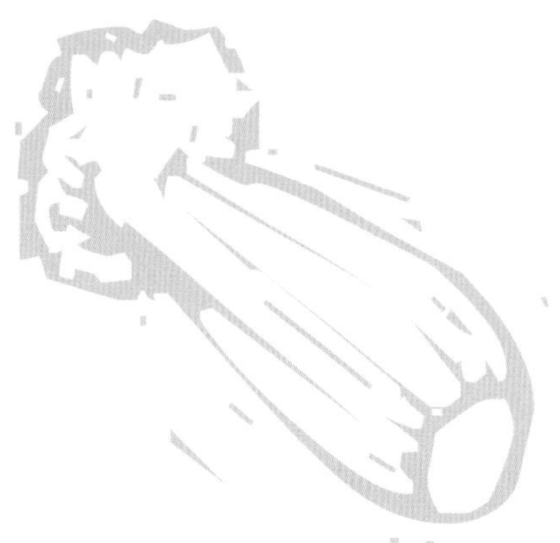

DRESSED-UP MENU

Basic Country Mustard

A Homemade Condiment from Hunter Angler Gardener Cook

If you find mustard fascinating, as I do, read the entire "How to Make Mustard" post online at Hunter Angler Gardener Cook. Hank Shaw, host of that blog, generously gave permission to reprint here his excellent Basic Country Mustard recipe from that post.

Allow two days or more for homemade mustard to mellow from fiery to fabulous. Mustard is the easiest condiment you will ever make at home.

If even "it's so easy" does not make you want to try making your own mustard, buy any of the fine Sunflower Sundries mustards, made in Mount Olivet, Kentucky, and available widely in Kentucky as well as online. You will still be awarded several local-ish virtue points.

Yield: About 1 cup
Prep Time: 12 hours

6 tablespoons mustard seeds
2 teaspoons salt
½ cup mustard powder
3 tablespoons vinegar (cider, white wine or sherry)
½ cup white wine or water

Optional
2 tablespoons honey [Kentucky sorghum or maple syrup work well, too]
2 tablespoons grated fresh horseradish
¼ cup minced fresh herbs (really any kind)

Grind the whole mustard seeds for a few seconds in a spice or coffee grinder or by hand with a mortar and pestle. You want them mostly whole because you are using mustard powder, too.

Pour the semi-ground seeds into a bowl and add the salt and mustard powder. If using, add one of the optional ingredients, too.

Pour in the vinegar and wine or water, then stir well. When everything is incorporated, pour into a glass jar and store in the fridge. Wait at least 12 hours before using. Mustard made this way will last several months in the fridge.

Note: Another favorite Kentucky condiment, ketchup, shines when made from scratch. Visit http://www.savoringkentucky.com/even-more-homemade for links to ketchup wizardry.

One more note: Hot Sweet Sorghum Pepper Relish (page 172) will please some Kentuckians—maybe you—on either a burger or a dog (or by itself on a spoon.)

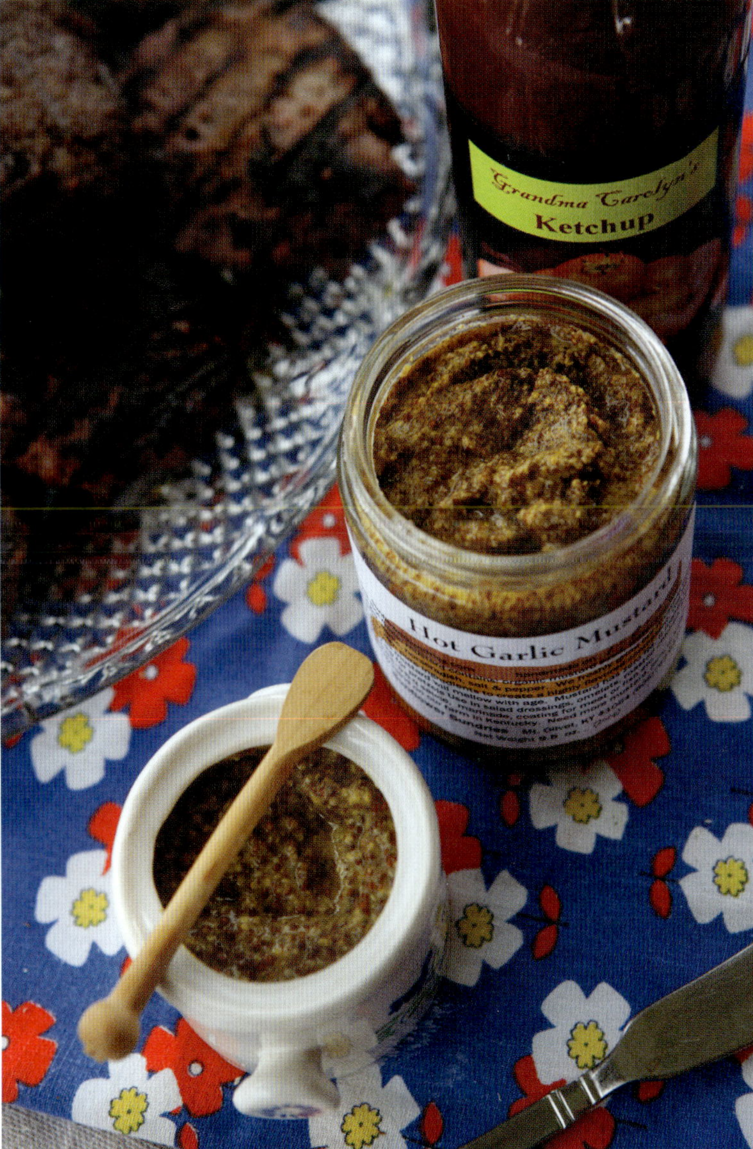

This is Kentucky condiment heaven: homemade Basic Country Mustard in front: Sunflower Sundries' great Hot Garlic Mustard in the middle; and excellent Grandma Carolyn's Ketchup from Georgetown in the rear. *Sarah Jane Sanders.*

Aunt Bea's Homemade Immediate Pickles

Aunt Bea moved to Wayne County from light-years-away Ashland, Kentucky, when I was eight or so. Thank goodness! She changed my life and the lives of many others, using those two timeless powers: love and food.

She grew a big garden and milked a Jersey cow that preceded her at her husband's beautiful farm. Her education as a home economics teacher showed in her neat kitchen—she always washed up dishes as she cooked, and urged me to do the same. She made picture-perfect loaves of graham bread and, my favorite, a vanilla "cream" pie baked in a graham cracker crust.

Her refrigerator stayed neat, too. No scary jars of red-brown-who-knows-what tucked in the back corners. Instead, in summer, the refrigerator held crunchy slaw, milk, buttermilk and butter in abundance. Thinly sliced cucumbers usually rested in salt water, awaiting the next meal.

I loved the fresh farm-and-garden smell of that refrigerator and have made versions of her cucumbers, as I remember them, ever since. Eventually, I realized Aunt Bea's cucumbers are a type of extremely quick pickle, made perhaps an hour or two before midday dinner. I never asked for a recipe, and so what follows is one of many versions of "Immediate Pickles" I make every summer, always relishing the love, freedom, good food and good scents that Aunt Bea brought into my life. Instead of refrigerating, I use ice cubes for crispness and chill.

These pickles taste amazing on their own and add crunch and flavor to dressed-up burgers and dogs as well. The basic recipe is simple and quick, with nearly endless variations available.

Yield: 4–8, depending on the pickles' use as a relish on top of burgers, mushrooms or dogs or as a salad

7–8 (about 4 pounds) mid-sized garden cucumbers or three seedless English cucumbers
1 tablespoon salt
about 3 cups ice cubes
1–2 tablespoons white, cider or rice vinegar
(more) salt and black pepper to taste

Prepare the cucumbers to be pickles. Use a vegetable peeler to remove about half their skin in long strips. Cut the cucumbers in half the long way. Scoop any seeds and their jellied surroundings out with a spoon. (Chickens love that goop, by the way, but if the seeds are still young and tender, eat them yourself. They're good for you but not good for pickles.)

Slice the cucumbers thinly in half moons. Put them in a colander and place in the sink. Sprinkle with about 1 tablespoon salt and toss lightly to distribute. Wait about 20 minutes and then give the now wetter cucumbers several good squeezes.

This helps remove some bitter flavors. Now top the cukes with ice cubes and leave them while you finish cooking the meal.

Just before serving, remove the remaining ice, squeeze gently to release a bit more water and put the cucumbers in a serving bowl. Add the vinegar. Stir the cucumbers well, and taste. You may need to add salt and more vinegar. You may want to add gratings of black pepper.

Vary these basic Immediate Pickles easily and often as summer progresses.

Know Your Cukes

Cucumbers have personalities. At least the good homegrown and locally grown ones do. Heritage cucumbers like lemon, 'White Wonder' and Armenia types feature natural sweetness and tender, crisp crunch. Conventional cucumbers tend to be crunchier and more appealing when they are small and too young to have formed seeds. Choose young, tender cucumbers when you can.

Options

Just before serving, add any of these:
fresh or dried dill weed (go easy—about ¼ teaspoon will add interest without overwhelming the quiet, cooling cucumber flavors)
1 tablespoon finely chopped onion greens or chives
¼ teaspoon toasted sesame oil
1 teaspoon fresh herbs from your herb garden, such as parsley, tarragon, mint, thyme, marjoram, basil, lovage, salad burnet
2 tablespoons thick sour cream.

Leftovers keep for four days. As cucumbers age in salt and vinegar, they become more translucent and less crisp.

Buttermilk-Maple Ice Cream

Growing up, homemade ice cream happened on Sundays a few times each summer and required planning well ahead. On Saturday, Mother made a custard of eggs, milk and cream from the farm, plus sugar and vanilla extract. I had a hard time staying away from that custard as it waited in the refrigerator for its big chill the next day.

On ice cream Sundays, we turned the wrong direction after church, away from home and toward Monticello, where we bought a giant block of ice from Beaver Industries. Strong guys ran it through a crusher and captured it in a burlap sack, which got nicely wet and melty in the back of the '49 Ford pickup.

You may guess the rest of the story: the men, mostly, fed ice and special chunky salt into the space between the ice cream churn's tall metal canister and the wooden bucket. Crank, talk, crank, talk, let the kids try a little, crank some more, talk as the crank gets hard to turn and then, joy: ivory-colored ice cream from the pale yellow custard, sometimes dolled up with fresh strawberries or fresh peaches—cool, sweet perfection.

Fast-forward to the time when miniature versions of those cranked machines worked with ice cubes, table salt and electricity. We burned through two of those before our now grown children bought us both a frozen cylinder-style machine and, most recently, a small gelato maker that does its own freezing.

With good, easy machines in hand, we have learned something remarkable: custard is the hard way to make excellent ice cream. Using lovely Kentucky cream and buttermilk, we now make ice cream that's easy to stir together and hard to beat.

Cuisinart includes a small recipe book with its ice cream makers. Our first married children surprised us one night by using the ice cream maker they had received as a wedding gift to make no-cook mint chocolate chip ice cream. It took about three minutes of measuring and stirring, plus twenty for the freezing while we ate our meal, and there it was: perfectly delicious.

Here's a fresh, slightly sophisticated ice cream that gets its tang from a little buttermilk and some of its sweetness from Kentucky maple syrup. Inspired by Cuisinart's Simple Vanilla ice cream, this stirs together in minutes and delights eaters about twenty-five minutes later. It is best served immediately but is still delicious after freezing.

Yield: Serves 8–10

1 cup buttermilk
⅔ cup sugar (raw or organic tastes especially good but any sugar will do)
⅓ cup Kentucky maple syrup
¼ teaspoon salt
3½ cups heavy cream
2 tablespoons pure vanilla extract

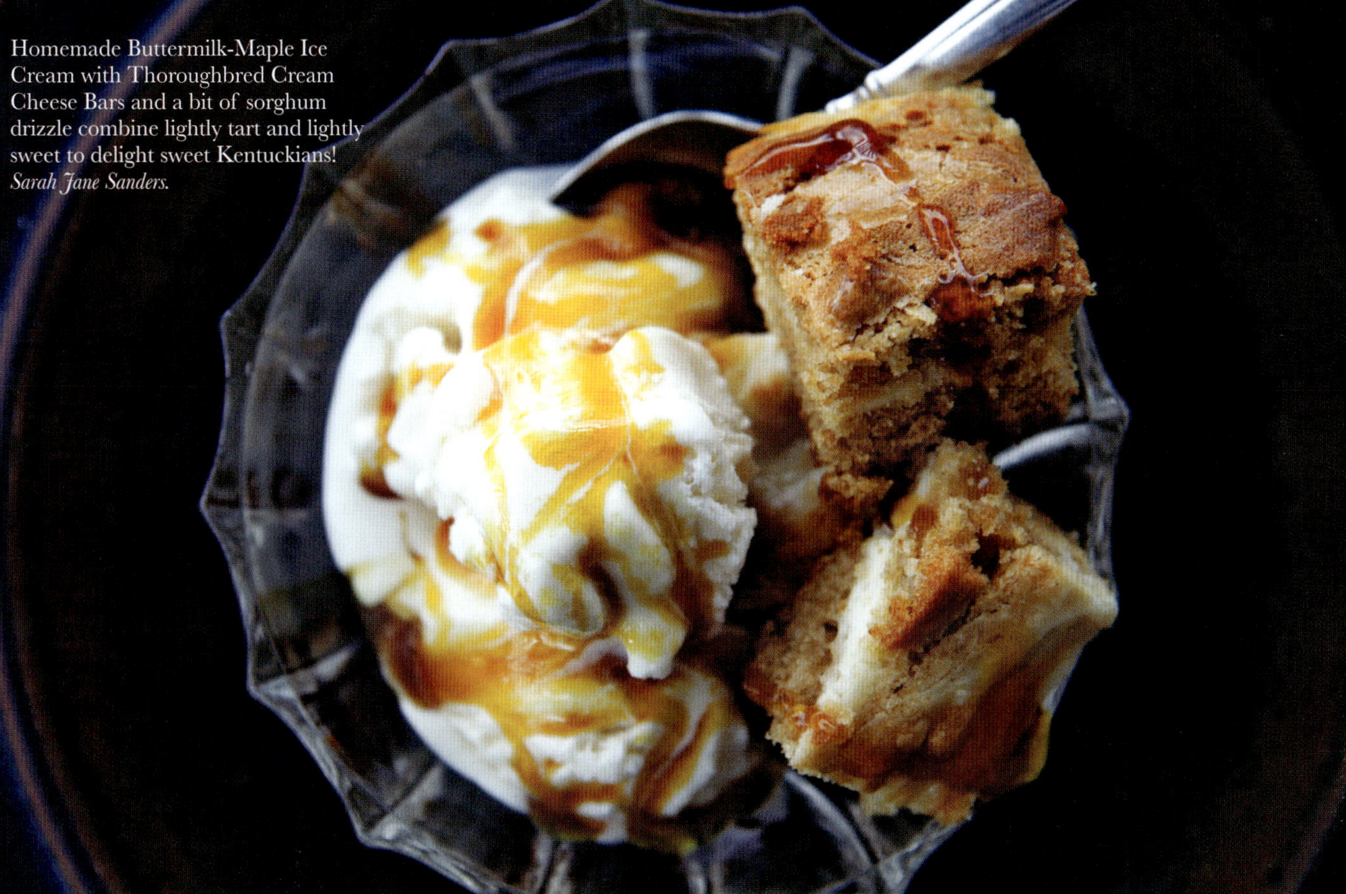

Homemade Buttermilk-Maple Ice Cream with Thoroughbred Cream Cheese Bars and a bit of sorghum drizzle combine lightly tart and lightly sweet to delight sweet Kentuckians! *Sarah Jane Sanders.*

Mix the buttermilk, sugar, maple syrup and salt together in a bowl or measuring cup that holds at least 6 cups liquid. When thoroughly mixed, add the cream and vanilla. Stir well. Follow the instructions that came with your ice cream maker.

Options

Use sorghum instead of maple syrup; add ½ teaspoon each ground allspice and cinnamon.

Add ¼ teaspoon almond extract.

Add fruit syrups or flavors—plan ahead. Make fruit syrups by cooking ¾ cup fresh fruit with ¾ cup sugar; then blend several minutes in a blender and strain through a fine mesh strainer. Chill thoroughly in the refrigerator before adding to the ice cream after it is nearly done, at about the 20-minute point in many countertop freezers.

No Ice Cream Maker? Here Are Good Options for Making Ice Cream Anyway

Make Brad Spence's Salted Butter Semi-Freddo (scrumptious.) Know the name of your egg farmer for this one, or use your own perfect eggs. (Recipe at http://food52.com/blog/7591-brad-spence-s-salted-butter-semifreddo.)

The online blog The Kitchn offers six ways to make ice cream with no machine. (They aren't as easy, but still...) http://www.thekitchn.com/how-to-make-ice-cream-without-an-ice-cream-machine-171060.

Thoroughbred Cream Cheese Bars

These beautiful caramel and ivory bars came from a longing to develop a sorghum bar cookie as delicious and perfect as the beloved hand-rolled cookies called Molasses Crinkles or Sorghum Crinkles. This recipe owes debts of gratitude to Sorghum Treasures *and* Sorghum Treasures II, *publications of the National Sweet Sorghum Producers and Processors Association, which inspired experimenting, and to* Cook's Illustrated, *which applied some of its focused research power to figuring out cheesecake swirl techniques that shine in this cookie.*

Yield: At least 48 individual squares

Cream Cheese Swirl
8 ounces cream cheese, softened (see note below)
1 cup sour cream
4 tablespoons sugar or Kentucky sorghum
¼ teaspoon salt
½ teaspoon vanilla extract
3 tablespoons all-purpose flour or gluten-free all-purpose baking mix

Sorghum-Peanut Batter
1½ cups all-purpose flour or gluten-free all-purpose baking mix
½ teaspoon baking soda
½ teaspoon baking powder
½ teaspoon salt
½ cup butter
½ cup brown sugar
½ cup Kentucky sorghum
⅓ cup peanut butter (any kind)
1 egg
1 teaspoon vanilla extract

Note: If cream cheese is cold, cut it into several pieces and microwave it in ten-second bursts until soft but not hot.

Preheat the oven to 350 degrees Fahrenheit. Make a foil sling to use in lifting the cookies out after baking. Place one piece of foil across a 9- by 13-inch pan; press it into the pan and leave several inches of overhang on each side. On top of that piece of foil, line the entire baking pan with heavy-duty foil, leaving some length on the ends, again to use as handles. Spray foil and any exposed pan surfaces with nonstick baking spray or butter and flour all the surfaces thoroughly.

In a large bowl, mix all the ingredients for the cream cheese swirl until just thoroughly blended. Set the swirl aside.

In a second bowl, mix together the flour, baking soda, baking powder and salt. Set aside.

In the bowl of a stand mixer or other work bowl, mix together the butter, brown sugar, sorghum, peanut butter, egg and vanilla extract; mix on medium-high for four minutes or beat well by hand until fluffy and light.

Add the flour mixture and stir lightly, by hand, or gently pulse in the mixer, until just blended.

Pour two-thirds of the tan cookie batter into the baking pan, and smooth gently toward the edges. This layer will seem small and will be thin when spread out, but will rise during baking.

Pour or dollop the cream cheese mixture over the tan cookie batter; spread it gently to within an inch of the pan's edge.

Dollop the rest of the cookie batter over the cream cheese mixture. It will not cover completely.

Use a table knife to make a few swirls in the top two layers to integrate the top cookie batter into the cream cheese more beautifully.

Bake for 15 minutes; rotate the pan, and bake 15 to 20 more minutes. In the center of the pan, the bars should be set. A toothpick inserted in the darker batter should come out nearly clean. An internal temperature of 180–182 degrees is another good guide to indicate doneness.

Put the pan on a wire rack to cool. Let the bars rest in the pan for an hour, and then use the foil handles to lift the bars onto a wire rack to cool for an additional hour—if you can stand the wait—before cutting carefully into small pieces.

Marksbury Farm Market, Lancaster (Garrard County), Kentucky

Pasture—grasses and plants for animals to eat—matters so much to the Marksbury Farm enterprises that blades of grass constitute the company logo. Preston Correll, who joined with three partners in 2010 to launch Marksbury Farm, a twelve-thousand-square-foot meat-processing facility with an affiliated butcher shop and farm store, said "Kentucky has some compelling advantages as an agricultural center, including the volume and quality of our pasture, and more importantly, the intellectual capital represented in the relatively large number of landowning, medium-scale farmers."

Pasture, an ancient agricultural component, presents a new frontier for Kentucky's thoughtful growers, chefs and eaters. Many farmers and advocates now assert that pastured foods like meats, eggs and milk in its many forms contribute to human health in crucial ways, including increased digestibility, reduced food sensitivities and improved nutrition. Pasture, with careful human management, builds soil vitality while also feeding farm animals. Human beings cannot digest grass directly—and who would want to? Yet we benefit, and the soil benefits, when animals eat grass and convert it into some of the best-tasting, nutrient dense, edible foods on the planet.

Preston underscores that Marksbury Farm's founders envisioned their company making positive impacts on the long-term well-being of Kentucky's land, people and economy. Marksbury's commitments include supporting producers in making decisions that take into account broad impacts. As Preston said, the company's concern is "not just, 'What is the best economic move here?' but 'How does this action affect my community, whose nourishment is my responsibility? How does it affect the health of my land? The stewardship of the organisms I own?'"

Marksbury Farm is changing how Kentuckians eat and farm. Farmers in the region benefit from being able to process their carefully raised animals near their farms in a state-of-the-art facility run according to principles of humane treatment for animals and ethical approaches to both farming and business. Marksbury's allegiance to family farms and family farmers and its central reliance on pastured animals stem from a commitment to a positive, permanency-oriented agriculture, one that makes it possible for Kentucky's families, communities, land and water to produce food for Kentuckians into the far future.

Home cooks, restaurants, independent grocers and institutions embrace Marksbury products because of their quality and the health benefits that come from eating pastured animals raised with no antibiotics, steroids or artificial growth hormones. Restaurants count on customers seeing Marksbury products on the menu and understanding quickly that the restaurant supports local growers and embraces Kentucky ingredients.

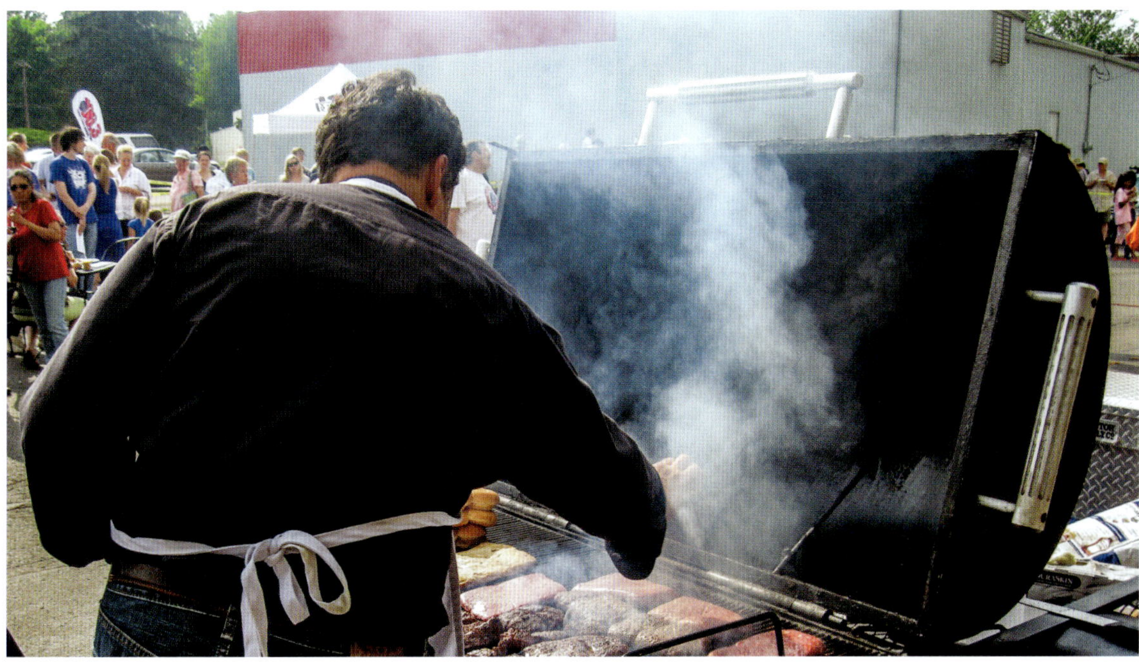

John-Mark Hack, partner and co-founder of Marksbury Farm Market, grills Marksbury burgers for a Good Food Co-op tasting event in Lexington. *Rona Roberts.*

Marksbury founders take pride in contributing to a new agricultural context, one in which smart, skilled medium-scale farms—sometimes called "ag of the middle"—can flourish. Marksbury co-founder and partner John-Mark Hack said the company's processing and marketing mean that "farmers don't have to be commodity producers. They can be food producers."

John-Mark offers the example of Todd Clark, a first-generation Fayette County farmer. Todd combines conventional production of tobacco with pasture-based farming of chicken, turkey, lamb, eggs and beef raised on nearly six hundred grassy acres. The animals, processed at Marksbury, sell widely throughout central Kentucky. John-Mark calls Todd "the prototype of the kind of American farmer we need if we're going to increase the market share of local food—producers who bring a highly developed skill set for land, labor and equipment management. People who know how to farm. That's what we need in the local food movement to expand it."

As owners of a young business, Marksbury Farm's leaders have built relationships with their growers, found customers for their custom-processing business and established new retail and wholesale markets for locally grown meats, all of which require skill, persistence and the patience to show up at hundreds of sampling venues to introduce locally processed meats to Kentuckians. Succeeding for the long term in an industry designed and dominated by industrial food manufacturers presents a particular structural challenge for Marksbury and similar small businesses working to bring the products of small and mid-sized farms to local plates: they must operate within a set of regulations designed to protect consumers from the dangers of meat production on a massive scale, even though many of those dangers derive from ways of operating that Marksbury intentionally avoids. John-Mark pointed out that Marksbury, which processes animals by the dozens or hundreds, must buy and pay steadily for the infrastructure, equipment, products, inspections, time and record keeping the federal government requires of plants that process animals by the hundreds of thousands. It is clear that these fixed costs raise the costs of locally grown meat; it is less clear to Marksbury's founders that the required investment increases food safety in their small operation.

John-Mark brings a wealth of agricultural policy and advocacy experience to his leadership role and to his work as founder of the Local Food Association, a new national trade group dedicated to "growing the business of local food." He said it has been most satisfying to demonstrate to regional farmers that "it's realistic for them to think about having their food grown sustainably, especially livestock."

The more we learn about soil, the more we realize its complexity and the incalculable variety of organisms in each cubic inch. We begin to understand that billions of relationships yield soil health and that soil health yields nutrients and flavor. We also recognize that diversity offers strength, a principle the four founders of Marksbury themselves embody. The four friends—two of whom are also cousins—bring to the Marksbury business their varied backgrounds in farming,

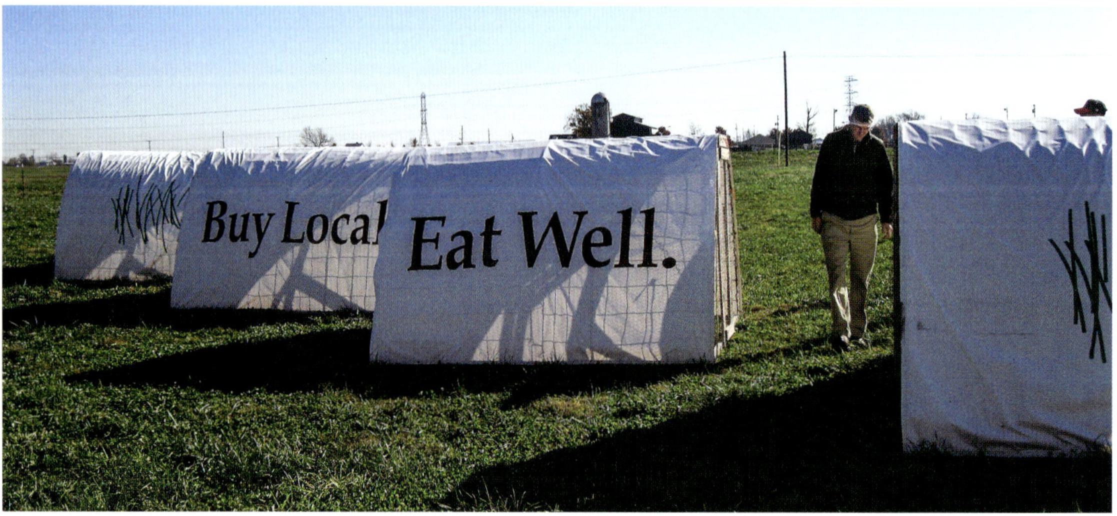

"Buy Local. Eat Well" is Marksbury Farm advice; we take it to heart. *Rona Roberts.*

banking, stone masonry, public service, agricultural policy, education, nonprofit management and trade association development.

A lot of effort and complexity and many relationships sustain Marksbury's commitment to a rebuilt local food economy in Kentucky. Because of the hard work of Marksbury's owners, growers and employees, Kentuckians get to carry out the seemingly simple directives of the Marksbury motto: "Buy local. Eat well."

Sunflower Sundries, Mays Lick (Mason County), Kentucky

"Every decision can be a decision of art," Jennifer Gleason said. Art may seem an unusual lodestar for a small business that makes high-quality foods and handmade soaps. Yet deep love of art and beauty powered Jennifer when she founded Sunflower Sundries in 1992. That same love continues to sustain her today as she and her husband, Jim Lally, produce memorably delicious traditional jams, coarse-grain mustards, handmade herbal soaps, pickled asparagus and heirloom 'Hickory King' cornmeal, grits and corn chips. "The anticipation of beauty keeps you going," Jennifer said about the source of the energy required to make every Sunflower Sundries product by hand, largely from ingredients grown on or near her farm.

Jennifer's lifelong inspiration has been to make things that people use every day and to make those products beautiful and of the finest quality. A year in India as an Ohio high school senior introduced Jennifer to a culture that nurtured and valued cottage industry and local production. Even before the trip, Jennifer said, she loved making things by hand and treasured self-reliance. Sunflower Sundries deliberately chose small-scale, local production methods that support doing business with friends, neighbors and local producers. Now, Jennifer said, "I'm living my dream every day."

Sunflower Sundries products sell in many Kentucky and Ohio retail outlets as well as online. Other than quality, beauty and handmade origins, two factors link the collection of products Sunflower Sundries offers.

The first is a commitment to a diverse array of products. Jim Lally said Jennifer realized around 1997 that she needed to offer a variety of products in order to appeal to more people and make her time investment worthwhile. She thought carefully about what else to offer after taking her handmade soaps to festivals, fairs and shows, where she discovered lots of other soap-makers showing up as well.

The second factor, Jennifer said, is the root of each product in her personal interests. "They were all initiated because I wanted them myself." Mustards? "That started when I was a child, because I loved vinegar, and vinegar is a main ingredient in mustard." Soaps? "I was using a bar of soap in the shower one day and I thought, 'That's one more thing I could make myself.' Self sufficiency has inspired me my

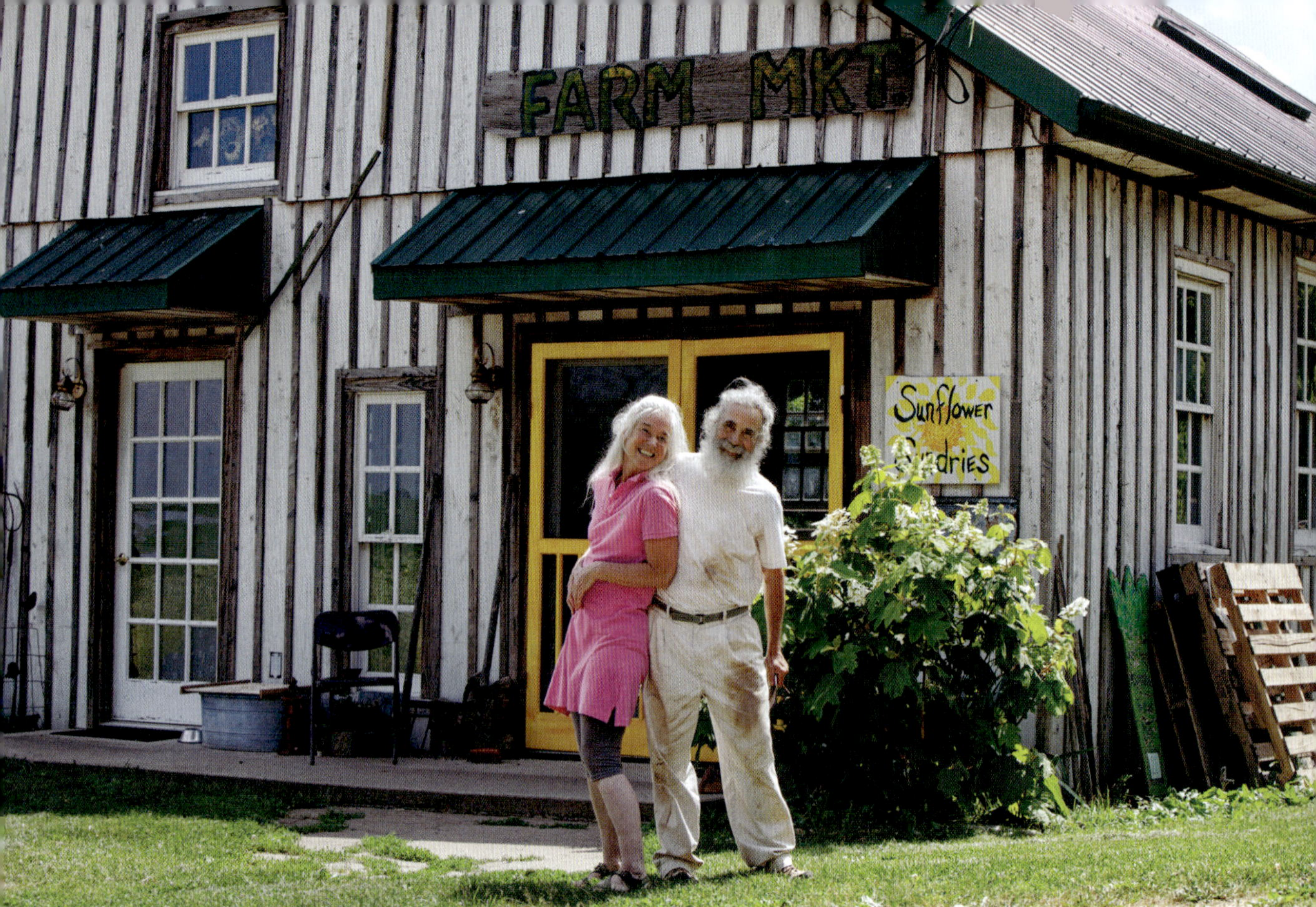

Jennifer Gleason and Jim Lally of Sunflower Sundries in Mays Lick love their place, their work and the beauty of every day and night. *Sarah Jane Sanders.*

whole life." Jams? "I had learned to love growing fruits and making jam from Jo Ann Gardner's book, *The Old-Fashioned Fruit Garden*."

Jennifer taught herself to make what she wanted to produce, both by reading and by hands-on learning from experts. A $4.95 pamphlet from Nichols Garden Seeds described soap making, and a regional soap maker provided coaching. A recipe for homemade mustard in a catalogue from Johnny's Selected Seeds launched her first handmade mustard. An Alice Waters recipe offered the starting point for her splendid pickled asparagus. For every Sunflower Sundries product, Jennifer said, "I want to be known for taste and quality."

In the late 1990s, Jennifer and Jim established a certified kitchen in the basement of their 1870 farmhouse. They pick the fruit at its ripest, when natural sweetness and flavors reduce the requirements for added sugar, allowing the intense flavors of the fruits themselves to delight eaters. Many of the fruits grow on the 154 acres Jennifer and Jim own; they freeze much of the perfectly ripe fruit for later cooking, which means Sunflower Sundries makes fresh jams year-round. Gooseberries, wild blackberries, wild raspberries, rhubarb, strawberries and peaches taste like the best versions of themselves in the Sunflower Sundries jam jars.

Sunflower Sundries' latest product, corn chips made from a legendary heirloom white corn called 'Hickory King,' uses sustainably grown corn from her farm and several others nearby. 'Hickory King' corn boasts innate qualities—shucks so tight around the tips of the corn ears that earworms cannot penetrate, for example—that make it a fine fit for Kentucky. These Hickory King Collective chips represent fifteen acres of Kentucky land now farmed in ways beneficial to the soil, the farmer and the community.

The chips join a stellar lineup of Sunflower Sundries foods, each distinguished from mass-market products by flavor, texture and nutrients. Four delicious mustards include no oil or eggs and keep indefinitely—but keeping them for long is unlikely because each mustard tastes so good you will find yourself cooking grilled sausages or making mustard-infused dressings regularly. Sunflower Sundries Hot Garlic Mustard on Kentucky brats and burgers should be your next favorite Bluegrass State taste.

Sunflower Sundries Soaps, too, made every five to six weeks by hand, please and surprise users. The light herbal scents—lavender, rose geranium or lemon grass, for

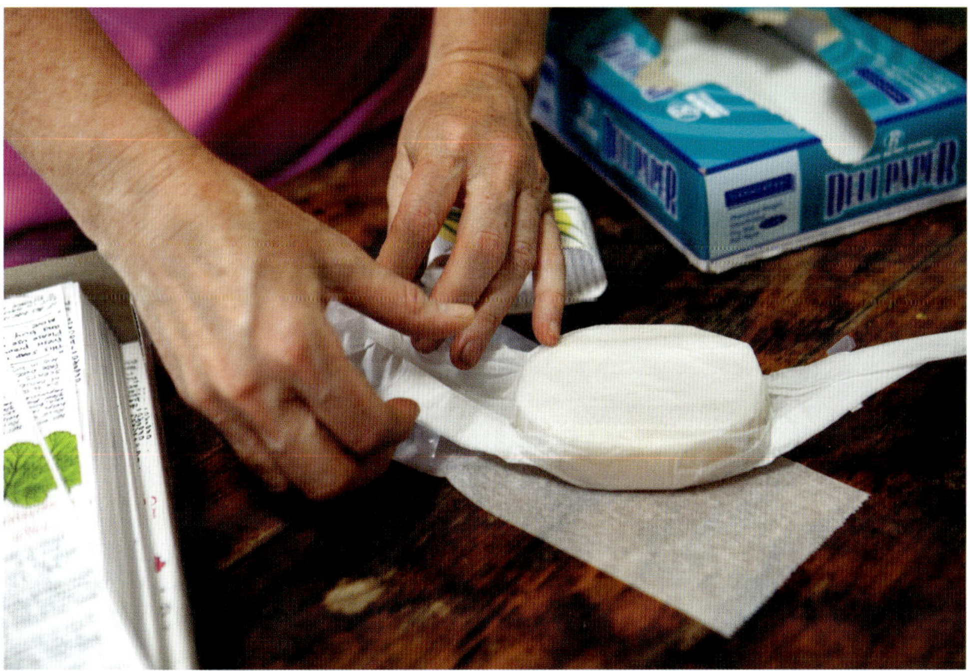

Jennifer Gleason demonstrates the hand-wrapped goodness of each bar of Sunflower Sundries soap. *Sarah Jane Sanders*.

example—derive from essential oils. The fine, textured soap lasts long, even with daily use. Soaps, Jennifer explained, require days to make and weeks to cure. "After twenty-three years, taking notes every single time, we know pretty well how to modify for difference in summer and winter temperatures, for example. But soap can be finicky. Whole batches can fail."

Knowing the story behind each oval bar makes Sunflower Sundries soap even more delightful. Jennifer notes one final benefit: by using handmade soaps with known, clean sources of fats, customers avoid commercial soaps, which tend to rely on used restaurant grease for their fat base.

"My life is completely creative every day," Jennifer said. "I have art, a garden that's my palette as well as my food. I get to make the best of the best. Sunflower Sundries: we're about 'Eat it! Use it!' We make people happy."

And then comes night. Jim said, "People come here during the day and say, 'It's so beautiful.' But they miss the best part. At night, we usually sleep outside. Right now the fireflies are everywhere, and the stars…they are so brilliant." In fact, Jennifer Gleason, inspired her entire life by handwork, also likes to track one of technology's most astonishing products, the International Space Station. Using a NASA app called "Spot the Station," Jennifer sets an alert that notifies her when the space station will be passing overhead in the night hours. And the next day? Perhaps she's shelling corn by hand, molding soap, picking gooseberries, hoeing Hickory King corn or all of the above.

Kentucky Breads: Corn, Wheat, Gluten-Free

In Kentucky's early days, bread choices amounted to "What kind of corn shall we have for breakfast this morning, dinner at noon and supper tonight?" According to *The Kentucky Encyclopedia*, answers might include "milled, roasted, boiled, or baked; served as hominy, mush, or grits; and dried, parched, or pickled."

These days, bread choices abound. Biscuits? Yeast rolls? Scones? Bagels and bialys? Croissants? Definitely.

Kentucky artisan bakers in a growing number of communities work to make excellent fresh bread and pastries available to their neighbors. Communities respond and change with the arrival of bread and pastries of the quality offered at marvelous places like Louisville's Blue Dog Bakery & Café and at Lexington's Sunrise Bakery, Bluegrass Bakery, National Boulangerie and the Midway School Bakery. Bread, meal and flour draw people together and create gathering places. These lively, lovely places in our towns, making delicious foods from Kentucky staples, support conviviality, boost connections and increase the important sense that we belong to a beloved community.

Bread, meal, flour and pastries literally shape our lives.

This shaping is not new. Because cornmeal or flour underpinned nearly every Kentucky meal in the 1800s, and because most families made regular trips to the mill to have their whole grain and corn ground, mills in the 1800s functioned like today's coffee shops. Mills served as good places to see neighbors, visit a bit and catch up on news. Sometimes communities embedded themselves around a mill. People built homes and churches, blacksmith shops, schools and stores near mills, taking advantage of the natural flow of potential customers. Central Kentucky and many other communities have many roads named for mills that once ran to or by them: Armstrong Mill, Clays Mill, Grimes Mill, Lemons Mill and Parkers Mill form a short list.

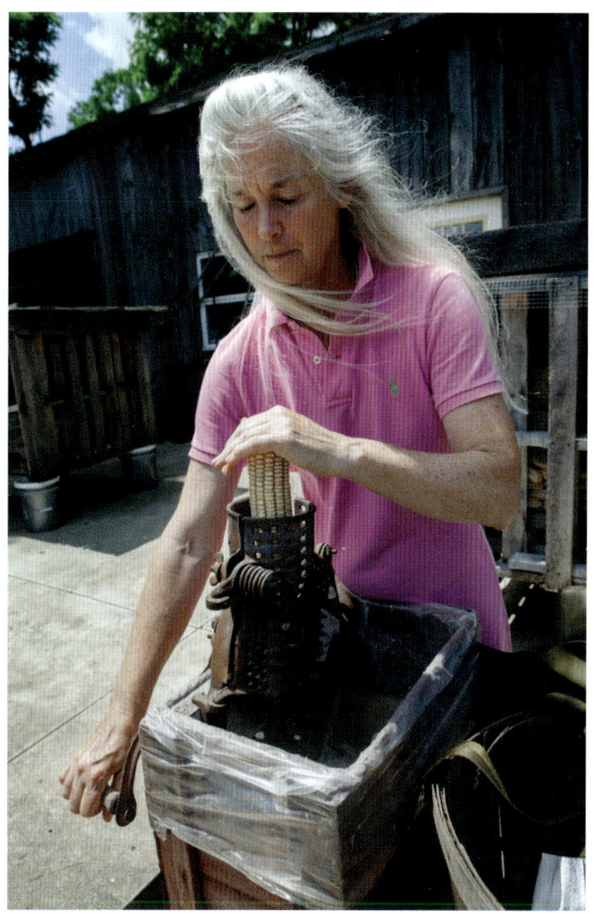

Jennifer Gleason of Sunflower Sundries shells organic Hickory King Corn with a hand-cranked corn sheller. *Sarah Jane Sanders.*

Twice yearly, the Kentucky Old Mill Association publishes *The Millstone*, a magazine devoted to the lore of Kentucky mills of all kinds, including textiles and gunpowder. Most articles focus on gristmills, those that ground corn and wheat into cornmeal and flour. Professional and skilled amateur researchers make the importance of Kentucky's milling history plain. By 1800, water-powered mills had appeared on many streams through Kentucky. Philip Weisenberger, fourth-generation owner of Weisenberger Mills in Midway, told a group of mill historians in 2002, "As a rule of thumb, there used to be a mill about every ten miles along a creek. Each served its own neighborhood."

National publications listed 696 mills in Kentucky in 1869 and 642 in 1882. As inventors and designers increased mills' capacities for power conversion and production, the number of mills declined. In 1930, Kentucky had 350 working mills, and today, few working mills remain.

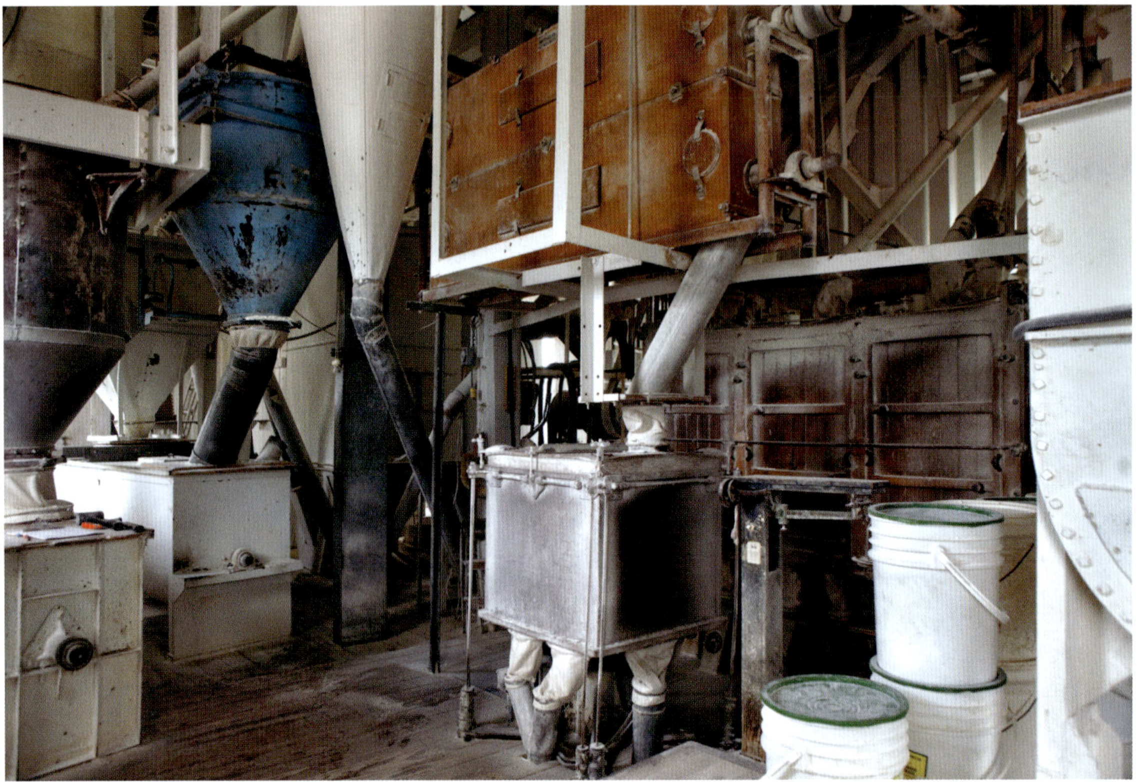

Weisenberger Mill, near Midway, grinds cornmeal and flour five days every week. *Sarah Jane Sanders.*

Historic Mill Springs Mill, established near Monticello, Kentucky, in 1877, grinds corn each weekend during the growing season, and Miller's Grist Mill, a portable electric mill, travels the festival circuit in Kentucky and nearby states. These micromills make it possible for a small number of Kentuckians and others to continue eating grains with unparalleled freshness and excellent texture. In 2014, Kentuckians do not yet have the benefit of state-centered mills that work to advance specific Kentucky-bred, Kentucky-grown, Kentucky-specific strains of wheat and other grains for Kentucky cooks and bakers. Perhaps we will. Asheville's Carolina Ground has begun playing those roles for North Carolina growers, bakers and cooks.

Kentucky farmers grow grain. They produced nearly forty-six million bushels of soft red winter wheat in 2013. Many Kentucky cooks can find and use Kentucky flour and biscuit mixes from a Kentucky mill. Two family-owned mills, each more than one hundred years old, mill Kentucky wheat five days weekly: Weisenberger Mill in Scott County near Midway and Hopkinsville Milling Company, which produces Sunflour brand cornmeal and flour. If you need fifty thousand pounds of flour or more, a third family-owned business, Siemer Milling Company, established in Illinois in 1882, mills millions of bushels of regionally grown wheat in Hopkinsville each year. Weisenberger and Hopkinsville Milling Company also grind corn into meal, grits and mixes.

Kentuckians with gluten-related illnesses and sensitivities benefit from yet another family-owned milling company, Bloomfield Farms, in Bardstown. Bloomfield Farms produces fine, quality non-gluten flours and baking mixes that are safe and delicious for use by people with celiac disease or gluten sensitivities. The top item on Bloomfield's online recipe list? Southern biscuits. Kentuckians who must avoid gluten can still enjoy favorite foods that have Kentucky ties.

Perhaps milling offers a satisfaction that passes easily from one generation to the next; however it happens, Dan Sutherland now runs Bloomfield Farms, which his great-great-great-grandfather William Sutherland founded in 1797. Of course the emphasis on gluten-free baking options came much more recently; manufacturing began in a new plant in 2010. Bloomfield continues milling with traditional flours, too, in a separate location.

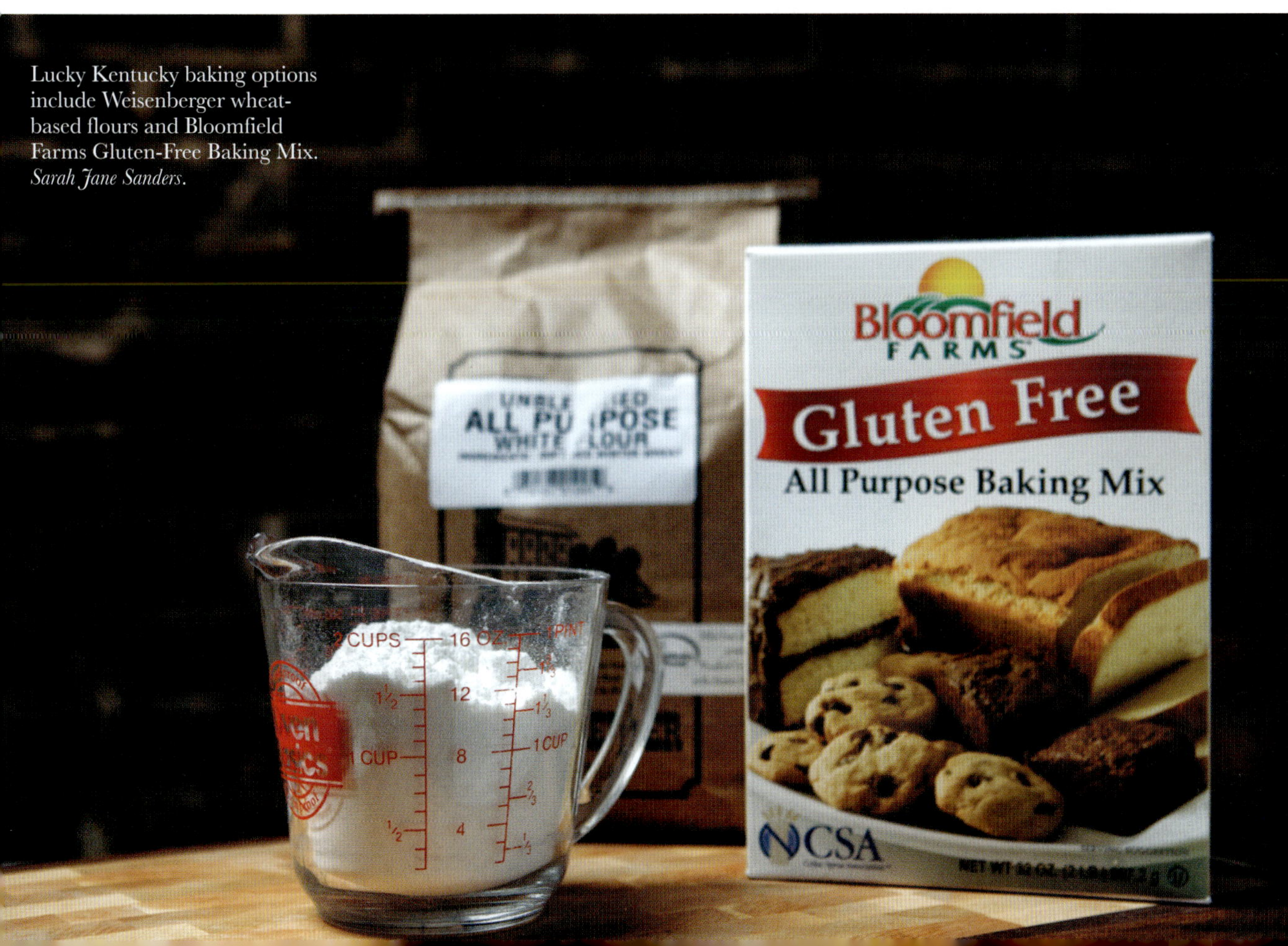

Lucky Kentucky baking options include Weisenberger wheat-based flours and Bloomfield Farms Gluten-Free Baking Mix. *Sarah Jane Sanders.*

Neither milling nor grain production has disappeared from Kentucky. Bread, flour, meal and grains matter as much as they always have. With the advent of the craft brewing industry and the expansion of the bourbon industry, the importance of grains and corn may even be increasing. With customer interest and support, we may spur more attention to growing varieties of grains that particularly thrive in Kentucky, to milling Kentucky's own grains and to ensuring that all Kentuckians, even those with food-related allergies and illnesses, get to enjoy favorite breads and pastries.

Meal 4

EGGS AND BACON GET MARRIED IN A MUFFIN CUP, AND WE HAVE THEM OVER FOR SUPPER, DINNER, BRUNCH OR BREAKFAST

Eggs and bacon sound like breakfast, until we realize that no ingredient in the kitchen stands as ready as the loyal, beautiful egg to offer protein on demand, in minutes, in thousands of variations. Here's a 'round-the-clock meal to delight people of all ages, in all seasons.

Everyday Menu
Goldenrod Eggs and Bacon
Herb-Spiked Vegetable Salad
Splendid Summer or Winter Squash
Kentucky Cheese Biscuits

For special occasions or holidays, dress this meal up by starting with Homemade Cream of Tomato Soup. Spoon Bread, Boone Tavern style, steps the meal up from biscuits, and the Butterscotch-Bourbon Pudding pleases adults and children alike (without making anyone tipsy.)

Dressed-Up Menu Additions
Homemade Cream of Tomato Soup
Boone Tavern Spoon Bread
Butterscotch-Bourbon Pudding with Kentucky Black Walnuts

Perfect Pairings

- *Cocktail:* The Salty Green River
- *Wine:* Elk Creek Vineyard's Riesling for its juicy acidity
- *Beer:* West Sixth Brewing's Lemongrass American Wheat for its bright contrast with the richness of eggs and cream
- *Tea:* Elmwood Fine Tea's Darjeeling Autumnal or Darjeeling Second Flush with the Butterscotch-Bourbon Pudding
- *Coffee:* Somerset Blend from Baxter's Coffee
- *Soundtrack for cooking:* [Some songs on all playlists have adult language and themes.] "She Loves My Troubles Away" (John Conlee), "Kentucky Gambler" (Merle Haggard), "Beautiful Girl" (Cunninlynguists), "The Monster and the Banjo" (Henry Hipkens), "Sittin' on Top of the World" (Blind Corn Liquor Pickers), "The Pill" (Loretta Lynn), "Kentucky Dirty" (Laura Bell Bundy), "Blue Grass Special" (Bill Monroe & His Blue Grass Boys), "Kentucky Mud" (Nappy Roots), "Kentucky Blackberry Blossom/I Walk the Line" (Reel World String Band), "Kentucky Mandolin" (Yonder Mountain String Band), "Sinners Hymn" (Henry Hipkens), "The Stamping Ground Set" (Reel World String Band), "Sixteen Tons" (Merle Travis), "Swanee River Boogie—Live" (Dr. John)
- *Soundtrack for eating:* "Anniversary Song" (the Swells), "Are You Lonesome Tonight" (the Carter Family), "Pretty Polly" (Coon Creek Girls), "Ashland Breakdown" (Noam Pikelny), "P.S. I Love You" (the Hilltoppers), "Paradise" (John Prine), "How About You?" (Rosemary Clooney and Bing Crosby), "Peggy Walker" (Dock Boggs), "Ya Da Da Doo" (the Swells), "Rocket Man" (My Morning Jacket), "Hillbilly Fever No. 2" (Red Foley), "You Make Me Feel So Young" (Rosemary Clooney), "Rose Colored Glasses" (John Conlee), "Sourwood Mountain" (Mike Seeger), "Hey There" (Rosemary Clooney), "Groove Yard" (Les McCann), "How Deep Is the Ocean" (the Swells), "Beautiful Dreamer" (Al Jolson, Bing Crosby)

The Salty Green River

This cocktail looks like a healthy juice drink—and its beauty lifts hearts and (human) spirits.

Yield: 1 cocktail

1 cucumber
10 fresh mint leaves
1 ounce freshly squeezed lime juice
⅛ teaspoon salt
¾ ounce sorghum or honey simple syrup (See "Simple Syrups," page 90)
1–2 ounces Hendricks Gin
ice cubes
club soda
mint sprig, cucumber slice or spear, lovage leaves, salad burnet (optional garnish)

Cut 7 thin slices from a fresh cucumber. Reserve one for garnish, if you want. Put the six cucumber slices and mint leaves in a cocktail shaker, along with the lime juice, salt and simple syrup. Muddle (press/push/prod, perhaps with a wooden spoon's handle) thoroughly. Fill the shaker with ice. Add the gin. (Use less alcohol, of course, if you prefer less strong drinks.) Shake 30 times.

Strain into a tall, ice-filled glass. Fill the remainder of the glass with club soda. Stir quickly. Garnish as you wish. Cheers!

Note: If you have a juicer, extract the juice of half a large cucumber and use up to ¼ cup in place of the cucumber slices.

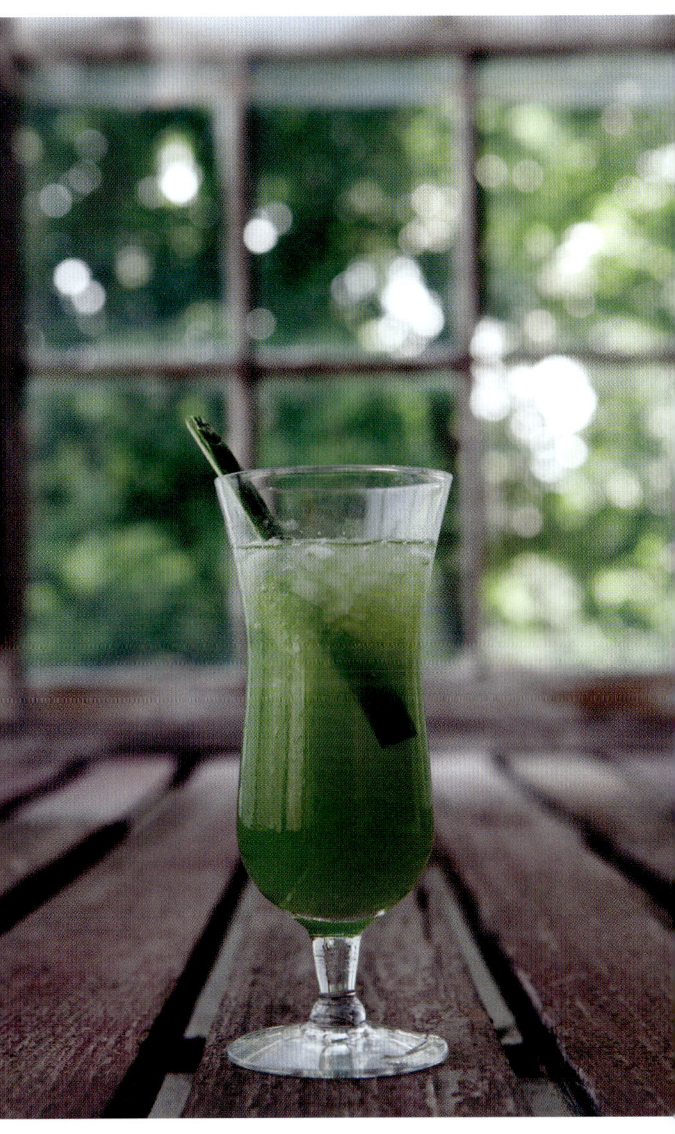

The Salty Green River cocktail is utterly refreshing. *Sarah Jane Sanders.*

EVERYDAY MENU

Goldenrod Eggs and Bacon

The ancestor of this family favorite came from my childhood when Mother made baked eggs in muffin pans, one of her several "eggs for supper" meals that I enjoyed. When my children were little, I promoted protein for breakfast, and we all liked things that came from muffin pans. We all liked bacon, too—imagine!—so somehow the bacon wrap appeared. I didn't realize the kids liked these eggs so much until they had their own kitchens and called back to ask how to make them. These really are a "make without a recipe" food, once you try it. Enjoy inventing your own house favorites. Since this goldenrod references the egg yolks' color, fear not the sneezes our lovely state flower (Solidago gigantea) sometimes provokes.

Yield: Makes 12 bacon-wrapped eggs; serves 8–12, depending on how many people eat two eggs

12 slices good Kentucky bacon
12 eggs
2–3 tablespoons heavy cream
2–3 tablespoons grated Heavenly Homestead Swiss, Kenny's Farmhouse Asiago or Ted, Good Shepherd Pyrenees or other rich Kentucky cheese
salt and black pepper
1–2 cups ultra-fresh baby spinach or chard leaves, cleaned and very dry (optional)
tiny snips clean, dry, fresh chives (optional)
hot sauce or hot salsa, or any other toppings you might like (optional)

Cook bacon until it is no longer transparent, and just starting to brown. It should be done, with crisp edges, but not stiff and crunchy.

While the bacon cooks, preheat the oven to 350 degrees Fahrenheit. Spray a 12-cup muffin pan with nonstick spray or rub each cup with a bland oil. Place a drop or two of heavy cream in the bottom of each muffin cup. If you are using the spinach or chard, put three or four small or torn leaves in the cup.

Use tongs to lift strips of warm, done-but-not-crisp bacon, one at a time, from the fat; shake each strip a little and then stand it on its edge in a muffin cup, making a kind of "bacon wall" around the outside of the cup. Break an egg into the center of each cup, over the greens and cream and inside the surrounding bacon strip.

Grate black pepper and sprinkle salt on each egg (go easy—the bacon is salty, too.) Put another drop or two of heavy cream on the top of each raw egg. If you are using chives, drop a few tiny snips on the top of each raw egg now. Top with a sprinkle of grated Kentucky cheese.

Bake for about 12 minutes; check with a toothpick or fork to see whether the yolk is done enough to suit you. The degree of doneness is a matter of personal preference. We eat ours well done, but soft centers have their appeal, too.

When you consider the eggs done, remove the pan from the oven. Some kitchen tongs can fit into each cup so you can lift out the baked egg-bacon. You can extract the eggs with a table knife and fork, too. You may need to run a table knife around each egg to make sure it is loose before removing it from the pan.

Serve immediately.

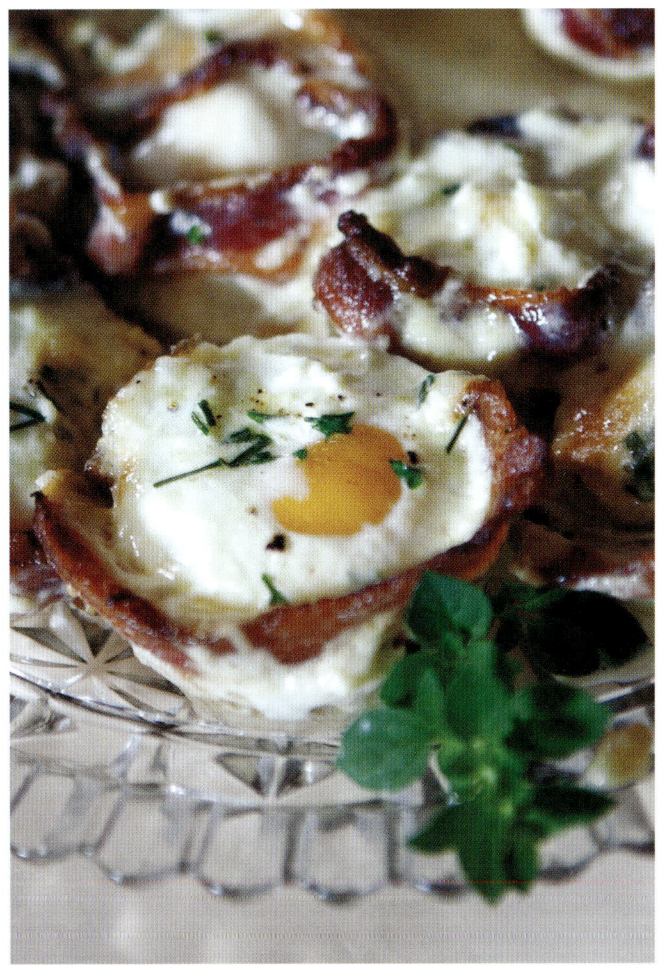

Goldenrod Eggs and Bacon is so easy to make and so satisfying it surprises even the cook. *Sarah Jane Sanders.*

Herb-Spiked Vegetable Salad

This is a "make what you have" salad, always different. Its simplicity and goodness will make you happy.

I always used to dread that time in early summer when the last of the spring lettuce disappears. A few years ago, I realized that leafy, flavorful, healthful herbs still abounded in my herb garden right through the hot months of summer and on into winter. Beginning with parsley, mint and lovage leaves as a base, I tried adding other vegetables, making a kind of chopped salad. Now "salad" is a year-round term for anything that gets a bit of vinaigrette, even when I have no fresh herbs. Salad never stops!

Yield: To serve 8 generously, prepare 8 cups of vegetables

Fresh herbs top the crunchy fresh vegetables in a work bowl, on their way to becoming Herb-Spiked Vegetable Salad. *Sarah Jane Sanders.*

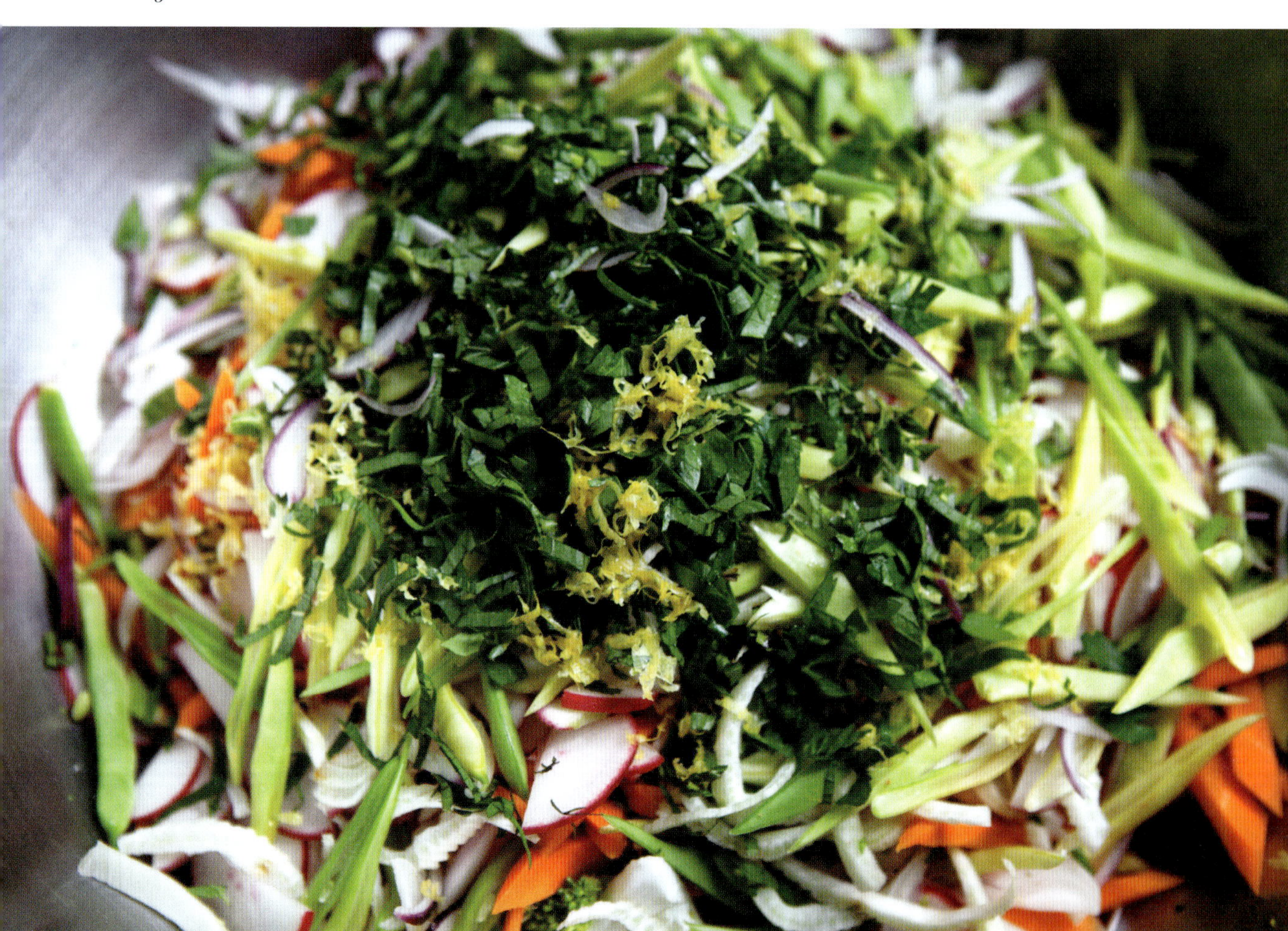

"Use What You Have" Guidelines

Collect, clean and chop any assortment of summer vegetables.

- Good options include cucumbers, carrots, lightly steamed or tiny raw green beans, assorted radishes, tender young summer squashes, kohlrabi, sweet baby turnips, broccoli, cauliflower, fennel, sweet or hot peppers (go easy on the hots) and tomatoes.

If you like, add savory, aromatic or piquant vegetables and herbs

- Good options include green or sweet onions, shallots, fresh young garlic or finely chopped garlic scapes, tarragon, oregano, marjoram, chervil, basil, mint, parsley, cilantro, lovage and salad burnet.

Top with a light dressing.

- Big hurry? Drizzle good olive oil over the vegetables, squeeze a half or whole lemon over them, salt, pepper, done.
- Three minutes for dressing? Make Lemon-Mustard Vinaigrette (page 67). Toss it over the vegetables. Taste, correct the seasonings and enjoy.
- Extra flavor hit? Remove the lemon zest with a fine grater before you squeeze the juice. Sprinkle the zest over the finished salad.

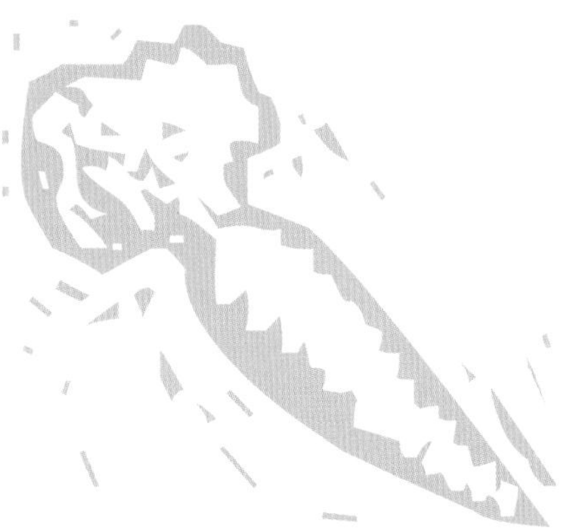

Splendid Summer or Winter Squash

Squash loves Kentucky, and Kentucky loves squash. Pattypan, zucchini, delicata, butternut, cushaw, 'Zephyr'—they grow almost like weeds in our beautiful land. Any time of year, if squash comes to a Kentucky table, we make it welcome—and we make it delicious. Here are a handful of non-recipe ways to prepare summer and winter squashes to add flavor and sustenance to your Kentucky plate.

Squash Basics

- Choose summer squashes in their baby or youthful stages for these recipes—no larger than the average banana. Wash the outsides of any tender-skinned squash well and shake or pat dry with a cloth before cooking.
- For winter squash, wash before peeling—if you must peel. Many winter squashes can be cooked in their skin, avoiding that painful prep step.

Ways to Prepare Summer Squashes Like Yellow Crookneck, Patty Pan, 'Zephyr' and Zucchini

Yield: Estimate ½ pound raw summer squash, or one good handful, per person

The Quick Tasty Broil

Split young summer squash lengthwise. (Slice firm mid-sized ones into circles or ovals.) Rub the cut sides with olive oil, sprinkle with salt, turn the cut sides up on a baking sheet. Broil for three minutes. Carefully remove to a serving bowl. Sprinkle with fresh lemon juice and freshly chopped green herbs. Chives, mint, oregano, dill and sweet marjoram work very well.

Timeless Black Skillet Fry

Chop small- to medium-sized squashes into dice-sized pieces. No need to be exact. Chop a small onion very fine. Heat a heavy skillet over medium heat. Add olive oil or bacon fat, up to 2 tablespoons. When you smell the fat, add the squash and onion carefully to the skillet. (Careful! Spatter!) Shake or stir with a wooden spoon. Add salt,

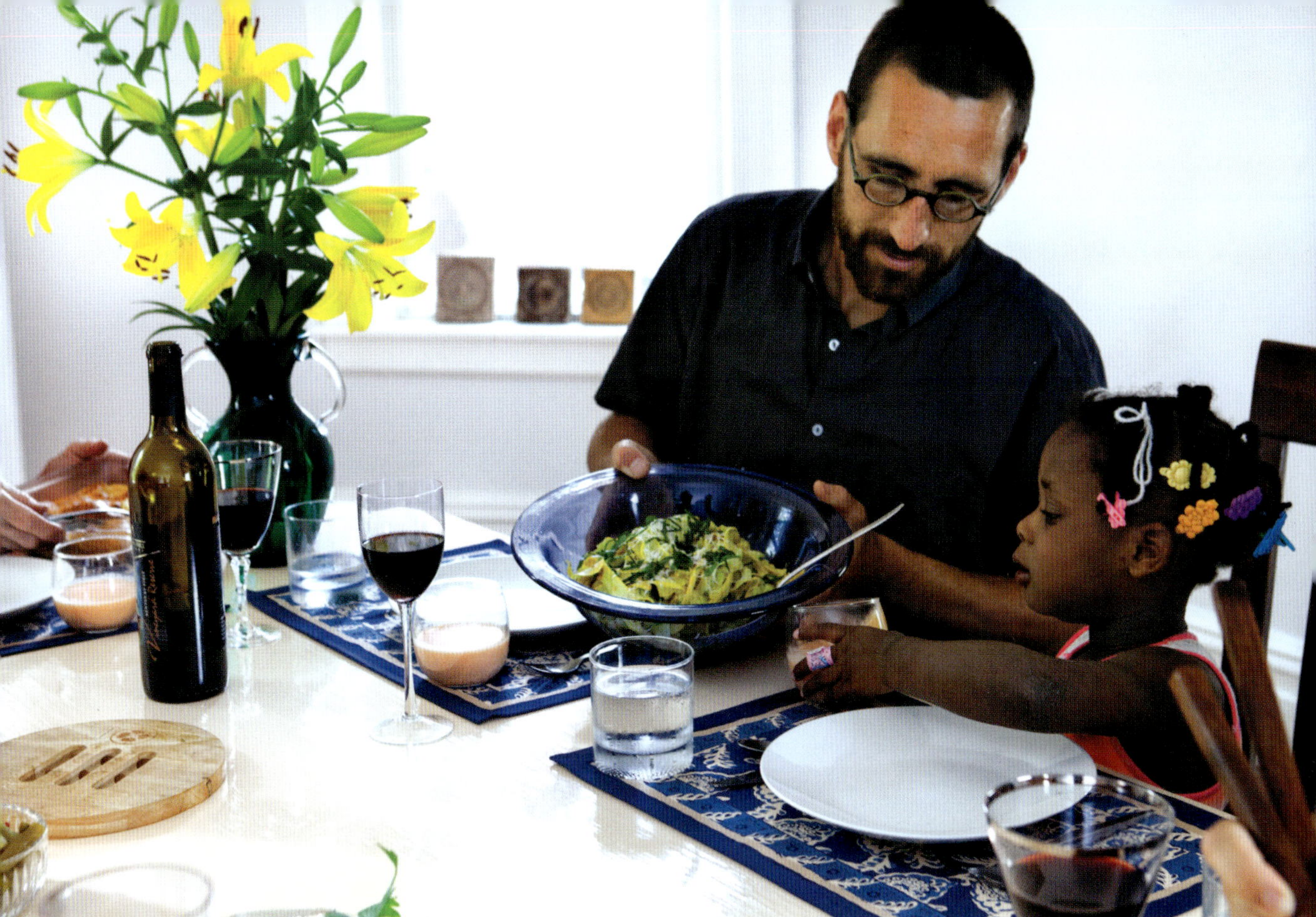

"May I please have some squash?" *Sarah Jane Sanders*.

pepper and 1 tablespoon cornmeal. Continue cooking for about five minutes until some of the squash pieces show light browning and a few turn translucent. Pour out of skillet into a serving bowl; serve immediately.

Put Squash Ribbons on It

With a vegetable peeler, make long ribbons down the length of medium-sized zucchini or "Zephyr" squash. Hello, squash ribbons! Now you have options. One good use is noodle replacement; pile a sauce on top and enjoy. Or heat a heavy skillet, add olive oil and then the squash ribbons, salt and pepper. Toss with spoons for one minute, then remove to a serving bowl, taste for salt, sprinkle with Bleugrass Chevre feta, Kenny's Farmhouse Kentucky Asiago, Sapori d'Italia's aged goat cheese, Good Shepherd Pyrenees sheep cheese or freshly chopped parsley. Serve.

Ways to Prepare Winter Squashes Like Acorn, Butternut, Cushaw and Kabocha

Bake Halves and Then Make Seasoning and Serving Choices

Preheat the oven to 375 degrees Fahrenheit. Line a heavy cookie pan or baking sheet with parchment paper or foil. Carefully, using a cutting board and a large chef's knife, cut the squash in half (or, if it's a 'Blue Hubbard' or cushaw, cut from the monster the amount you plan to use for this meal). Scoop out seeds and add to your compost, save the seeds for next year's garden or, if you are a better person than I am, clean the seeds, roast them and eat them. Rub the squash's cut surfaces with olive oil or butter. Turn cut side down on a heavy baking sheet. Bake on a middle oven shelf for 45 minutes, or until the squash feels soft when pressed with the back of a spoon. Remove from oven.

Make Seasoning and Serving Decisions

- Divide the squash among those eating and invite them to add butter, salt, pepper, maple syrup or sorghum as they please.
- Do the hard work for your eaters. Wear an oven mitt and hold the hot squashes while you scoop the soft, sweet baked flesh into the serving dish. Mash well or add a little cream or coconut milk and use an immersion blender to yield a super-smooth texture. Add salt, pepper and other seasonings as you wish. Butter is always good. For more choices, go either savory or sweet. Good savory options include lightly sautéed onions or garlic. Straddle the sweet-savory fence by adding ground cinnamon, cardamom, cumin and a hint of cayenne. Go straight to sweet comfort with ground cinnamon, nutmeg, allspice or coriander and sorghum, maple syrup or honey. Serve immediately.

Note: oil-rubbed wedges of winter squash do fine at 400 degrees Fahrenheit if you are in a hurry.

Kentucky Cheese Biscuits

Even people who don't like biscuits—all two of them—perk up when cheese biscuits appear. The inspiration for these delights comes from Mrs. Lettice Bryan, who published an astonishing book, The Kentucky Housewife, in 1839. Mrs. Bryan's "Short Biscuit," "Saleratus Biscuit" and "Lard Biscuit" serve as these biscuits' ancestors. Mrs. Bryan's book proves that Kentucky cuisine included remarkable scope and breadth even in the first fifty years of statehood.

Yield: Serves 8 with plenty for sorghum and butter-topped "biscuit dessert," or serves 12

4 cups all-purpose or pastry flour
1½ teaspoons baking powder
¼ teaspoon baking soda
1 teaspoon salt
¾ cup butter or lard, cold enough to be quite firm
4 ounces grated Kentucky cheddar or other hard aged cheese (about 1 cup, loosely packed)
1½ cups buttermilk

Note: A food processor makes this easy. If you do not have one, enjoy the satisfying, traditional handwork of rubbing or "cutting" the fat into the flour mixture.

Preheat the oven to 400 degrees Fahrenheit.

Put the flour, baking powder, baking soda and salt in the work bowl of a food processor fitted with a work blade. Whir for 5 seconds to blend.

Cut the butter or lard into small pieces and add to the food processor. Add the grated cheese. Pulse 6 to 8 times.

Add the buttermilk all at once. Pulse 5 to 7 times, or until the mixture just holds together in a ball.

Flour a board, counter or large piece of waxed paper. Put the biscuit dough on the floured surface. Pat it out with a lightly floured hand until it is an oblong about ⅓ inch thick.

Use a biscuit cutter to cut as many small rounds as possible. Do not twist the cutter if you want taller biscuits. Simply push straight down and pull back up.

For soft-sided biscuits, place the biscuits touching one another on an ungreased baking sheet. For biscuits that brown all over, leave an inch of space between the biscuits on the pan.

Bake in the top third of the hot oven for 10 minutes. Check the color. If light gold, they are done. Some people like biscuits a bit more brown; if you do, allow one more minute. Then remove from the oven and serve piping hot. Don't forget the butter and sorghum!

DRESSED-UP MENU

Homemade Cream of Tomato Soup

Saturdays on the farm, especially when adults work away from the farm during the week, can hardly contrast more with the playful, rest-and-connect Saturdays many of us enjoy in the city. Farm Saturdays mean getting up early, doing laundry, hoeing a week's worth of garden weeds, feeding animals, cleaning house, figuring out why the tractor won't start, canning or freezing whatever is ripe and tackling small repair projects in the barn, fields and house.

Instead of lingering over brunch at a favorite restaurant, farm families need a quick, good lunch, and no one has time to cook it. Mother's solution? Turn homegrown, home-canned tomato juice into Homemade Cream of Tomato Soup. Add grilled cheese sandwiches served on sheets of waxed paper. Enjoy. Then back to work.

These days, when a big number of Mother and Dad's loved ones gather at midday, we may choose Homemade Tomato Soup, grilled cheese and salad for our shared feast. Like several other foods from Mother and Dad's house—homemade applesauce and Sorghum (Molasses) Crinkles come right to mind—Cream of Tomato Soup pleases people all along the age spectrum.

When you begin a baked eggs meal with this soup, it becomes an occasion, encouraging friends and family to linger around your table.

Yield: Serves 8

4 cups whole milk
⅓ cup butter
⅓ cup all-purpose flour (replace with white rice flour to make this soup gluten free)
3–4 cups tomato juice
1 teaspoon salt
1 teaspoon black pepper

Heat the milk gently in a small saucepan or in a glass dish in the microwave until it is very warm.

In a separate large saucepan, melt butter over medium heat. Whisk in flour. Lower heat slightly. Whisk steadily until the mixture turns light gold.

Carefully and slowly, pour in the hot milk. (Whisk, whisk.) Continue whisking until the mixture smooths out and thickens.

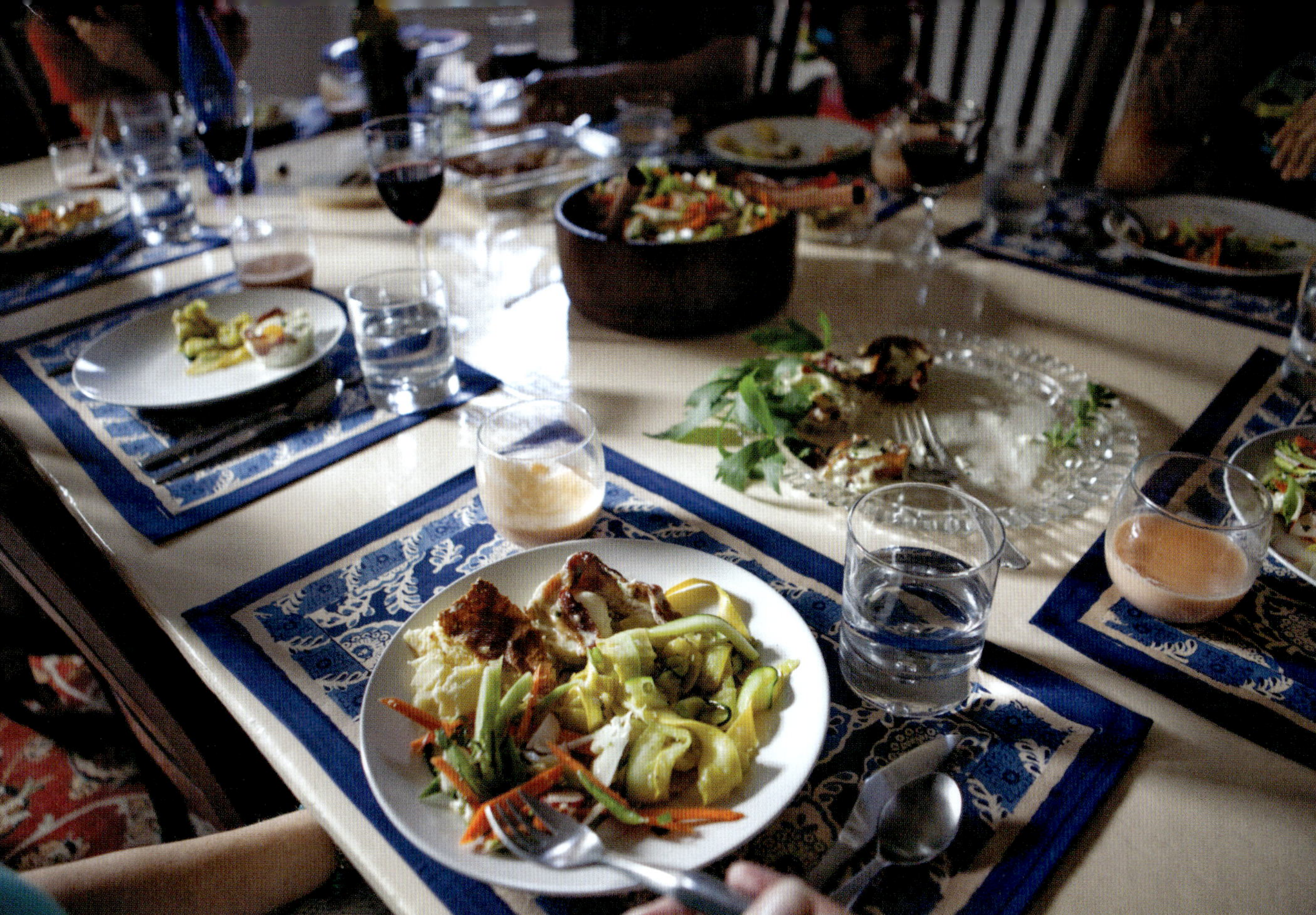

Beautiful plates of food from Kentucky's bounty are especially fresh and delicious when friends surround the table. *Sarah Jane Sanders.*

Very slowly, drizzle the tomato juice into the saucepan. Add salt and pepper. Taste for seasonings and adjust as needed. If the soup becomes unpleasantly thick, add a bit more tomato juice. Turn heat to low. Heat until very warm. Do not boil. Serve.

Options

Add 3 tablespoons finely chopped onion to the butter.

Top with a few chopped fresh herbs. Basil, parsley, oregano, chervil, chives, dill, marjoram and thyme work well.

Top with 1 tablespoon whole fat Greek yogurt or sour cream

Boone Tavern Spoon Bread
The 1950s Recipe

Spoon bread makes believers out of cornmeal doubters. It also makes poets out of food writers and historians. In his fine Southern Food, *John Egerton quotes Redding S. Sugg Jr. as saying spoon bread is "the apotheosis of cornbread." Later, Egerton says, "Spoonbread is the lightest, richest, most delicious of all cornmeal dishes, a veritable cornbread soufflé."*

Spoon bread's big lift in Kentucky came when Boone Tavern manager Richard T. Hougen began the practice of serving it warm, with butter, to each arriving diner at that Berea College–affiliated restaurant. Hougen managed Boone Tavern from 1940 to 1975; he also wrote three cookbooks.

Hougen's recipe, titled "Southern Spoon Bread," appears with variations in many places these days. The recipe included in his acclaimed 1955 cook, Look No Further, *works particularly well if you have a stand mixer and if you plan to serve spoon bread to guests. This spoon bread neither rises nor falls as dramatically as some that require beating egg whites and egg yolks separately.*

Yield: 8 small or 6 medium servings

3 cups milk
1¼ cups cornmeal
3 eggs [beaten]
1 teaspoon salt
1¾ teaspoons baking powder
2 tablespoons butter [melted]

[Heat milk to boiling in a saucepan on medium high.] Stir meal into rapidly boiling milk. Cook until very thick, stirring constantly, to prevent scorching.

Remove from fire and allow to cool. The mixture will be cold and very stiff. Add well-beaten egg[s], salt, baking powder and melted butter. Beat with electric beater for 15 minutes. If hand beating is used, break the hardened cooked meal into the beaten eggs in small amounts until all is well mixed. Then beat thoroughly for 10 minutes using a wooden spoon. Pour into well-greased casserole. Bake for 30 minutes at 375 degrees. Serve from casserole by spoonfuls.

From Richard T. Hougen, *Look No Further: A Cookbook of Favorite Recipes from Boone Tavern Hotel, Berea College, Kentucky* (New York: Abingdon Press, 1955).

Note: This recipe can be doubled, tripled and even quadrupled to feed spoon bread to a crowd. Thanks to Kentucky food and foodways researcher and author John van Willigen for the find. Among many other locations, the recipe is included in *Kentucky's Cookbook Heritage: Two Hundred Years of Southern Cuisine and Culture* (Lexington: University Press of Kentucky, 2014).

What could top spoon bread better than sorghum and butter? *Sarah Jane Sanders.*

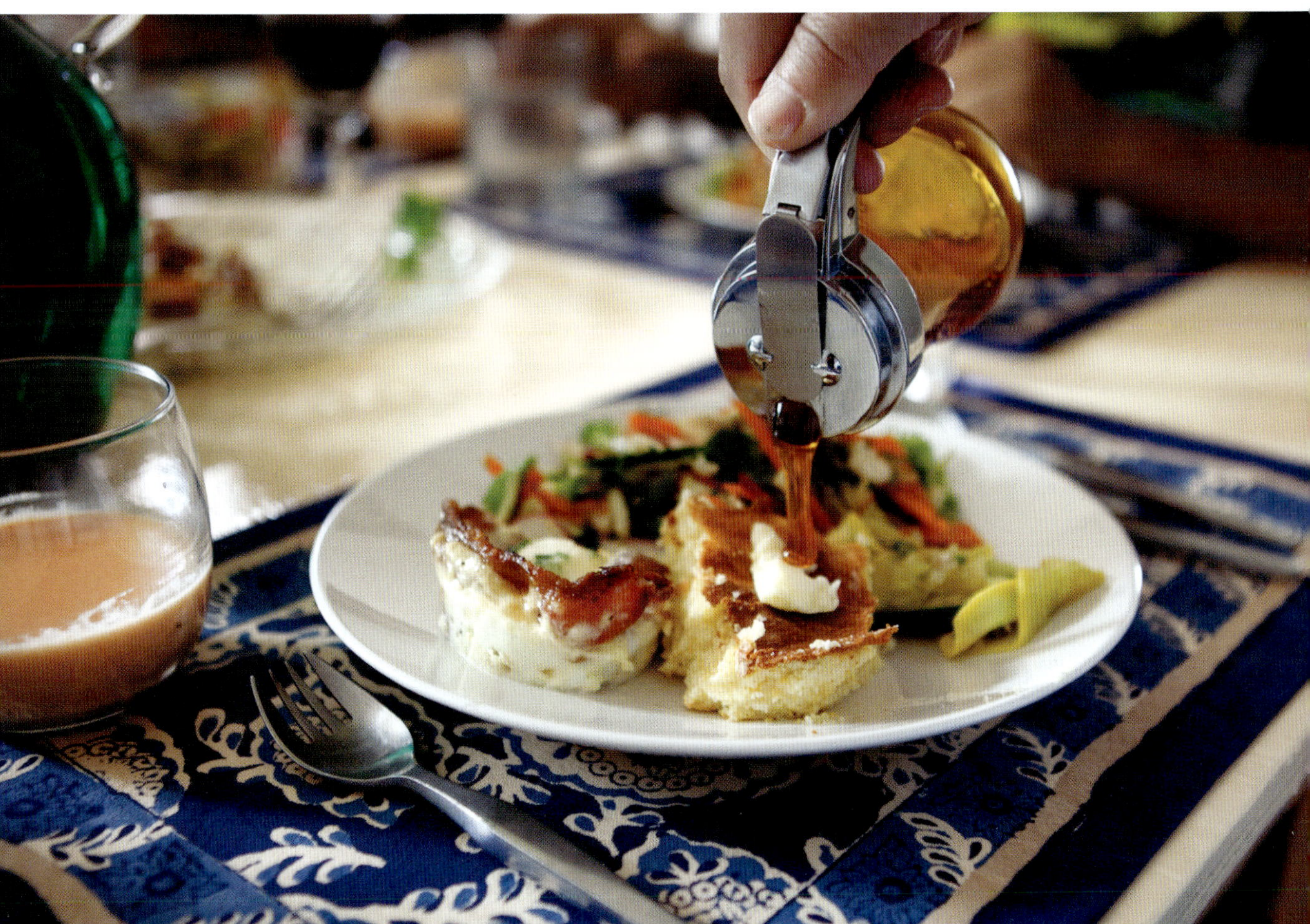

Butterscotch-Bourbon Pudding with Kentucky Black Walnuts

Caramel can scare people to death: the way white sugar turns into a clear syrup, then turns gold and then—"Uh-oh! It's burned black and smoking! Help!" Butterscotch, though, accomplishes a milder taste trick more simply, using brown sugar, butter and other goodness. You do pay attention, just enough attention, to this superbly comforting pudding as it cooks, but no smoke alarms will sound. Promise!

Leave the bourbon out if you prefer.

Yield: This rich dessert is great in smaller than usual amounts. It makes 10 servings, about ⅓ cup each.

2 tablespoons butter
1 cup loosely packed light brown sugar
4 tablespoons cornstarch
2 cups milk
½ teaspoon salt
⅛ teaspoon ground allspice
2 eggs
½ teaspoon vanilla extract
1–2 tablespoons good Kentucky bourbon (2 tablespoon for more pronounced bourbon flavor and more adult eaters)
½ cup chopped black walnuts
flaky sea salt, such as Maldon, for sprinkling on top to produce a salty butterscotch flavor (optional)

In a large, heavy-bottomed pan, brown the butter over low heat (see "Browned Butter: A Cook's Best Friend," page 39).

Remove from heat immediately; add the brown sugar.

In a small bowl or four-cup measure, stir together the cornstarch and 3 tablespoons of the milk to make a smooth slurry; add the rest of the milk to the slurry. Whisk together thoroughly. Pour the milk-cornstarch mixture, salt and allspice into the pan. Whisk well. Return the pan to medium heat, and stir almost constantly, especially once you see steam starting to rise. The mixture will thicken quite quickly after that and can burn or scorch easily. Keep whisking! When the mixture has boiled at least a minute and is quite thick, remove it from the heat again.

In a small dish, beat the eggs lightly until well blended. Scoop about ⅓ cup of the hot butterscotch mixture into the small dish with the eggs and stir well. This warms the eggs and keeps them from curdling when you add them to the hot mixture.

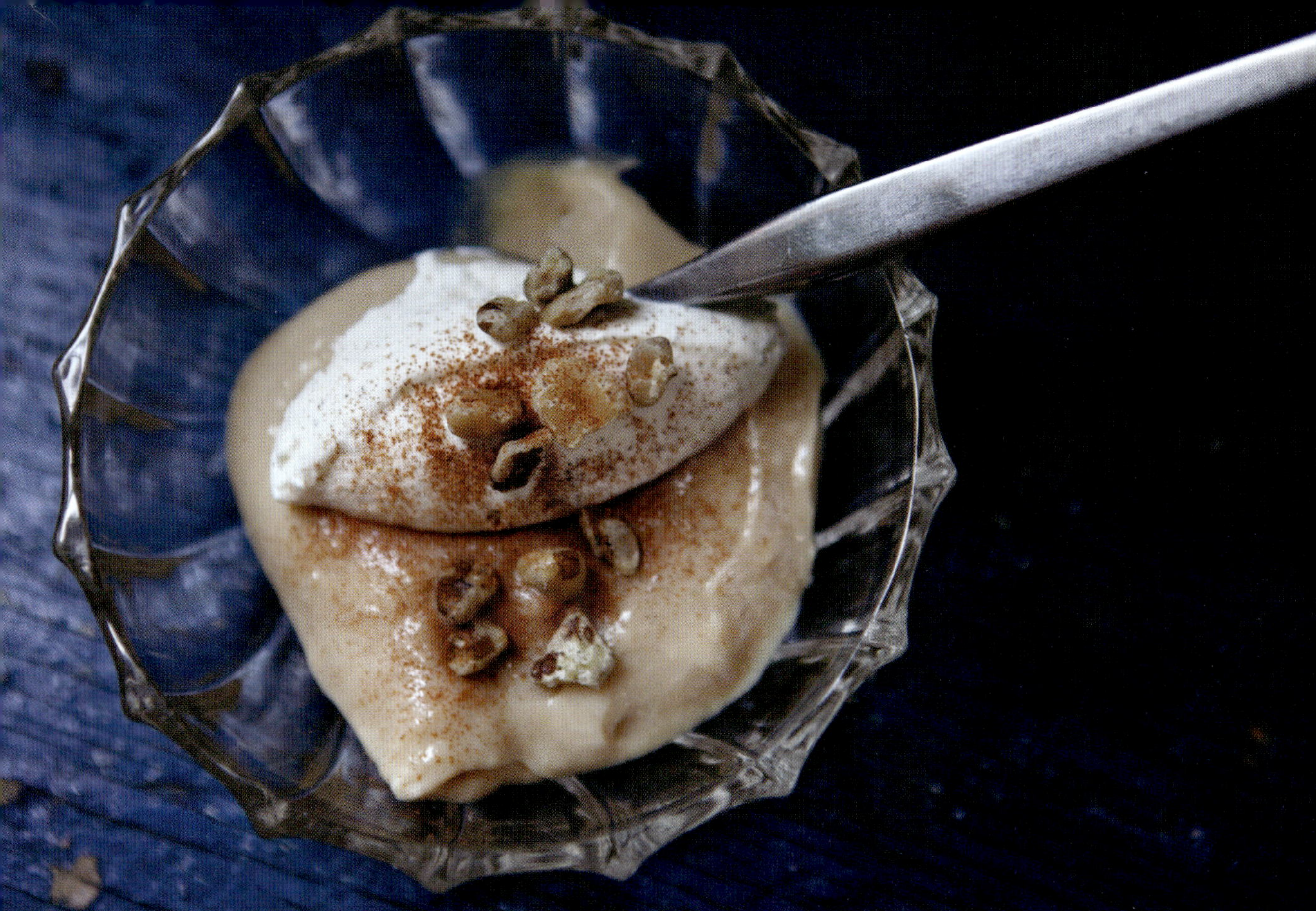

Butterscotch-Bourbon Pudding with Sorghum-Bourbon Whipped Half-Sour Cream and Kentucky black walnuts is a dessert in which caramel tastes rise to the heights. *Sarah Jane Sanders.*

Pour the warm egg mixture into the saucepan. Whisk thoroughly. Return to the heat. Cook three minutes. Remove from heat. Cool five minutes. Add the vanilla and bourbon and stir until completely integrated.

For greatest happiness, serve warm. Scoop ⅓-cup servings of pudding into cute individual dishes. Top with a good sprinkle of chopped fresh Kentucky black walnuts or flaky sea salt.

To serve later, top with waxed paper or plastic wrap and chill.

Options: Before topping with black walnuts, add a dollop of Whipped Half-Sour Cream (page 43) flavored with 2 teaspoons good bourbon. This pudding is also miraculous over or under sliced bananas that have been lightly browned in butter.

Heavenly Homestead Cheese, Windsor (Casey and Russell Counties), Kentucky

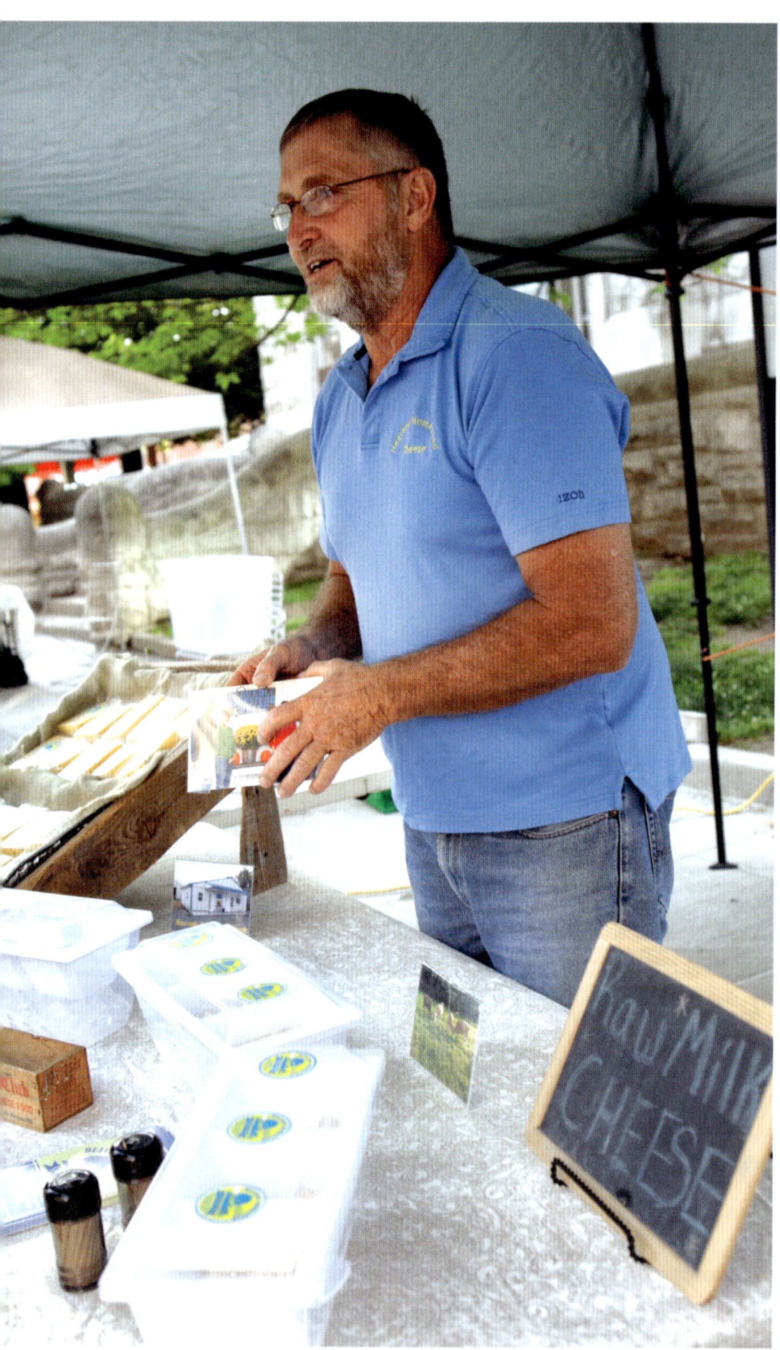

Terry Huff, of Heavenly Homestead Cheese in Windsor, shows customers at the Lexington Farmers' Market pictures of his farm and family. *Sarah Jane Sanders.*

Terry Huff loved milk cows growing up, when his family separated fresh milk and cream, selling the cream to a nearby Carnation plant. He enjoyed milk cows so much that he has kept them for most of his adult life, devising ways to keep them around him even when he held down demanding full-time jobs that required considerable commutes. For decades, he got up early, stayed up late and worked through weekends because of a passion for milk cows.

Around 2005, Terry built a herd of Jersey cows, a type known for high-quality cream and for producing milk that contains a specific genetic array that delivers a particularly human-friendly, healthy form of protein called A2/A2 beta-casein. The business plan involved selling fluid Grade A milk to the dairy industry. Milk prices fell, and Terry said he found himself working off the farm in order to support the milk operation. Eventually, heartbreakingly, he sold that herd.

In late 2009, Terry went to a workshop at the Hardin County Cooperative Extension Office (Elizabethtown) on micro-processing milk. Experienced cheese makers made presentations there, including Kenny Mattingly, founder of Kenny's Farmhouse Cheese in Austin, and Susan Miller, the founder of Bleugrass Chevre. Terry saw cheese making as a way to get to keep cows and make enough money from their milk—once it became cheese—to sustain the operation. He worked with health inspectors and regulators to build a cheese barn that he could keep clean and that would pass inspection. He rebuilt his herd of twelve cows, mostly Jerseys, and is at work breeding a herd that yields milk that offers the greatest possible benefits to the human body.

Terry; his wife, Marti; his daughter Lindsey Perkins; and her husband, Dustin Perkins, all play roles in Heavenly Homestead. Recently, the family welcomed a new member when Lindsey and Dustin adopted a child from Bulgaria. Marti, Lindsey and Dustin all work full time off the farm.

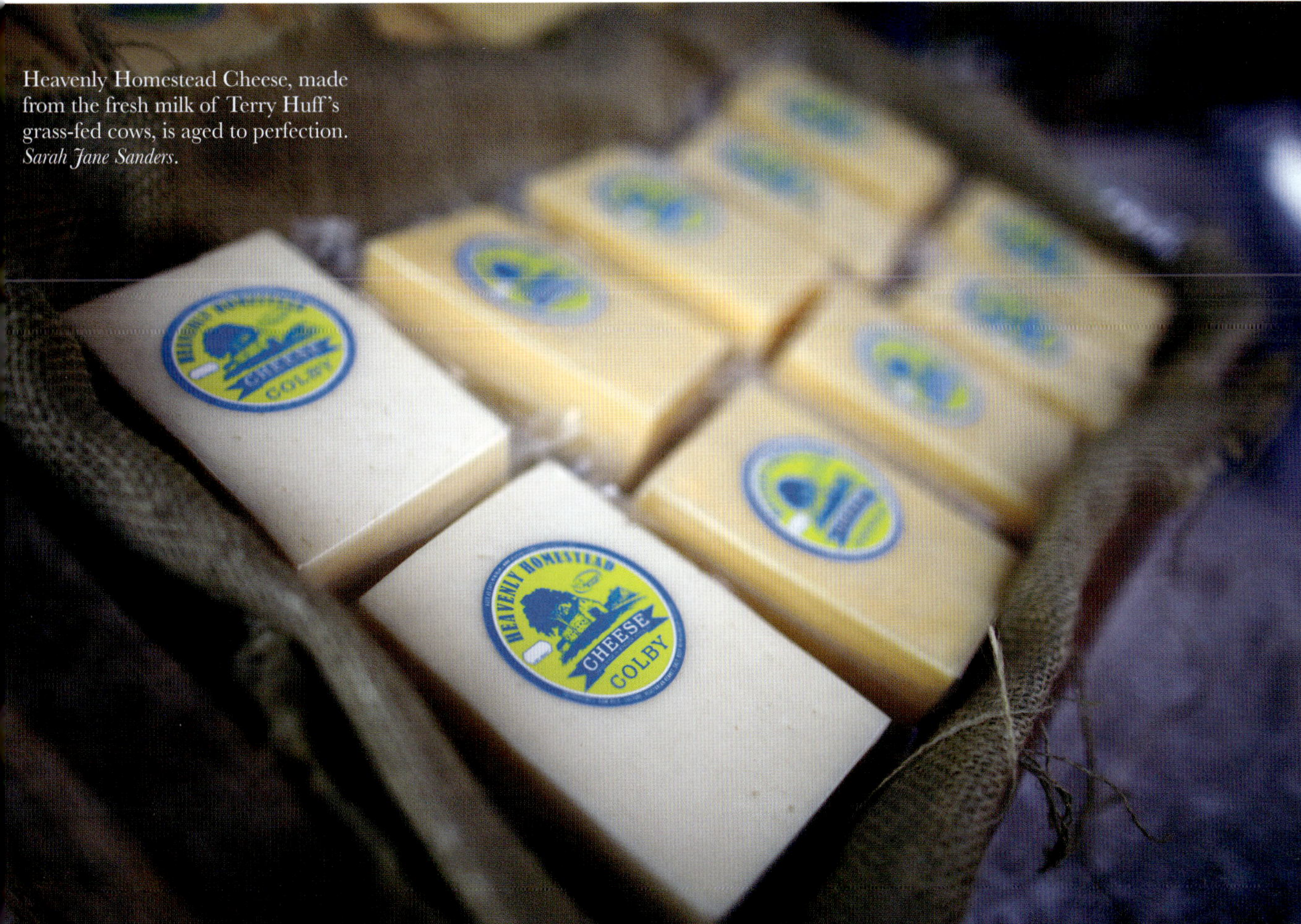

Heavenly Homestead Cheese, made from the fresh milk of Terry Huff's grass-fed cows, is aged to perfection. *Sarah Jane Sanders.*

One component of cow's milk is a protein called beta-casein. Each cow's milk contains one of three different types of beta-casein, depending on genetic differences. Jersey cows are among the old breeds of milk cows that produce milk that is high in a type of beta-casein, A2 (or A2/A2), that some consumers and health advocates consider beneficial to human beings.

In 2012, Heavenly Homestead Cheese began selling to the public. A cheese buyer at Good Foods Co-op, Lexington's large natural foods grocery, introduced Heavenly Homestead to customers this way: "Every cheese that Heavenly Homestead makes tastes just the way it should. Cheddar tastes like cheddar. Monterey Jack tastes like itself."

Each Heavenly Homestead cow yields enough milk to make eight hundred to one thousand pounds of cheese each year. That's with a nice winter vacation, because Heavenly Homestead's cows take a break in winter, when they eat hay instead of fresh grass. Terry said, "We never feed silage, corn, soy beans or any byproducts of any kind. We feed a little barley that a neighbor grows for us, mixed with wet molasses. We hope to be feeding barley sprouts by July 2014 because barley helps cows get the minerals and nutrients out of their other food."

Raw milk cheese production requires aging the cheese for at least sixty days before selling it on the premise that any potentially harmful microbes will yield in that time to salt, acid and other factors. Pointing to packages of Tomato & Basil Cheddar for sale at Lexington Farmers' Market, Terry said, "That cheese right there is getting pretty strong, as it's been aging for a year or so. It's still alive, so it keeps changing." Upon tasting, it fills the mouth with layers of rich flavor, all delicious.

Like nearly all Heavenly Homestead cheeses, the Tomato & Basil Cheddar is sunny yellow. Terry said, "Grass-fed cheese has a strong color. It comes from the beta-carotene in the grass. If cows are eating green grass, the cheese from that milk won't be white. If you've got grass-fed cheese, it will be straw-colored. There is no mistake about it. It's not something we put in it. It's a natural process." Cheese made from the milk of cows that are fed hay or silage will be white.

It is Kentuckians' great good fortune that Terry Huff's affection for cows led him to cheese making as a way for his cows to pay their own way in an economy that otherwise is unfriendly to small dairy herds. We are also fortunate that he wants to share his knowledge of cows, and of cheese, to help us all know the signs of goodness and quality as Kentucky cheese making rebuilds.

Weisenberger Mill, Midway (Scott County), Kentucky

Philip Weisenberger, forty, knows a bit about persistence and focus. Philip's great-great-great-grandfather August Weisenberger, an immigrant from Baden, Germany, bought the present Weisenberger Mill on South Elkhorn Creek in 1865 and began grinding Kentucky corn and soft red winter wheat. Six generations of Weisenbergers later, the same creek and the same mill now work nine hours a day, five days a week, producing about one thousand bushels of ground Kentucky corn and wheat each week. "We like doing something really well and sticking to it," Philip said.

Weisenberger Mill offers a textbook example of a "living company," a business that changes with its environment in order to thrive across centuries instead of decades. After more than 150 years, Weisenberger Mill has adapted a bit while continuing its core work of grinding wheat and corn into different types of flour, grits and meal. Now the company offers more than seventy products that include mixes for everything

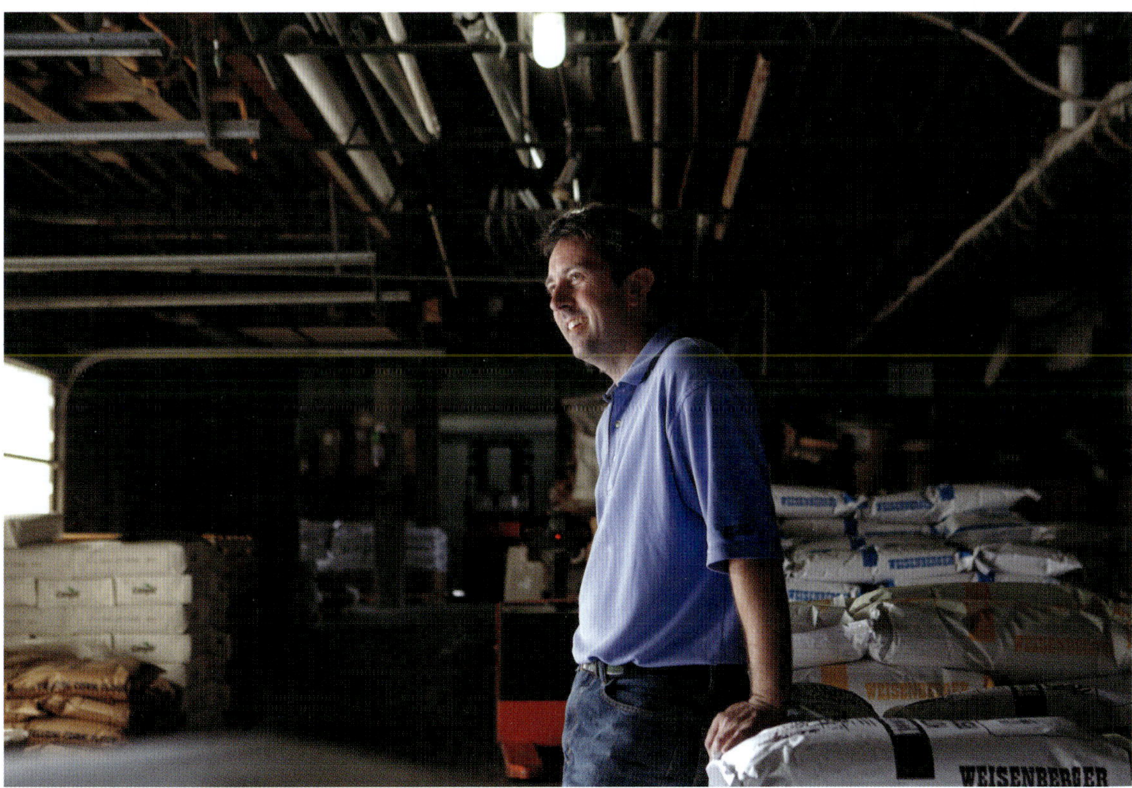

Philip Weisenberger, sixth-generation owner of Weisenberger Mill near Midway, started working in the mill when he was twelve years old. *Sarah Jane Sanders.*

from funnel cakes to pizza crust. Individual customers can order online. Philip said, "Forty years ago, we had forty people working here. Now we have six, including Dad [Mac Weisenberger] and me."

The present mill itself features equipment installed in 1913, when the Weisenbergers dismantled the original mill and reused its stones to form concrete for the new structure. That commitment to "adapt and reuse" fits perfectly with the habits and values that sustain Weisenberger Mill.

Philip said, "I used to wonder why we didn't do things differently. Now I'm so glad we do things the way we always have."

Standing inside the historic mill as it grinds corn for cornbread mix and wheat for several types of flour, one connects to more than 150 years of Kentuckians' dependence on these elemental foods. Kentuckians prefer white corn—Texans and New Englanders prefer yellow—so Weisenberger grinds white corn from Hardin County (Elizabethtown) four days a week; Mondays are for yellow corn. Both corns are "dent" corns, high in soft starch.

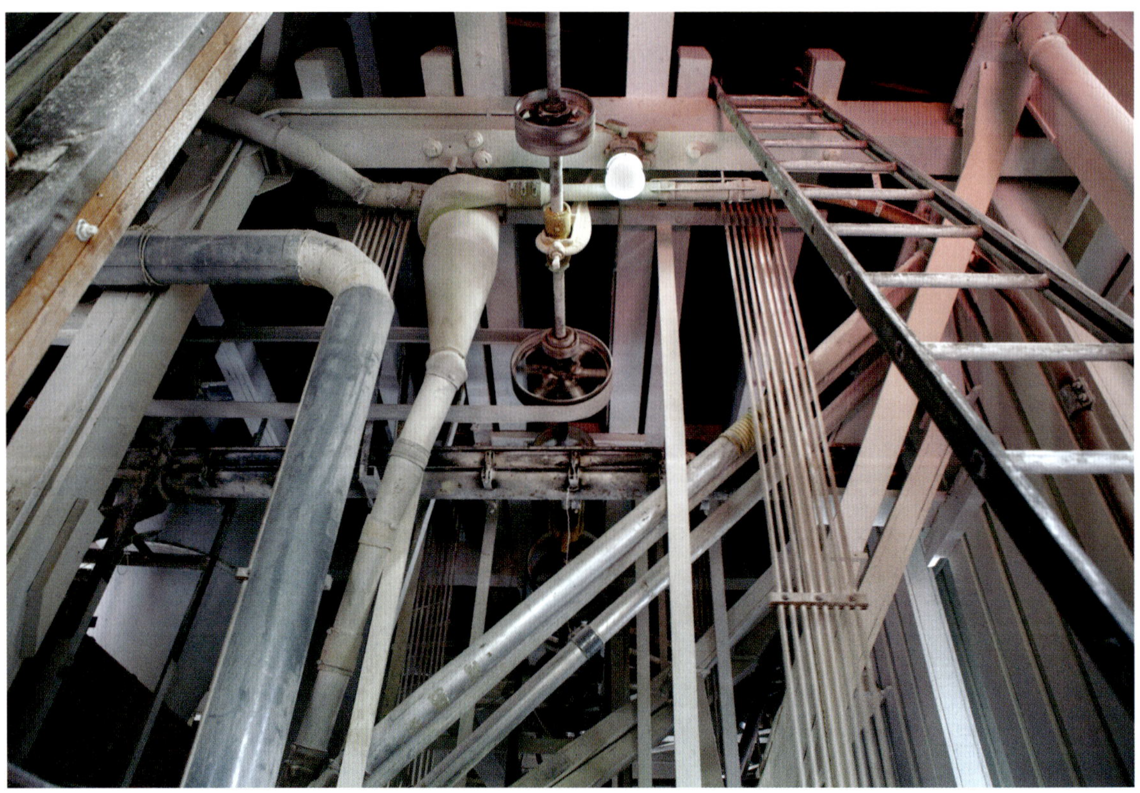

The dramatic machinery of Weisenberger Mill is powered by electricity generated with South Elkhorn Creek's water power. *Sarah Jane Sanders.*

All corn and all wheat ground at Weisenberger Mill grow in Kentucky, just as they did when August Weisenberger first bought the mill. None of the white corn comes from genetically modified plants; in late 2014, the same will be true for the yellow corn.

As it has for generations, Weisenberger Mill runs on water power from South Elkhorn Creek. Today, in a system built in 1913, water diverted from the wide creek powers an electrical turbine; the generated electricity powers the many shafts and pulleys that, in turn, power the milling machinery.

Recently, as many Kentuckians look to support local businesses and build stronger community economies, bags of Weisenberger Mills flour and cornmeal often come with Kentucky Proud stickers that announce the Kentucky county of origin and the grower's last name: "Milled from wheat grown in Fayette County, Kentucky, at the James farm."

Philip said, "Most of our sales are in food service—schools and restaurants, cafeterias, institutional kitchens. We do a lot of wholesale." Asked whether Weisenberger Mill sets its prices to include a premium for artisanal quality and workmanship, Philip said, "No, we don't charge one. Maybe we should."

While serving customers, keeping an eye on the front office, listening for the phone and giving visitors an insiders' tour, Philip recalled his grandfather Phil's advice: "Always leave a good taste in the customer's mouth. He meant it both ways, the product and the service." Phil Weisenberger can be assured that his son Mac and grandson Philip took that advice seriously and carry it out every day.

Kentucky Proud

Kentucky Proud is a marketing and branding program that identifies foods raised or made by Kentuckians in Kentucky. Participating producers and restaurants receive economic benefits for participation. The Kentucky Department of Agriculture manages the Kentucky Proud program, which also maintains a list of Kentucky farmers' markets and sponsors the annual Incredible Food Show in Lexington.

Kentucky Cheese: Nearly Lost but Now It's Found Again

Kentucky has good grass and lots of it. At one time in the early 1960s, cows eating that grass poured billions of pounds of Kentucky milk into at least eighteen commercial cheese factories around the state, making Kentucky third in the nation in cheese production, behind Wisconsin and Missouri.

In 1962, the Kentucky Crop and Livestock Reporting Service reported construction of four new cheese plants and an increase of nearly 15.00 million

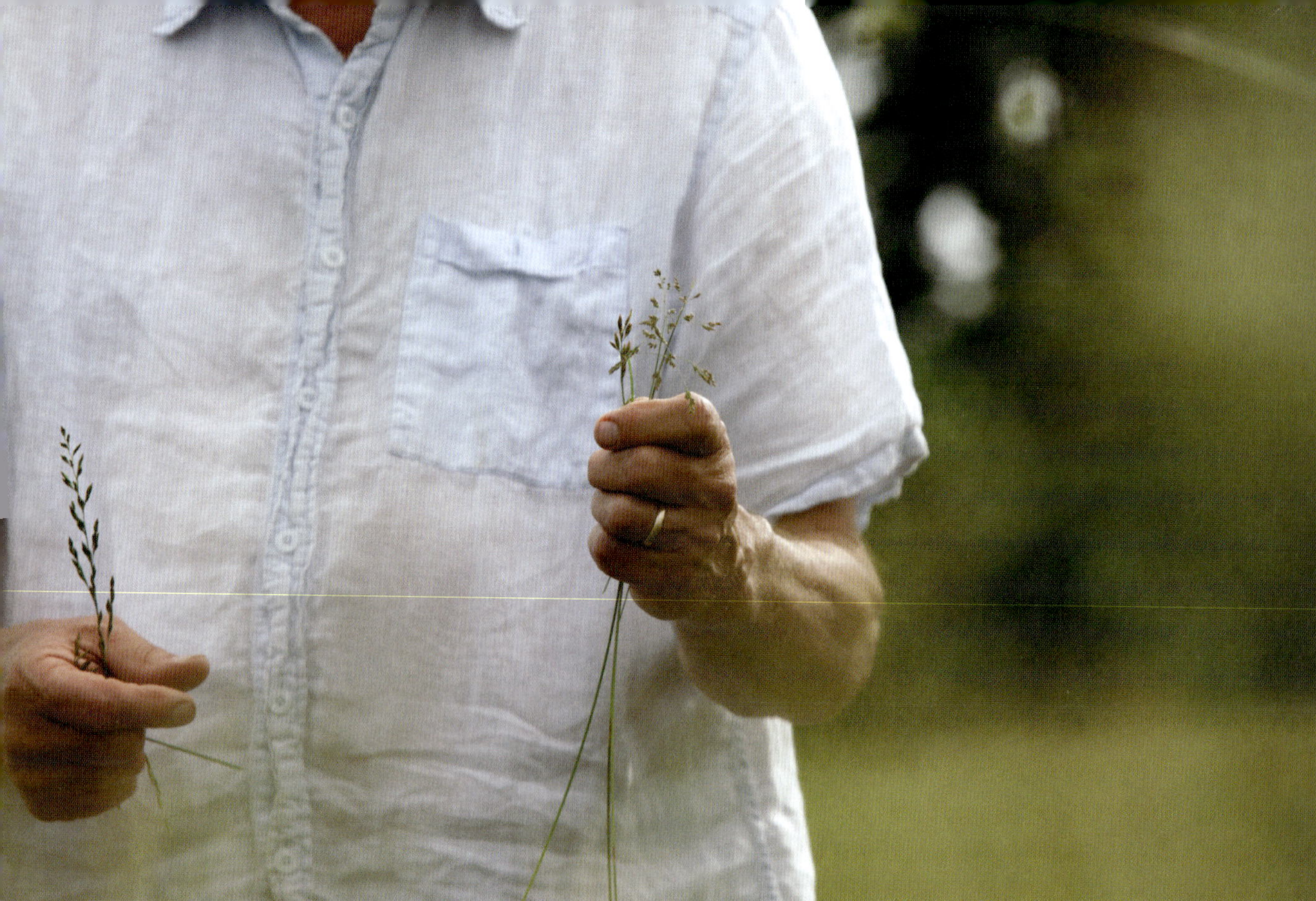

Mac Stone of Elmwood Stock Farm holds grasses, the key to the perfect nutrition found in many Kentucky foods, particularly cheese. *Sarah Jane Sanders.*

pounds of cheese since 1960, bringing total Kentucky cheese production in 1961 to a record 65.00 million pounds, made from 28 percent of the total milk Kentucky cows produced—2.26 billion pounds. Kentucky dairy farmers received $21,102,858 for the milk.

By contrast, the Kentucky Farm Bureau's summary of state and national statistics shows Kentucky's milk production for 2012 at 1.12 billion pounds, down about half from 1961 levels. Maury Cox, executive director of the Kentucky Dairy Development Council, said 80–90 percent of Kentucky milk now goes into bottles, not cheese. Commercial cheese making in Kentucky has shrunk to three locations.

Many factors contributed to this change, including changes in milk pricing, regulatory constraints, transportation efficiency concerns and industry consolidation. Large-scale cheese making now depends on intensive dairy production—one owner with lots of cows eating grain in small spaces instead of lots of farmers owning lots of cows eating grass on lots of acres.

New energy and enthusiasm for Kentucky cheese now appear because of new producers, "microprocessors," who mostly use their own pastured animals' milk and follow practices developed by European cheese-making artisans. These Kentucky cheese makers have begun reclaiming the state's potential for converting green grass to exquisite cheese.

Kenny Mattingly stands out as the pioneer of the new style of Kentucky cheese maker, one who not only makes good cheese from Kentucky milk, but also educates customers about the benefits of grass-fed cows, minimal processing and small-scale production. In 1998, Kenny and his family made 4,000 pounds of Kenny's Farmhouse Cheese from their own cows' milk in Austin, Kentucky. The Mattinglys now produce more than 100,000 pounds of cheese a year.

For two decades Kenny's smiling, generous presence at food tasting events has warmed Kentucky eaters to the notion of locally made cheese from locally grown milk. Kenny has worked to introduce his cheeses to Kentucky chefs, who then share the cheese—and the good news about Kentucky's cheese comeback—with their customers, who go looking for Kenny's in stores and, increasingly, find it and other Kentucky cheeses where they shop.

Most important, Kenny shares encouragement and information generously with others in the commonwealth who aspire to be cheese makers. Terry Huff of Heavenly Homestead Cheese, one of Kentucky's newest crop of cheese makers, said "I can't say enough good about Kenny. He helps everybody, and he helped me."

Like Kenny Mattingly, Susan Miller of Bleugrass Chevre, the first retail goat cheese maker in Kentucky, works to cultivate and support new cheese makers, whether their milk is from goats, cows or sheep. For the first and second Kentucky Cheesemaking Schools, in 2010 and 2011, Susan hosted hands-on workshops at her dairy in Fayette County. Bleugrass Chevre's fresh feta and creamy cheeses in several flavors rightly enjoy a fervent following at Lexington Farmers' Market locations and retail stores in central Kentucky.

Sanford and Colleen Dotson of Bath County (Owingsville) launched Good Shepherd Cheese, Kentucky's first sheep cheese company, after hearing Susan Miller speak at an early Kentucky Proud Incredible Food Show, an annual event in Lexington. The Dotsons' finely crafted Pyrenees-style sheep cheese has won countless converts to the flavors and goodness of sheep cheese.

Each Kentucky cheese maker offers distinctions that make Kentucky cheese plates beautifully flavorful and diverse. Giovanni Capezzuto of Sapori d'Italia in Nicholasville makes the state's only aged goat cheese, following heritage Italian methods. Patrick and Leeta Kennedy of Cloverdale Creamery (and Stone Cross Farm) in Taylorsville (Spencer County) make aged raw milk cheeses in traditional English styles. Ed Puterbaugh of Boone Creek Creamery in Lexington (Fayette County) applies his training as a microbiologist to making dozens of styles of cheese by hand, using

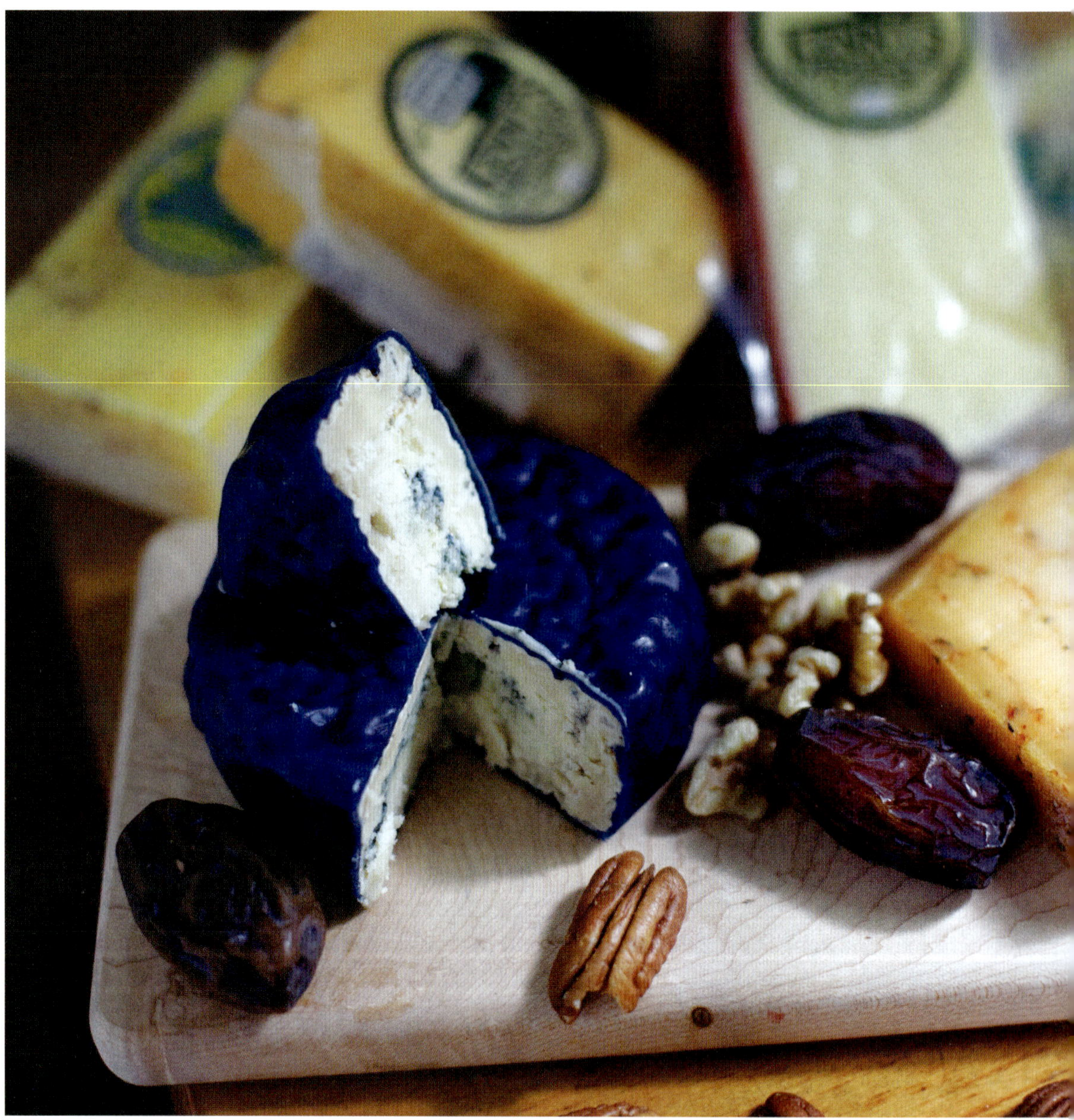

Kenny's Farmhouse Kentucky Bleu wears a bright blue wax coating on this Kentucky cheese plate, full of wonderful flavors. *Sarah Jane Sanders*.

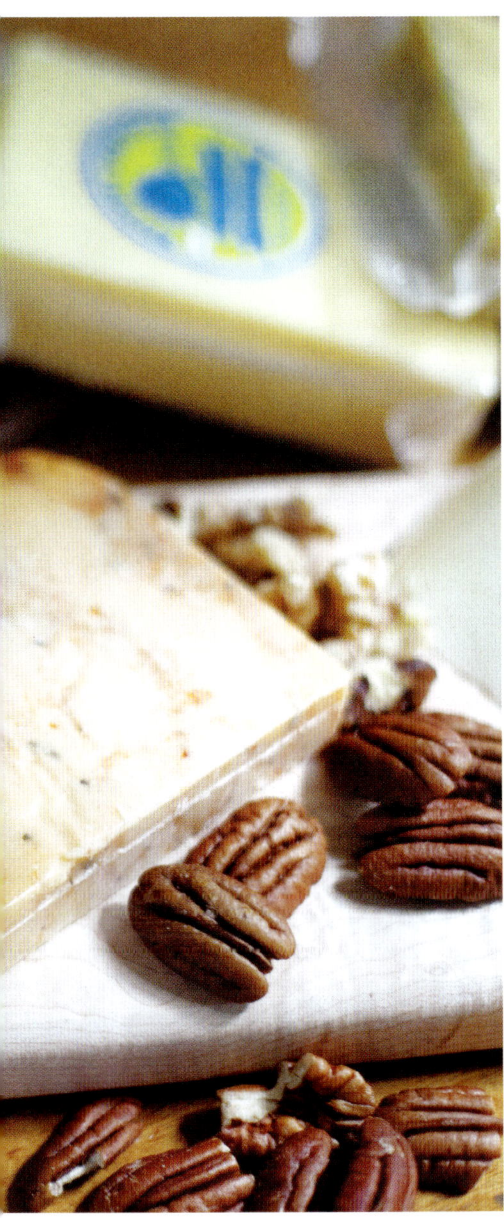

Kentucky milk, in one of the few urban cheese making operations in the United States.

Kentucky's cheese makers are gaining experience, and it shows in the increasingly complex, deepening flavors and finer textures of their cheeses, year after year. The cheese makers' "caves" (ripening rooms) are also doing their parts as they become increasingly filled with beneficial microbes that deepen cheese flavors and improve cheese quality.

With a new Kentucky Cheese Guild planned for 2014, Kentucky's new approach to making great cheese takes another step toward its own ripening. This calls for a celebration; most likely some exquisite Kentucky cheese will be involved.

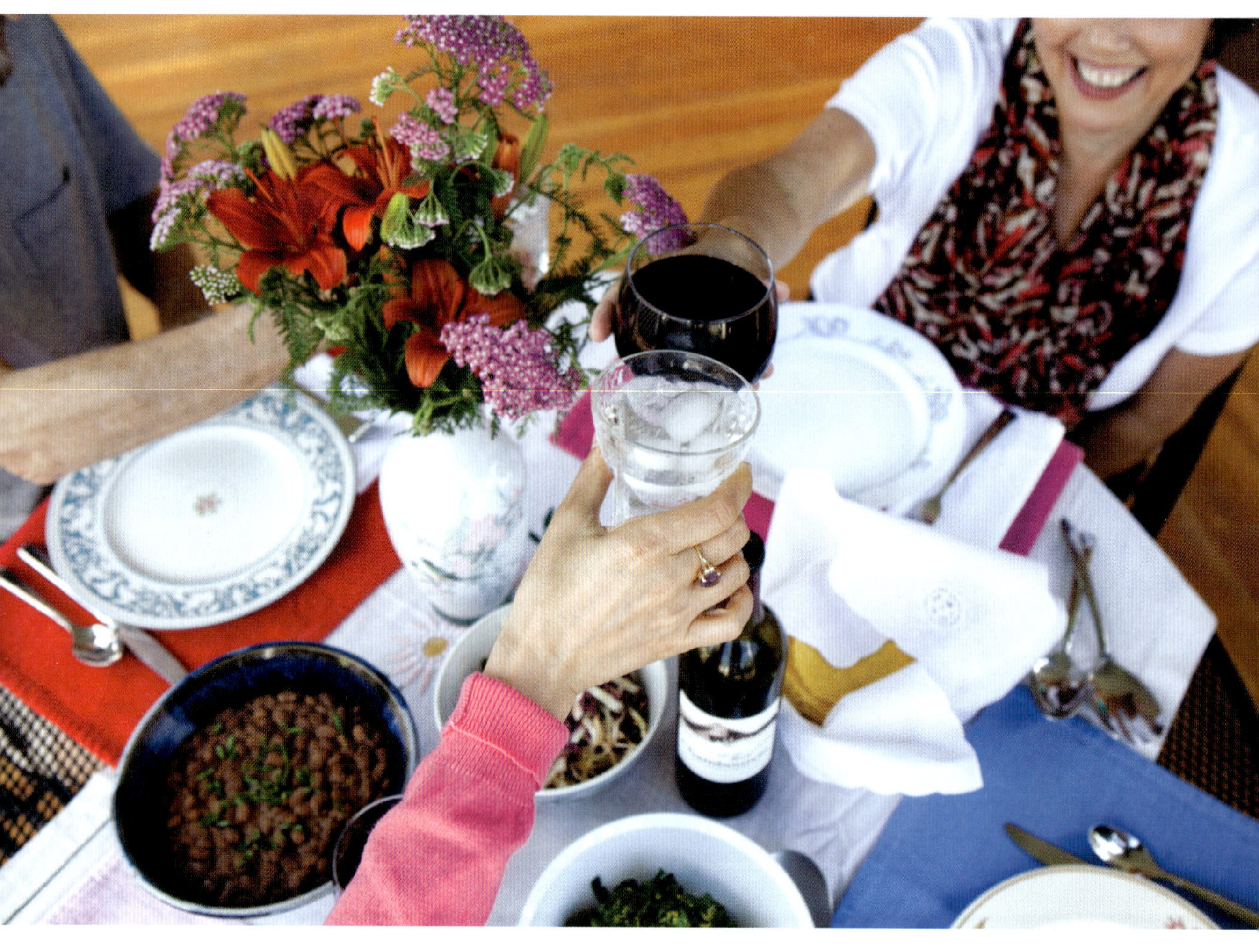

Friends says "Cheers" to a rich (but not expensive) Kentucky meal and to the wealth of friends who share it. *Sarah Jane Sanders*.

Meal 5

COUNTRY SPLENDOR: PERFECT SMOKY PINTO BEANS, GREENS AND GOODNESS

Everyday life is the best. And everyday food from Kentucky makes the tongue and tummy happy. Make this rich, dark, warming food well, and notice your popularity rise.

Everyday Menu

Perfect Smoky Pinto Beans from Scratch
Smoky Pintos, Quick Method
Slow-Cooked Kentucky Greens
Quick Kentucky Greens with Garlic
United We Stand Corn Muffins
Fresh and Tangy Slaw

For special occasions or holidays, dress up wonderful beans and greens by adding more side dishes with tart, fresh flavors; they lighten and leaven the meal. Finish with a splendid fruit crisp made of Kentucky's state fruit, the blackberry, or any other Kentucky fruit. The sweetening relies on small amounts of three Kentucky sweeteners to keep the taste spotlight on the real star—pure fruit flavors, with all their wonder and complexity.

Dressed-up Menu Additions

Pickled Commonwealth Beets
Tomato-Feta Salad
Sliced Cantaloupe with Fresh Berries and Mint
Sweet Sorghum Hot Pepper Relish
State Fruit Crisp

Perfect Pairings

- *Cocktail:* The Levisa Fork
- *Wine:* Horseshoe Bend Rosé of Cabernet Franc for its lusciousness and excellent ability to highlight the smoke and salt in this meal
- *Beer:* West Sixth Pay It Forward Cocoa Porter or the latest Country Western (a collaborative beer made by West Sixth Brewing Company and Country Boy Brewing)
- *Tea:* Elmwood Fine Tea's Kentucky Blend black tea, hot with the berry crisp or iced with everything
- *Coffee:* CaffeMarco's Yirgacheffe for its lemony lightness with the berry crisp
- *Soundtrack for cooking:* "Blue Smoke" (Merle Travis), "Don't Come Home A-Drinkin' (With Lovin' on Your Mind)" (Loretta Lynn), "Co-Dependent with You" (Reel World String Band), "Cocaine Blues" (Merle Travis), "Green Pastures" (Emmylou Harris & Ricky Skaggs), "Cotton-Eyed Joe" (the Chieftans, Ricky Skaggs), "Hello Stranger" (the Carter Family), "Come On-A My House" (Rosemary Clooney) "Darkest Hour Is Just Before Dawn" (Emmylou Harris & Ricky Skaggs), "I'm a Man of Constant Sorrow" (the Stanley Brothers), "Have Mercy" (the Judds), "I Got Rhythm—Live" (Lionel Hampton)
- *Soundtrack for eating:* "Blue Eyed Kentucky Girl" (Loretta Lynn), "Blue Moon of Kentucky" (Bill Monroe & His Blue Grass Boys), "My Old Kentucky Home" (Louis Armstrong), "Fallin' in Love" (Henry Hipkens), "Bury Me In Bluegrass" (Reel World String Band), "A Week in a Country Jail" (Tom T. Hall), "Midnight" (Red Foley), "You're Lookin' at Country" (Loretta Lynn), "My Sunny Days" (the Kentucky Headhunters), "Spanish Flang Dango" (Lily May Ledford), "Tiptoe Lightly" (Reel World String Band), "Stranger Things Have Happened" (Henry Hipkens), "Swanee River" (Dave Brubeck), "Take Me Back to Renfro Valley" (the Osborne Brothers, Mac Wise), "That's What Angels Do" (Laura Bell Bundy), "Hard Times Come Again No More" (Deborah Rentz-Moore, Lydia Brotherton, Ensemble Phoenix Munich)

Opposite: The Levisa Fork cocktail is a wonder: vanilla drenched, bourbon blessed, orange finished. *Sarah Jane Sanders*.

The Levisa Fork

Like sitting on the front porch glider, peacefully watching the river flow, this homey, vanilla-scented cocktail eases and pleases before an earthy meal.

Yield: 1 cocktail

¼ whole vanilla bean, split, seeds intact
1 section orange zest, about an inch long
¼ ounce sorghum simple syrup (see "Simple Syrups," page 90)
2 dashes orange bitters
1½ ounces Kentucky bourbon
ice
vanilla bean and orange "wheel" for garnish (optional)

Working directly in the serving glass—a rocks-style glass works perfectly—muddle (press/turn/push/press) the vanilla bean and orange zest well with the sorghum simple syrup and the bitters. This jumpstarts the drink's richness as the vanilla bean seeds and orange peel oils release flavors and aromatics into the mixture. Add ice to fill the glass. Add bourbon and stir. Garnish, if you like, with the vanilla bean and orange wheel on the side of the glass.

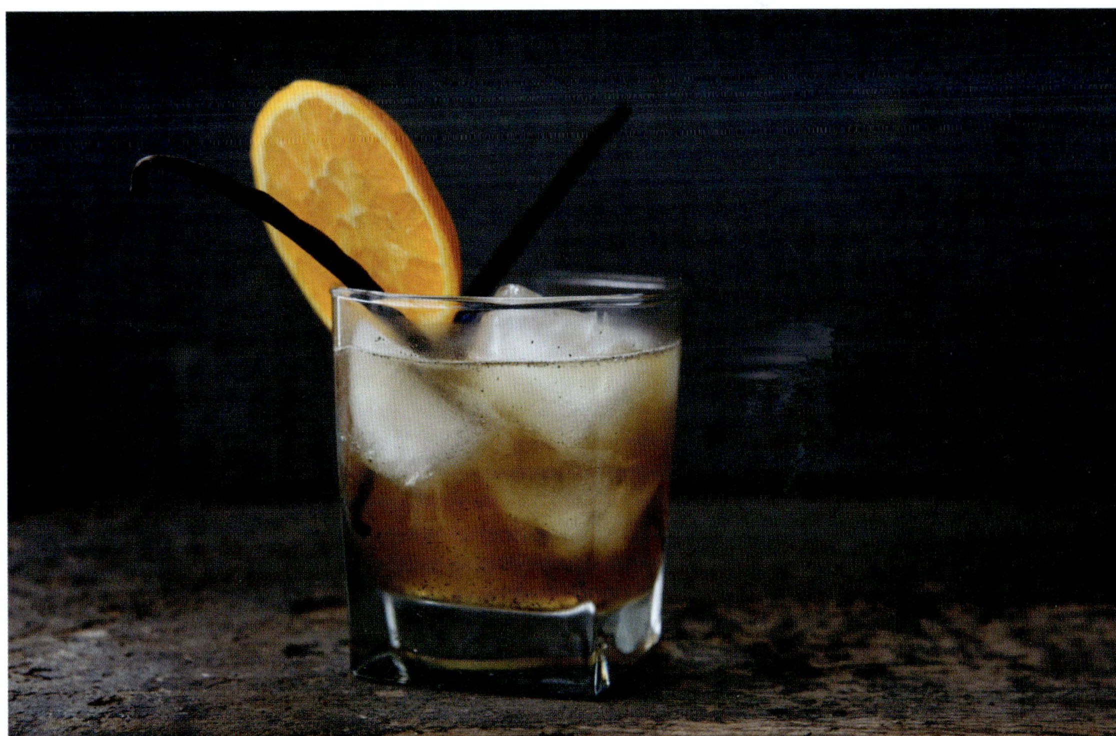

EVERYDAY MENU

Perfect Smoky Pinto Beans from Scratch

Honestly, at least fifty types of cooked pinto or soup beans merit that "perfect" assessment. The most perfect of all, for most Kentuckians, will always be the beans served at a beloved childhood table. Fortunately, we can see in the rearview mirror that dreary era when the "Food Police" outlawed pork in cooked beans and stews. Today's Kentucky pork, often cured with nothing more sinister than celery powder, merits high praise for flavor and nutrients. And real chicken broth works well, too—especially when those chickens come from Kentucky's pastures.

Here are two fantastic ways to make cooked pinto beans, which we also call "soup beans" in parts of the Bluegrass State. In either recipe, you get to control the degree of actual soupiness.

Yield: Serves 8 generously

1 pound (about two cups) pinto beans, brine-soaked (see "About Cooking Navy Beans From Scratch," page 103)
Kentucky smoked pork for seasoning: a Colonel Newsom or Scott Ham hock, a bacon rind or 8 slices bacon, cut into 1-inch pieces (bacon works whether cooked first or not, so you choose)
½ teaspoon baking soda
salt, to taste after beans are nearly cooked
dried hot red pepper, one or two bay leaves and a large white or yellow onion, either whole or quartered (optional)

Put the brine-soaked beans in a slow cooker or large pot. Add water to cover, then 2 cups more. Add the smoked pork, baking soda and other optional seasonings. Cover.

Cook on low heat until just right. Beans, stoves and slow cookers vary so greatly it is not possible to predict cooking time precisely. Some guidelines are 1) for stovetop cooking, do the first test at 90 minutes; plan on about 3 hours cooking or 2) if you are using a slow cooker, cook on high heat and do the first test after 2 hours; plan on at least 4 hours cooking time.

Serve in individual soup bowls or in one large bowl. Choose garnishes from "Classic Toppings for Greens" (see page 161) because these toppings go beautifully with pinto beans as well.

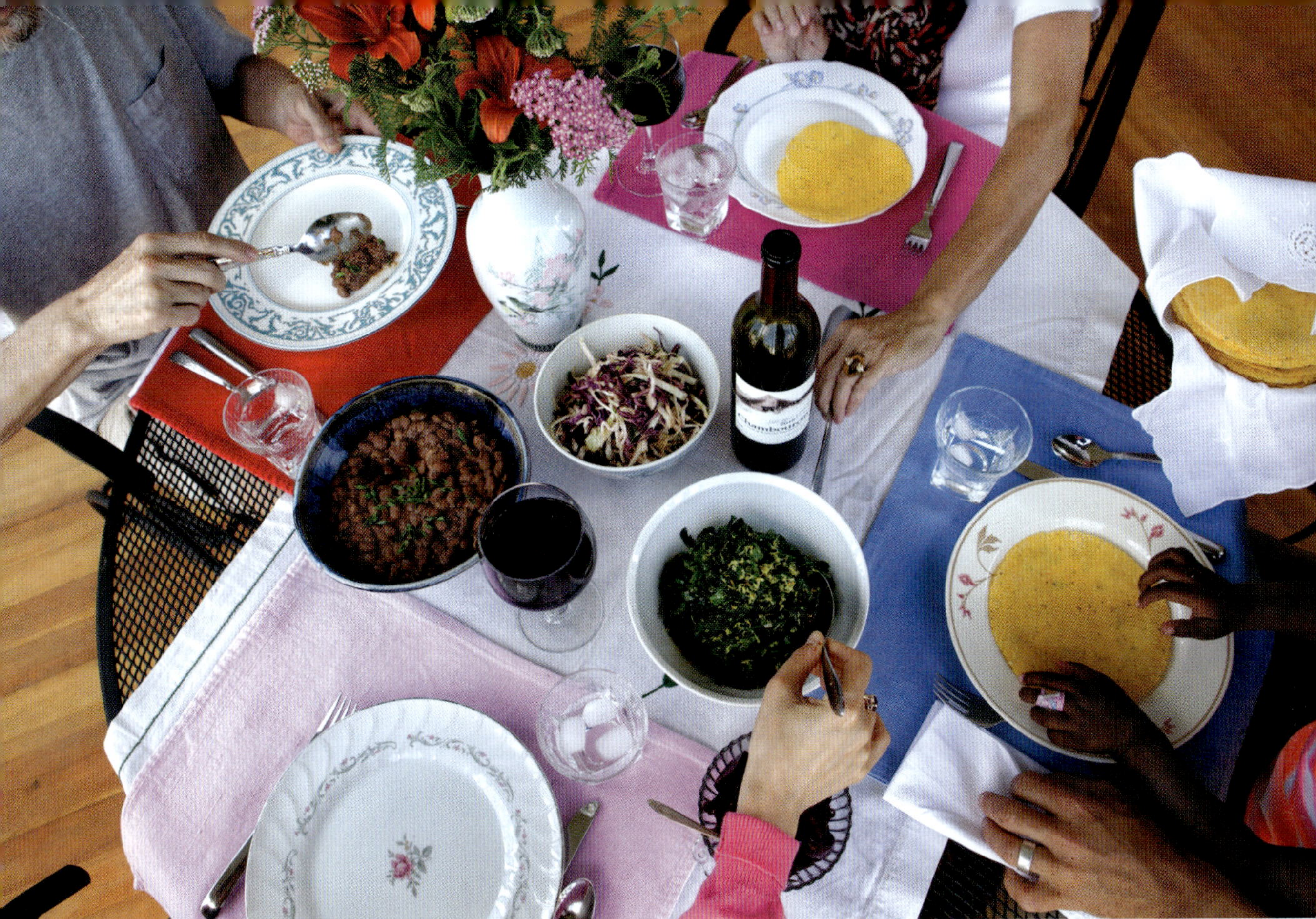

Tortillas, beans, slaw and greens are wonderful eats from Kentucky's timeless abundance. *Sarah Jane Sanders*.

Flavorful Beans without Pork

If you want delicious, pork-free beans, replace some or all of the cooking water with chicken broth and don't add the pork (of course!). Use homemade broth if you have it (see page 59) or buy an unsalted commercial broth. Add a whole or quartered yellow onion, studded with five or six whole cloves. Add a couple bay leaves and, if you like heat, include a dried hot pepper or a teaspoon or so of hot pepper flakes. Taste carefully for salt when the beans are nearly done and adjust as needed.

When Are Pinto Beans Done?

For any pinto beans, you will be the judge of how done they get and how soupy you want them to be when you serve them. These factors are a bit entwined, but we will separate them here.

Here's how to test the beans' doneness. Fish out a couple of beans, cool them slightly and taste/feel. Assess.

- *If they are cooked through but not yet creamy*, they are almost done. Remove any large piece of seasoning meat; let it cool if necessary; pull or cut into small pieces and return to the pot. Cook for another 30 minutes. Add salt if needed. The beans should now be mostly intact, with a few burst open; all should be creamy and moist in your hungry mouth.
- *If they are still crunchy in the middle*, cook another hour and then test again. Repeat until the beans reach the magic stage: cooked but not yet mushy. Add salt if needed. Beans and cookers vary; allow lots of time. This step can take several hours.

In addition, you can manage the degree of soupiness to your satisfaction.

- *To decrease soupiness*. If you use a slow cooker, you will almost certainly end up with a lot of extra juice surrounding your finished beans. Either serve soup and beans together as "soup beans" in bowls or, for a less juicy side dish, remove beans from the soup with a slotted spoon into a serving dish. You can also mash a cup or two of beans with a potato masher, or anything you like, and return the mash to the soup to thicken it
- *To create MORE soup*. If you are cooking on a stovetop and want the beans soupy, you may need to add boiling water one or more times during cooking. If you want the beans creamy but not too runny, for serving on a plate instead of in a bowl, allow the beans to absorb the cooking liquid toward the end of their cooking time. Stir gently often and keep a close watch to prevent sticking.
- *To infuse flavors from the soup into un-soupy beans*. If your beans make lots of soupy liquid and you want to enjoy the flavor of that liquid with less soupiness, separate the beans and soup by pouring the beans through a colander over a large saucepan. (Be careful!) Cook the soup at a low boil until it reduces by ½ to ⅔. Before you add this concentrated flavor-upper to the cooked beans, taste a bit to be sure it is not too salty. Add as much or as little as you like to reach the bean-to-soup ratio that suits you best.

Smoky Pintos, Quick Method

Yield: Serves 8 generously

1 large onion, diced
2 tablespoons bacon fat or olive oil
4 (15-ounce) cans cooked pinto beans (look for ones with no added chemicals other than salt)
2 cups water or chicken stock
additional salt, to taste (optional)
4 slices cooked, chopped bacon, or other smoked pork bits (optional)
1 dried red pepper (optional)

In a large, heavy-bottomed pot, sauté the onion in the bacon fat or olive oil until it is lightly browned on the edges. Add the remaining ingredients, including any add-ins.

Cook slowly 30 minutes. Taste and add salt, if needed.

Make adjustments as needed to manage soupiness. (See "When Are Pinto Beans Done?" page 158)

Serve in individual soup bowls or in one large bowl. Offer add-your-own toppings for beans and greens if you like (see "Classic Toppings for Greens," page 161)

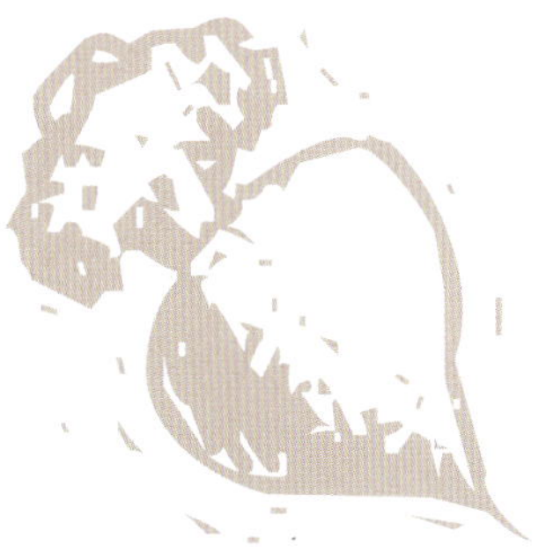

Stellar Greens

Kentucky's first cookbook author Mrs. Lettice Bryan said of "Turnip Sallad," or cooked turnip greens, "They should always be boiled with bacon, it being the only good way they can be prepared." What tasted good in 1839 tastes good today. We have also learned new ways to make cooked greens wonderful, in addition to employing trusty bacon.

Even for mature greens, stick with cooking times of around thirty minutes maximum. No need to cook a good green leaf until it loses its integrity. Here are recipes for medium-cooked greens, as well as a garlic-infused, quick-sautéed version. Try new options, and experiment on your own.

Much as Kentuckians love long-cooked greens, this green, crunchy quick-cooked Lacinato kale with Blue Moon garlic and garnishes has its own fan club. *Sarah Jane Sanders.*

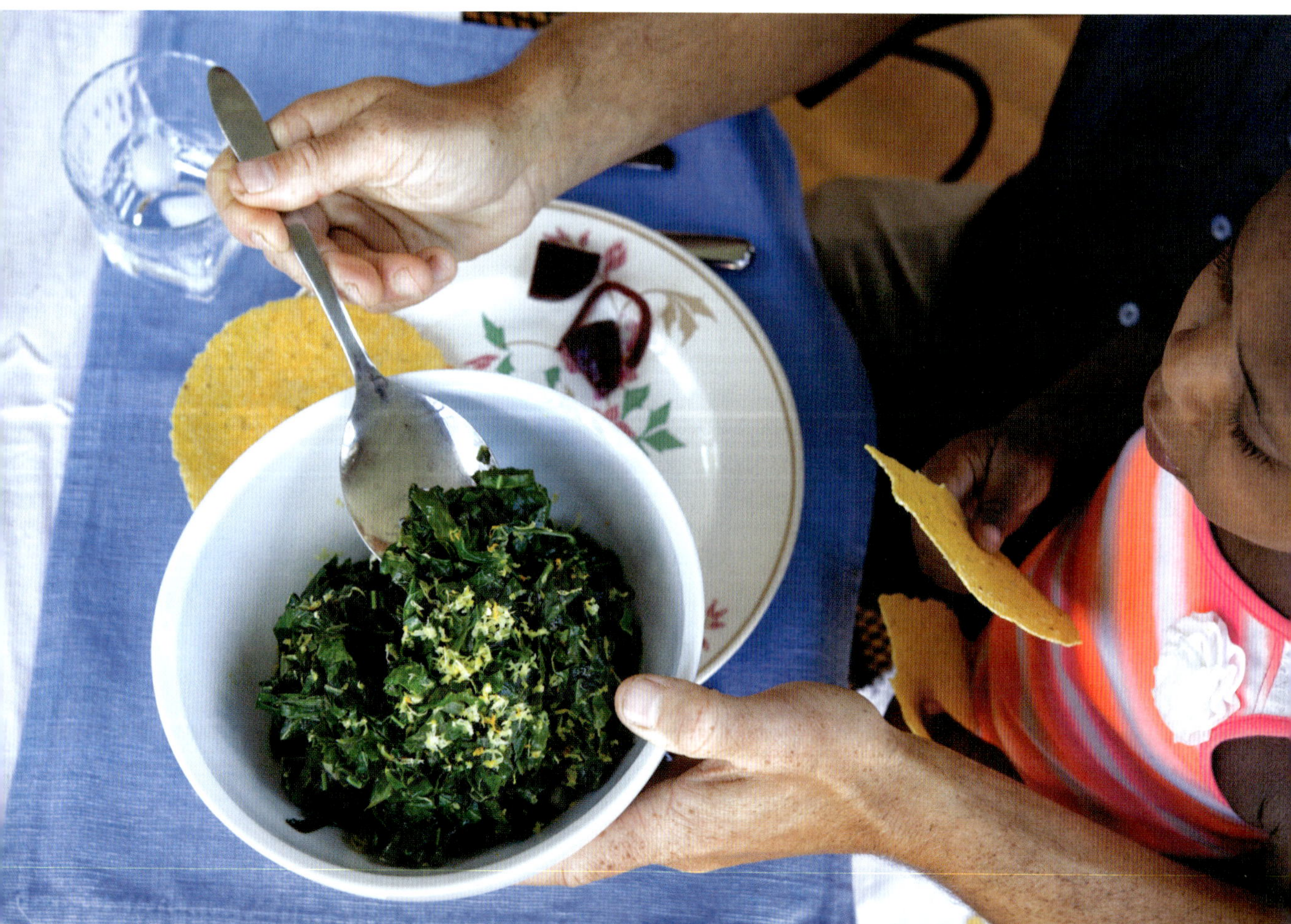

Slow-Cooked Kentucky Greens

Yield: Greens shrink fantastically during cooking. Six pounds of greens, once cleaned and de-stemmed, should serve 8 people as part of a larger meal.

1 Kentucky country ham hock, or about 4 ounces good Kentucky bacon, salt pork or other smoked pork
6 pounds washed, de-stemmed greens—either use a single type of green or any mix of kale, collards, turnip greens, young poke, mustard greens, beet greens, bok choy or other Asian greens, dandelion greens, chard or other types (see "How to Wash and Prep Greens," page 100)
salt and pepper, to taste

In your largest stockpot or slow cooker, set the rinsed pork to simmer in a gallon of cool water. Cook 1–2 hours.

Tear the greens into bite sized pieces. Leave them damp. Add the greens to the porky broth. Cook 30 minutes.

Remove the pork, and when you can handle it, take it apart into bite-sized pieces and return it to the pot.

Cook 5 more minutes.

Taste, correct seasonings and serve with any of the traditional toppings in their own small dishes alongside.

Classic Toppings for Greens

Enjoy any of these toppings for Kentucky greens, alone or in combination:

- cider vinegar
- sliced or whole fresh green onions or chopped mature onions
- diced or sliced fresh hot peppers
- sliced pickled jalapeños
- hard boiled eggs
- invent new toppings: fresh herbs! Chopped sun-dried tomatoes!

Quick Kentucky Greens with Garlic

Yield: 5 pounds of greens, cleaned, de-stemmed and quick-cooked, should serve 8 people as part of a larger meal.

5 pounds washed and spun or towel-dried, de-stemmed greens—either use a single type of green or any mix of kale, collards, turnip greens, young poke, mustard greens, beet greens, bok choy or other Asian greens, dandelion greens, chard or other types

3 tablespoons good olive oil

4 or more cloves of fresh Kentucky garlic, such as Blue Moon, sliced thin or minced fine

½ teaspoon red pepper flakes (optional but highly advised)

Using a sharp knife and a cutting board, make stacks of de-stemmed greens and slice across their leaves to make thin slivers, about ⅛ inch wide. Don't worry if the width varies some.

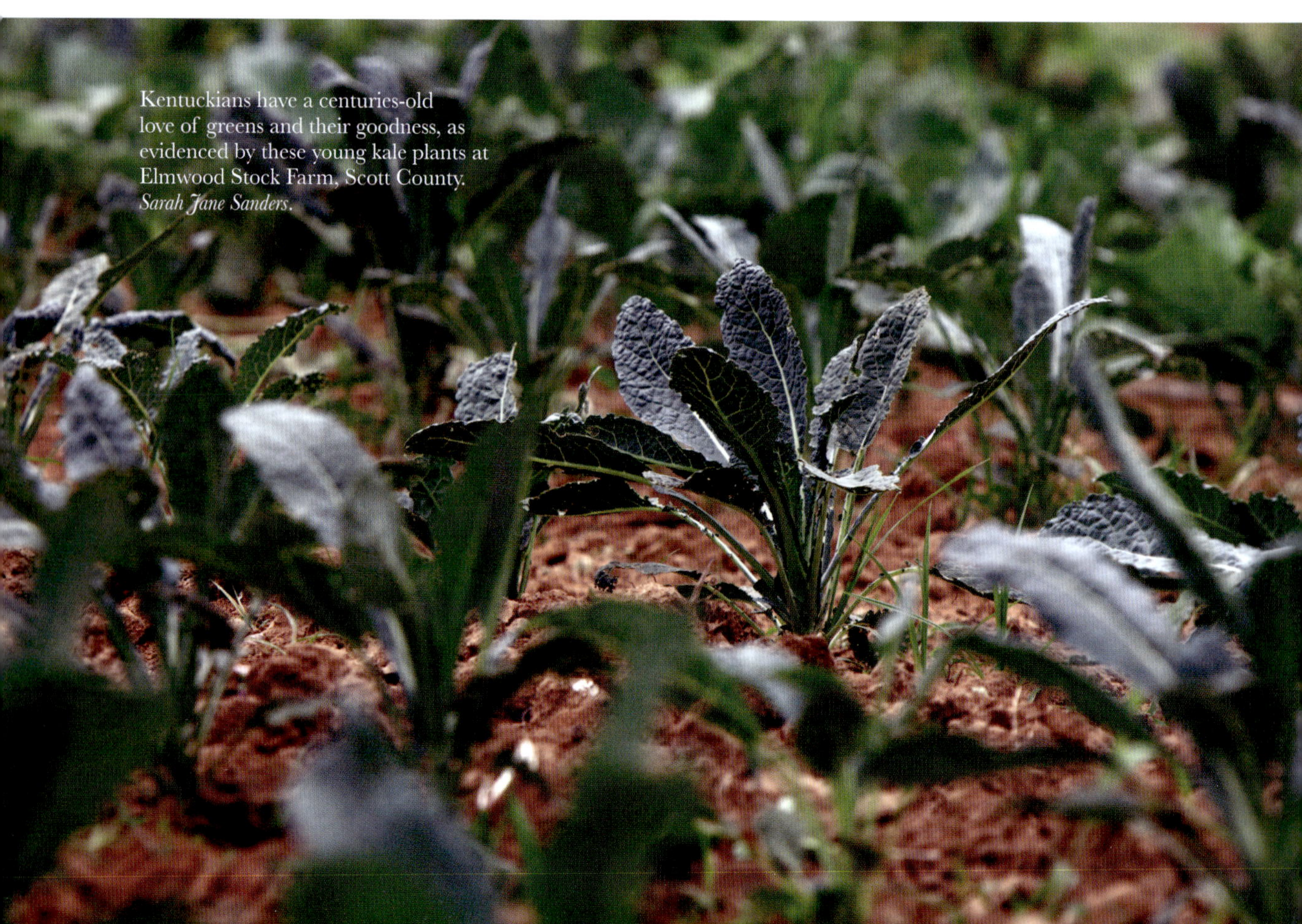

Kentuckians have a centuries-old love of greens and their goodness, as evidenced by these young kale plants at Elmwood Stock Farm, Scott County. *Sarah Jane Sanders.*

Heat the oil on medium in a large, heavy skillet that has a lid. When you can smell the oil, add the garlic and red pepper flakes, if using. Stir for 30 seconds.

Add the greens (spatter, spatter) and stir to distribute the oil through the greens. Cover the skillet with its lid; turn the heat to low. Cook two minutes. Uncover; turn the heat to high, stirring the greens constantly, until they are wilted, still quite green and tender with a little bit of resistance if you poke them with a fork (or bite a slightly cooled sample green with your teeth).

Serve greens immediately.

Cornbread in Small Packages: Tortillas or Muffins

For most of Kentucky's history, cornbreads from home have been best. With the rare exceptions of spoon bread and a few delicious corn muffins, I have never eaten a restaurant-produced cornbread that I would want to try again. Fresh tortillas offer a new option.

In most towns in Kentucky, we can now buy freshly made tortillas daily, and they are scrumptious. We may eventually become good at making tortillas at home, but for now, local stores like Lexington's Tortilleria Ramirez offer packages of fifty or one hundred warm, handmade tortillas that taste wonderful with Kentucky pinto beans, greens and side dishes.

When Mexico and Kentucky meet on your plate, you dunk fresh tortillas in pinto bean soup or roll a few pinto beans in a tortilla, add lime-scented slaw and hot pepper relish and indulge. Or perhaps you butter and salt the tortillas and eat them separately from the soup and sides. The timeless corn and beans theme will sound forth! This is a great combination. Add Kentucky hot sauce like Sav's Piment or Screaming Mimi's at will.

United We Stand Corn Muffins

Recall that Kentucky is a border state, and many towns are famous for hospitality to strangers. What if we reach out to embrace a big world of corn muffins by adding—gasp—some flour and a bit of Kentucky sweetener to lighten and entice friends of another cornbread persuasion? Here's a new way to bridge the North-South Cornbread Divide with a muffin that tones down the northern sugar and lightens up the southern texture, while centering on those core Kentucky flavors: corn, bacon and onion.

Yield: 12 mid-sized muffins

1 cup all-purpose flour
1 cup cornmeal, yellow or white; use bolted meal if you want a smoother texture and unbolted if you prefer more crunch
2 teaspoons baking powder
½ teaspoon baking soda
½ teaspoon salt (increase if the bacon is not salty)
½ cup corn kernels
4 slices thick-cut bacon, fried crisp and chopped fine
2 tablespoons finely chopped fresh chives or green onions or grated onion
2 eggs
½ cup milk
½ cup buttermilk
2 tablespoons bacon fat or melted butter
2 teaspoons Kentucky sorghum, maple syrup or honey (optional)

Preheat oven to 400 degrees Fahrenheit.

Mix together flour, cornmeal, baking powder, baking soda and salt in a large bowl. Add corn kernels, bacon and chives or onion. Stir lightly.

Add all wet ingredients to the bowl: milk, buttermilk, eggs, fat or melted butter and sweetener.

Stir wet and dry ingredients together just until mixed.

Spoon into 12 greased or sprayed muffin tins.

Bake 15–20 minutes, or until spotted with light brown on top.

Fresh and Tangy Slaw

Slaw can bore you and your taste buds, or it can make them rub their sleepy eyes and say, "Whoa, Nellie! What's this freshness?" This slaw, made from familiar ingredients with just one exotic touch of lime, brightens any meal. It makes a fine complement to the richness of beans, greens, and cornbread.

Yield: Serves 8 generously

1 lime, zest grated and juice squeezed (or substitute 4 teaspoons rice or cider vinegar)
1 clove garlic, very finely diced
1 teaspoon cumin
1 scant teaspoon mild or hot chili powder (your choice)
1 tablespoon Kentucky sorghum, honey or maple syrup
salt and pepper, to taste
¼ cup olive oil

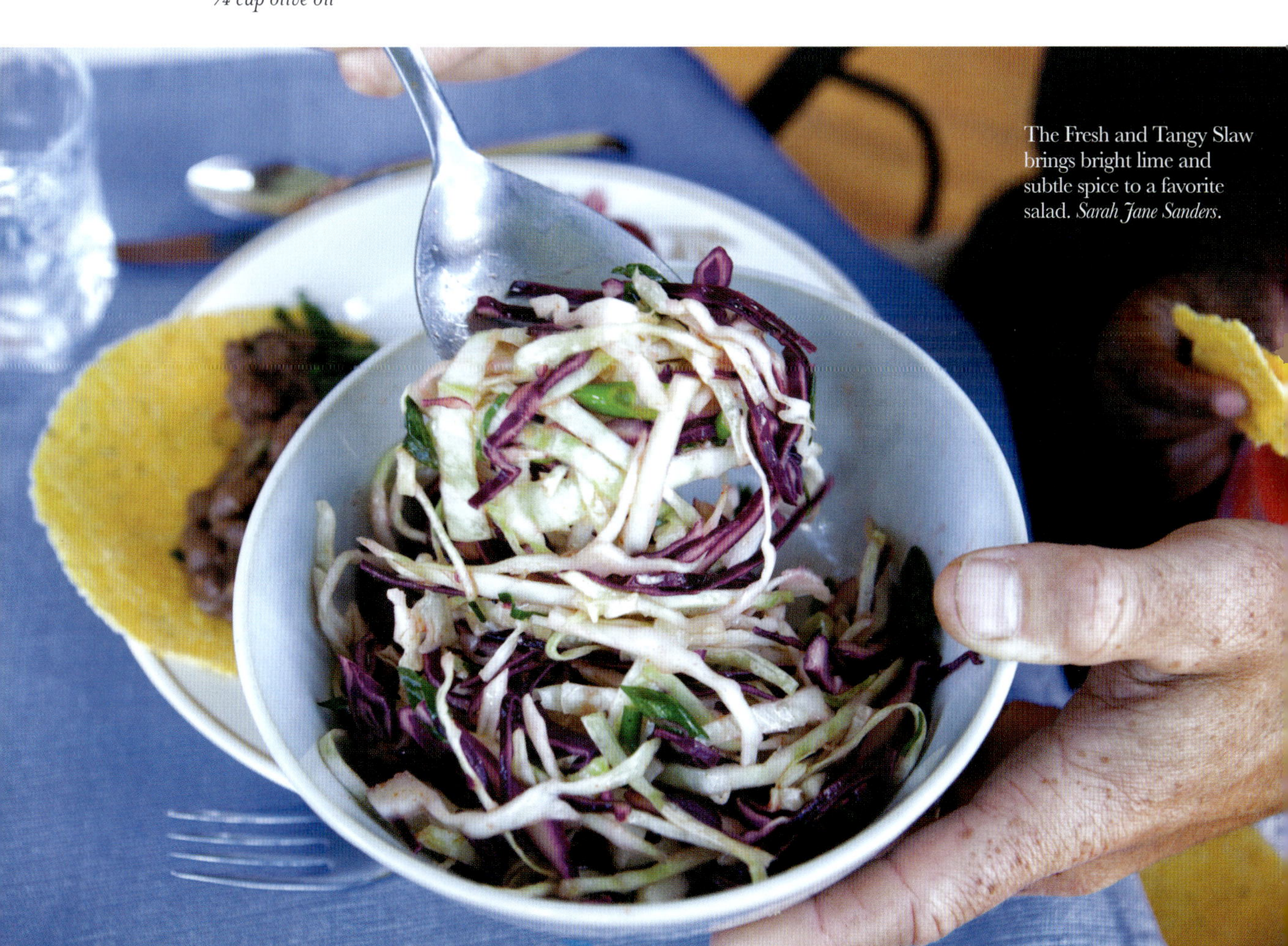

The Fresh and Tangy Slaw brings bright lime and subtle spice to a favorite salad. *Sarah Jane Sanders.*

1 head fresh cabbage, either green or red, or half a head of each, about 2½ pounds total, finely shredded (not grated)
2 green onions, finely chopped, or 2 tablespoons finely chopped chives
fine slivers carrot or sweet red pepper for color
¼ cup or more chopped fresh cilantro or parsley (optional)
hot pepper high notes from 1 jalapeño or serrano, finely chopped; ¼ teaspoon or more ground cayenne; or ½ teaspoon or more crushed red pepper flakes (optional)

In a small bowl or measuring cup, mix the dressing ingredients thoroughly: lime zest and juice (or vinegar), garlic, cumin, chili powder, sweetener, salt, pepper and olive oil. Alternatively, blend this mixture in a blender for 1 minute. Set aside.

In a large bowl, mix the cabbage(s), onions, carrots or red peppers and any added herbs or hot peppers. Pour the dressing over the salad and stir it well.

Enjoy any leftovers; refrigerate for up to 1 week.

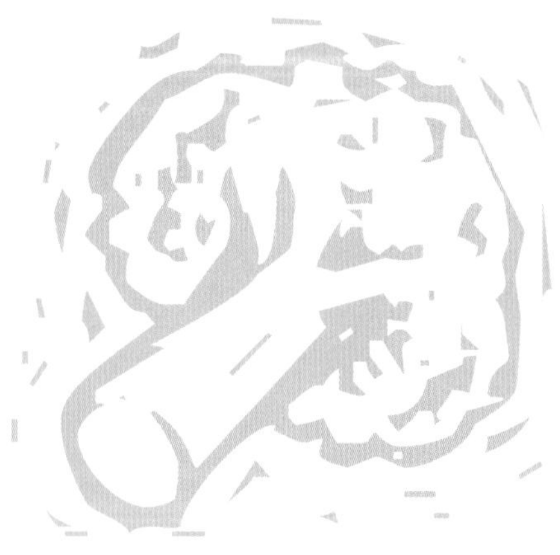

DRESSED-UP MENU

Pickled Commonwealth Beets

Pickled beets tickle both the adults in our house. Through mysteries of settlement and migration we cannot quite trace, the umpteenth-generation commonwealth of Kentucky Protestant and the second-generation commonwealth of Massachusetts Jewish mill towner both grew up in households where pickled beets graced the tables.

For years near the end of his long life, my dad grew a sizable row of beets in his Wayne County garden with one main purpose: to pickle and can a year's supply for his Massachusetts son-in-law. Dad made pickled beets as Mother had taught him—by taste, rather than by recipe. We have run lots of trials and settled on this approach to making sweet-tart Pickled Commonwealth Beets that both of us find delicious.

Yield: 1 gallon pickled beets (4 quart jars or 2 half-gallon jars)

3 quarts (about 12 cups) scrubbed, fresh whole beets, tops removed; any size works, but ideally the beets are of similar size so they cook evenly
1 tablespoon mixed pickling spices
3 cups cider vinegar
3 cups reserved beet liquid
2 cups sugar
1½ teaspoons salt
2 medium yellow or white onions, thinly sliced vertically and then into half-moons

Put the beets in a very large stockpot; cover with cool water and add 3 cups more. Cover and cook over medium-low heat until the largest beet can be pierced through with a slender knife or ice pick without much resistance. This can take 45–60 minutes.

Remove the pot from the heat. Set a strainer over a large bowl or measuring cup. Pour the red cooking liquid through the strainer until you have captured three cups of hot beet liquid. Set that aside. Drain and discard the rest of the liquid from the beets. Let the beets cool for 15 minutes in the sink or in a large mesh strainer.

Tie the pickling spices into a loose bundle in a piece of cheesecloth or clean fabric.

As the beets cool, prepare the liquid that pickles them. In a large saucepan over medium-high heat, cook the vinegar, reserved beet liquid, sugar, salt and pickling spices in their little packet. Once the mixture reaches a boil, cook one minute to be sure the sugar dissolves. Remove from heat.

Add the sliced onions to the hot pickling liquid; stir well. Leave them to soften a little as you prepare the beets.

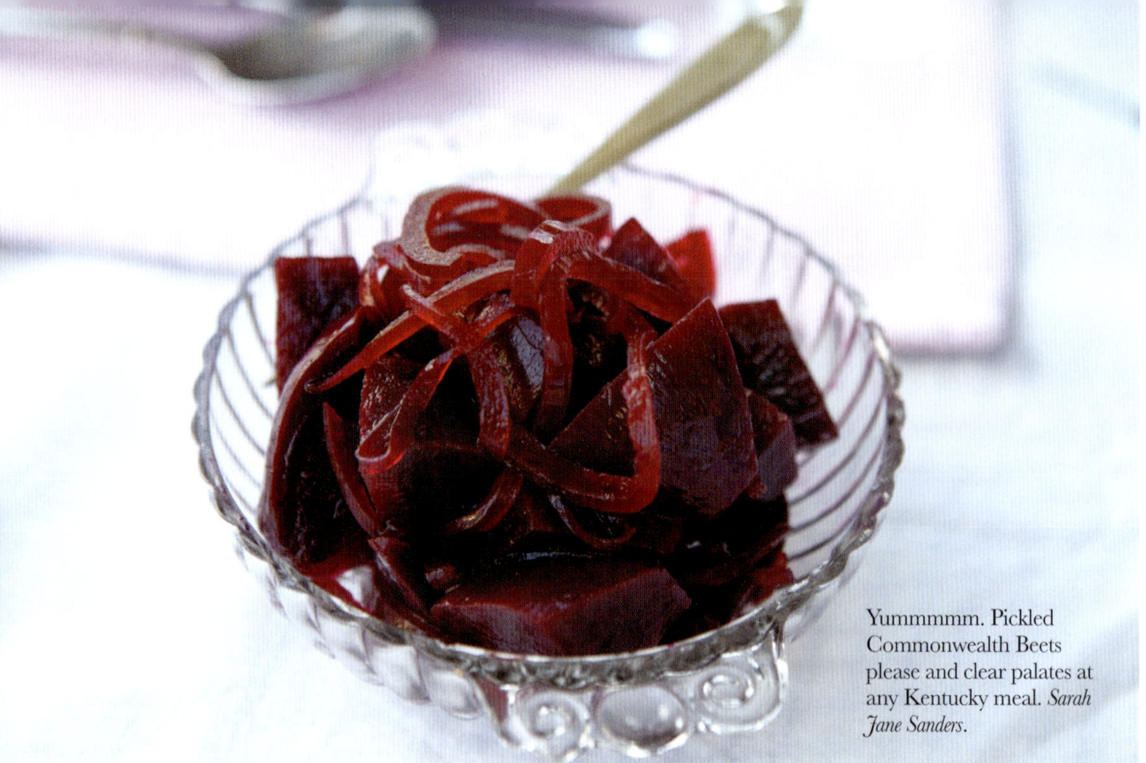

Yummmmm. Pickled Commonwealth Beets please and clear palates at any Kentucky meal. *Sarah Jane Sanders.*

Pickled Beets Bonus: Pickled Eggs

After you eat the beets from a jar, do something amazingly easy and good: use the lovely beet-purple liquid to pickle hard-boiled eggs. Hard boil 4–5 eggs per quart jar. Cool and peel the eggs. Carefully slip the whole, peeled eggs into the pickling liquid and return the jar to the refrigerator. Eat the eggs within one week. They are best after three days.

Peel the beets. Usually you can simply squeeze a beet a little and its rough skin remains in your hand as a slick, clean beet emerges. Use a knife to clean any beets that have rough spots or stubborn skin.

For medium and large beets, chop into pieces that are no larger than half an egg or cut the beets into your family's favorite shape and size. Small beets stay whole.

Fill clean jars about ⅓ full with prepared beets. With tongs, fish some softened onions from the pickling liquid and layer on top of the beets. Repeat the layers, stopping just below the top of the jars' rounded shoulders. Add hot pickling liquid to cover or nearly cover the beets. Discard the pickling spices.

Set lids loosely on the jar(s) of beets. Cool completely. Then fasten the lids in place, not too tightly, and store in the refrigerator. Pickled beets keep at least 8 weeks (although not in the house of pickled beet lovers.)

Note: Yes, you may can these beets instead of refrigerating. Canning will make them stable and safe at room temperature for some years. Watch this three-minute video online for good canning guidance: Tips for Water-Bath Canning For Dummies (http://bit.ly/1pGOR7W).

Tomato-Feta Salad

You always remember your first time eating a tomato-feta salad—or at least, I remember mine. A friend who cooked beautiful, unusual food served a tomato-feta salad during a summer meal. The ways the flavors played with one another made me imagine a lot of ingredients and secret techniques must be involved.

Surprise! Four ingredients make this salad, although you can add more if you want. You don't need to measure, although I will suggest some amounts to get you started. No peeling, no seeding and salad in three minutes! This salad is as good as the quality of its basic ingredients.

Yield: 8 servings

3 pounds sweet, fully ripe summer tomatoes, all one type or mixed (you will need about 2 very large Brandywine or other heirloom tomatoes or 5 to 6 medium-sized tomatoes)
2 ounces good feta cheese, such as Bleugrass Chevre feta
1 tablespoon good balsamic vinegar, such as Stuarto's Fig Balsamic
1 teaspoon salt (a crunchy salt, such as Maldon, is good in this dish)

Wash and core the tomatoes. Chop them into tablespoon-sized chunks and put them in a medium-sized bowl.

Crumble the feta into the bowl.

Sprinkle the balsamic vinegar over the bowl; add the salt.

If you want no add-ins, your salad is done. Stir well and serve in bowls with spoons. It is a wonderfully juicy salad, and all those juices deserve to be savored.

Possible add-ins: black pepper, chopped fresh parsley or cilantro, torn basil leaves, fennel fronds, fresh summer corn kernels (roasted, grilled or raw), finely chopped chives or scallions, olive oil, thinly sliced raw sweet onion or shallots, grilled or roasted onion rings, red pepper flakes and more.

My personal favorite version adds two ingredients: a small dollop of olive oil and a heavy grating of fresh black pepper.

Sliced Cantaloupe with Fresh Berries and Mint

Perfect cantaloupe needs nothing, not even salt, to bring its perfection to the taste buds. Even perfection, though, can be dressed up a little. This recipe works beautifully for many kinds of cantaloupe and its excellent melon cousins.

Although growing melons can be tricky, some Kentuckians seem to be especially good at it. Sam Livesay at Briary Creek Farms in Eubank (Pulaski County) brings a wide array of delicious melons to the Lexington Farmers' Market each summer, including several varieties of Crenshaw, canary melon, honeydews, Persian melons, Casaba and more. A sweet-tart drizzle dresses up good melon for eating with the main course, as a stand-alone refresher or a scrumptious light dessert.

Yield: Serves 8

¼ cup Kentucky maple syrup or honey
1 tablespoon lemon juice
½ teaspoon vanilla extract
⅛ teaspoon salt
1 excellent cantaloupe or similar melon, about 3 pounds
1 cup fresh, whole, clean berries (any type—raspberries, blackberries, blueberries, serviceberries, etc.)
1 tablespoon finely chopped fresh mint
1 cup red raspberries, fresh or frozen, for the drizzle, see note (optional)

Note: If you choose to include raspberries in the drizzle for their color and flavor, allow 90 minutes for steeping the optional cup of raspberries with the sweetener and cooling the mixture before proceeding with this recipe. Place 1 cup red raspberries in a small saucepan, and add the maple syrup or honey. Carefully, slowly stirring, bring to just under a boil. Let steep until cool, then strain through a fine sieve into a small bowl or measuring cup, pressing lightly to extract juice. Proceed with the rest of the recipe.

Mix together sweetener (whether raspberry-steeped or not), lemon juice, vanilla extract and salt. Stir well. Set aside.

Melon Scrub Sense

In recent years, we have learned the hard way that washing the outsides of melons—even when we are going to peel them, too—makes good safety sense. If you grow your own melons or buy from a trusted farmer, you may need to wash because of good old healthy soil that clings to the outsides. If you buy commercial melons, wash—even *scrub*—the melon all over before cutting and peeling. Scrubbing assures that any nasty bugs go down the drain instead of hitchhiking into the melon on your knife.

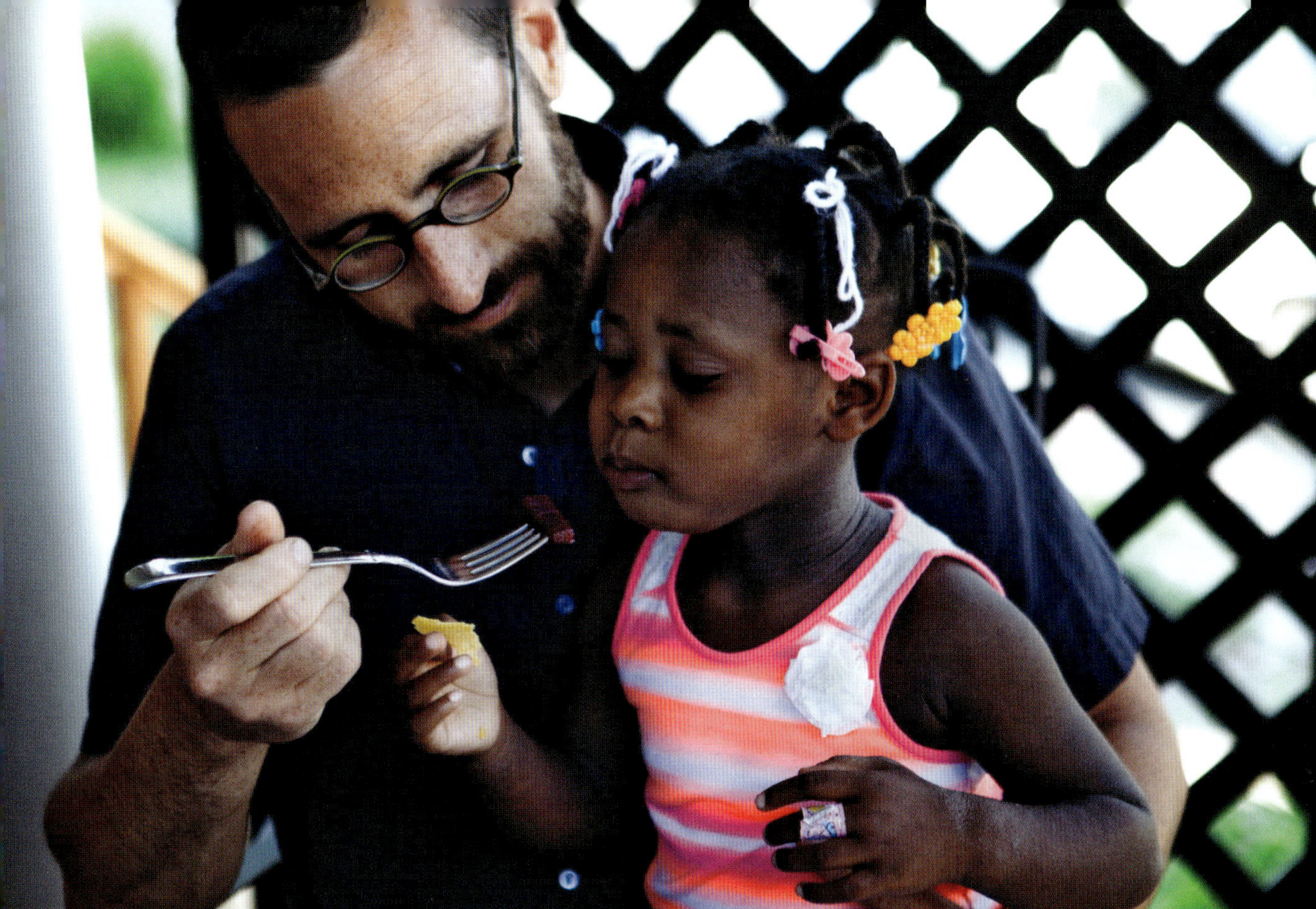

"I want to try it!" *Sarah Jane Sanders.*

Cut the washed melon in half; remove seeds for your compost or some friendly chickens.

Working with each half, or with quarters if that is easier, cut away the skin and any whitish, tough layer just beneath it. Slice the melon into chunks or, for a pretty presentation, into ultra-slim wedges. Arrange on a lovely platter. Sprinkle the berries around. Drizzle a little of the prepared syrup over the fruit. Top with mint.

Sweet Sorghum Hot Pepper Relish

Relish means "great enjoyment"—how appropriate for something pointedly hot, sweet, sour and salty all at once. Relish and salsa are first cousins, although relish has longer keeping powers in the refrigerator. Stir some of this relish into finely chopped peaches or cantaloupe, if you like, to create instant fresh fruit salsa.

2 cups (about ½ pound) hot green peppers (such as jalapeños, hot bananas or serranos), stemmed and seeds removed, for a milder relish
2 cups (½ pound) sweet red peppers (or replace with hot ones if you want doubly hot relish), stems and seeds removed
1 medium-sized onion (about ½ pound), quartered
1 scant tablespoon salt
½ cup cider vinegar
⅓ cup Kentucky sorghum
1 tablespoon whole mustard seeds, any color
½ teaspoon salt

Options: zest of one lemon, peeled in strips and cut in ⅛-inch slivers, to be added during cooking; 1 additional tablespoon sugar, if you prefer slightly sweeter relish

Note: Protect your skin while you cut fresh hot peppers by putting a plastic bag over the hand that holds the peppers during cutting. Move the cut peppers to the food processor or container using the plastic covered hand and your knife. Carefully remove and discard the plastic bag and wash the knife and cutting board well with soapy water.

Chop peppers and onion fine; a food processor with a steel blade works well for this. Pulse it slowly, just until the veggies look nicely shredded, about 5–7 times.

Place the pepper mixture in a mesh strainer, stir in 1 tablespoon salt and let macerate for at least two hours. Pour cool water through the vegetables and press them gently to remove as much water as possible.

In a medium saucepan with a heavy bottom, bring the vinegar, sorghum, mustard seeds and ¼ teaspoon salt to boil over medium heat; stir well. Add the strained vegetables and lemon zest, if using. Stir well, cover and simmer on low for 15 minutes. Stir a few times to keep the mixture from sticking. The juices will thicken slightly. Remove from heat and taste. If you want a hint more sweetness, add 1 tablespoon sugar; if you want sharper tastes, try another ¼ teaspoon salt. If you add sugar, cook two more minutes. Now let the relish rest until it reaches room temperature. Move to a glass jar for storage. This relish will keep several weeks in the refrigerator.

State Fruit Crisp

Fruit crisps make a fine finish to any meal. They are quick to make and easily delicious without being ruinous to good health. By using fresh fruits like blackberries—Kentucky's state fruit—or any combination of fruits you freeze or can at their peak, the glorious tastes of Kentucky summers can fill your dessert plates year-round.

No blackberries? Raspberries, gooseberries, plums, currants, cherries, blueberries, pears, strawberry-rhubarb, grapes and—of course—apples create flavors so varied you never get bored. Treat this recipe as a guideline; fruits vary in sweetness and juiciness, but the crisp will taste wonderful almost no matter what. Using a variety of sweeteners makes the fruit taste bright and exciting in this recipe and reduces the overall amount of sugar in this dessert; double the amount of one of the sweeteners if you like sweeter desserts.

Yield: Serves 8

Fruit Filling

5–6 cups fresh or frozen fruit (whole small berries, pitted cherries or finely sliced or chopped pieces of larger fruits; peel or not as you wish)

2 tablespoons Kentucky sorghum

2 tablespoons Kentucky honey

2 tablespoons Kentucky maple syrup

1 tablespoon sugar

juice and zest of half a lemon

¼ teaspoon salt

1 tablespoon small tapioca pearls or corn starch, tapioca flour, all-purpose flour or gluten-free all-purpose baking mix (optional, for thickening)

Topping

½ scant cup unbleached flour or gluten-free all-purpose baking mix

2 tablespoons sugar

2 tablespoons cold unsalted butter, cut into small pieces

¼ teaspoon salt

¼ teaspoon allspice, nutmeg, cinnamon or cloves (optional)

Note: For extremely tart fruit like gooseberries, increase sweeteners by 1 tablespoon each.

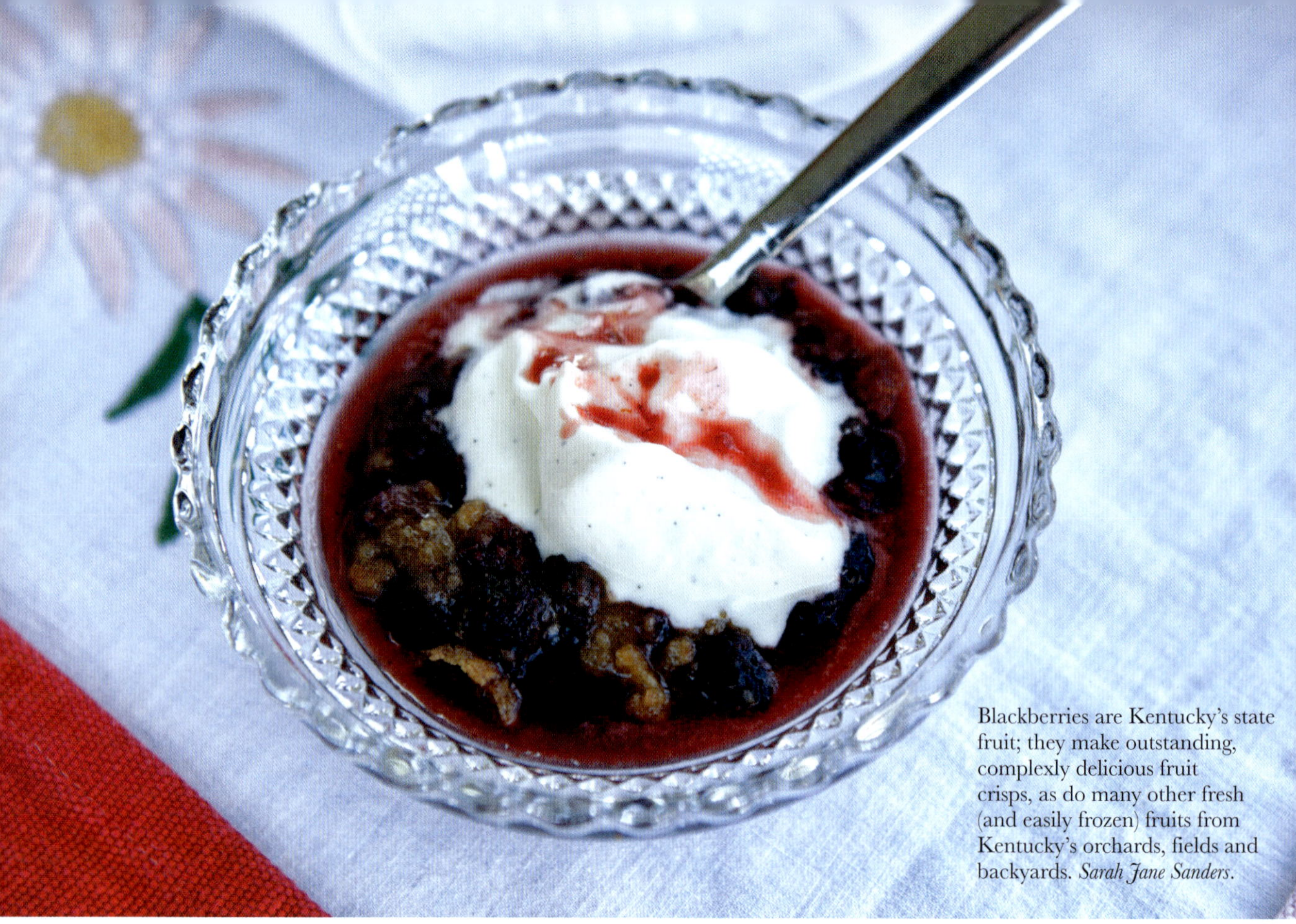

Blackberries are Kentucky's state fruit; they make outstanding, complexly delicious fruit crisps, as do many other fresh (and easily frozen) fruits from Kentucky's orchards, fields and backyards. *Sarah Jane Sanders*.

In a large bowl, mix the fruit, all the sweeteners, lemon juice and zest and salt. If using a thickener, add it now. Stir until very well mixed. Let the fruit rest and macerate while you make the crisp topping.

Preheat the oven to 350 degrees Fahrenheit.

In a separate small bowl, mix together the flour, sugar, butter, salt and optional spice for the crisp topping. Alternately, pulse these ingredients about five times in a food processor fitted with a stainless steel blade. Whether using your hands or a machine, aim for a texture that is like sand mixed with a few pea-sized pebbles. Do not over-process; err on the side of chunkiness.

Butter or use nonstick spray to prepare a standard pie plate or any non-aluminum baking dish that easily contains the fruit, with room for the topping and some delicious juiciness. Put the fruit mixture in the baking dish and sprinkle the crisp topping mixture all over it.

Bake for 50–60 minutes, until the top shows many spots of thick bubbly juice and the crisp topping has some golden brown tips here and there. If you start with frozen fruit—you guessed it—baking may take 70–90 minutes. Serve warm or at room temperature with Whipped Half-Sour Cream (or use all heavy cream) from page 43 or top with Buttermilk-Maple Ice Cream (page 110).

Blue Moon Farm, Poosey Ridge (Madison County), Kentucky

For people who moved to the commonwealth of Kentucky from other states, Leo and Jean Pitches Keene put a lot of faith in Kentuckians. More than twenty years ago, Leo and Jean began thinking that Kentuckians might learn to savor garlic, which is not a plant or a flavor rooted deeply in Kentucky foodways. Kentuckians have justified that faith by embracing fresh, pungent garlic for its own self and for its ways of enhancing some time-honored foods from Kentucky's land. One good example is quickly sautéed garlicky greens (see page 162).

It all began in a grocery store. Leo said, "We were living in Mount Sterling. We would buy garlic at the grocery store in these little paper coffins and then get home and find out it was not usable. It occurred to us that we might be able to grow this stuff. So we grew a little."

In 1988, Jean and Leo had settled on Blue Moon Farm, sixty-five acres in Madison County that included about six acres of rich, river bottomland. At first, they grew elephant garlic and tried a mail-order business, selling through magazine ads. Their first ad yielded one customer—and he continued faithfully buying Blue Moon garlic until his death more than fifteen years later.

In 1993, Jean and Leo went to an early Hudson Valley Garlic Festival in Saugerties, New York, near Jean's birthplace. The event included a day for garlic growers to meet with one another. "There were a lot of them," Leo said, "And some of them were doing pretty well." Even more eye opening, when the festival opened the following day, Leo said, "About five thousand people showed up, and they were grabbing everything anybody had to sell."

Not long afterward, small farm champions in Kentucky organized a Harvest Festival in Louisville that featured pairings between growers and chefs, including a pairing that showcased Blue Moon's garlic. Louisvillians showed interest in garlic; soon Lexington Farmers' Market buyers had their own opportunities to taste and smell Blue Moon garlic. Over time, Blue Moon became a fixture at the Lexington Farmers' Market.

Leo and Jean began expanding both the market season and number and type of foods they grew and sold. Leo said, "In the beginning we did not start until June. We didn't know then about baby green garlic." Neither did their customers. Now, tender baby garlic may be the main reason Lexington Farmers' Market shoppers count the days until the first Saturday in April, when the main market season kicks off.

Bluegrass garlic aficionados—yes, we finally saw the light—cherish the procession of garlic types that follows. It's May? Time for garlic scapes, the slender-tender, otherworldly flower stems of hard-necked garlic varieties. Scapes are easy to clean, chop and eat; they offer a subtle garlic taste that lacks garlic's usual bite. In June, garlic fans can buy large heads of young garlic, still boasting tender skins. 'California Early'

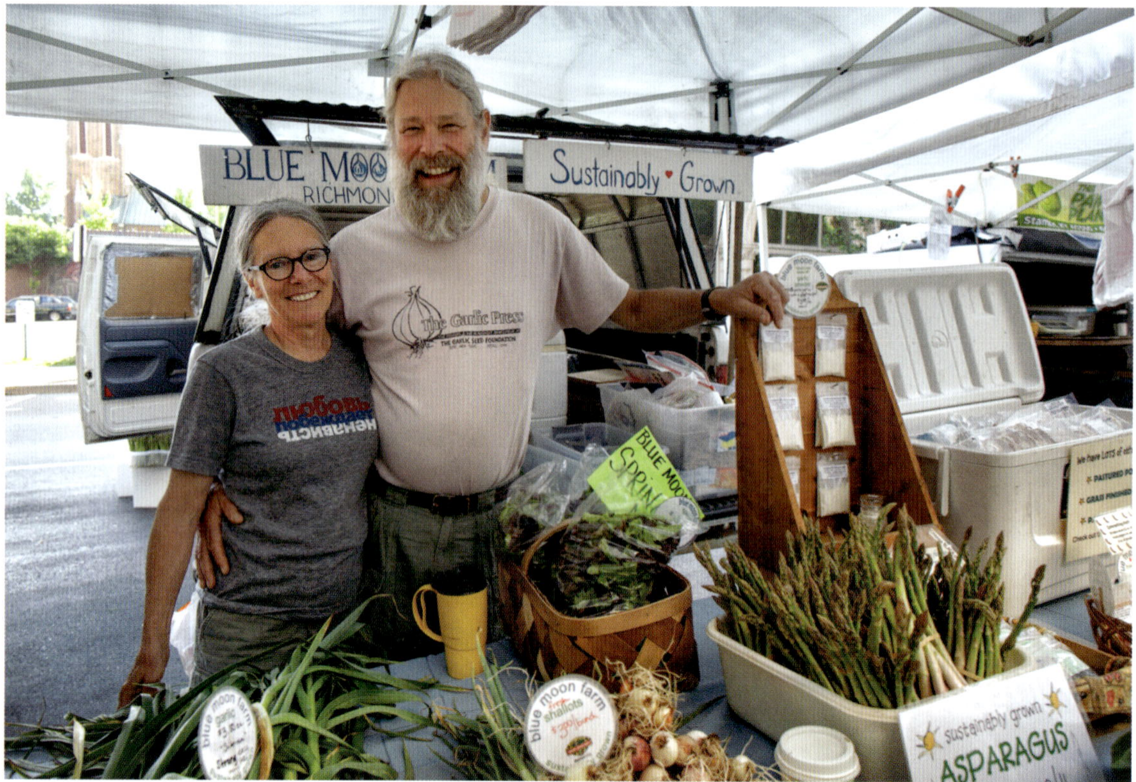

Jean Pitches Keene and Leo Keene of Blue Moon Farm in Madison County brought fresh, fine locally grown garlic to Kentucky more than twenty years ago. *Sarah Jane Sanders.*

and 'Lorz Italian' varieties usually come to market first. Finally, July brings the fully mature garlic, with fat cloves filling out the heads' papery skins. The most beloved variety? A hard-necked type called 'Music.'

In addition, Kentucky's new garlic fans learn more each year from Leo and Jean about how to use garlic—"Even the roots are edible," says Jean—and how to grow garlic in our own home gardens. Pickled garlic scapes, slow roasted cloves or whole heads, braised whole baby garlic, garlic powder and garlic scape pesto now fill crucial spots in central Kentucky menus. Blue Moon developed garlic scape pesto some years ago as a "value-added" product, a way to extend the fresh garlic season year-round for customers, as well as increase farm income.

Once they began coming to the Lexington Farmers' Market early in the growing season, Jean and Leo realized they could also grow and sell additional early season crops. As with the decision to try growing garlic for themselves, success with growing lettuce for themselves led to a realization: "We realized we were planting lettuces for ourselves, and we could just plant more and come earlier and sell it."

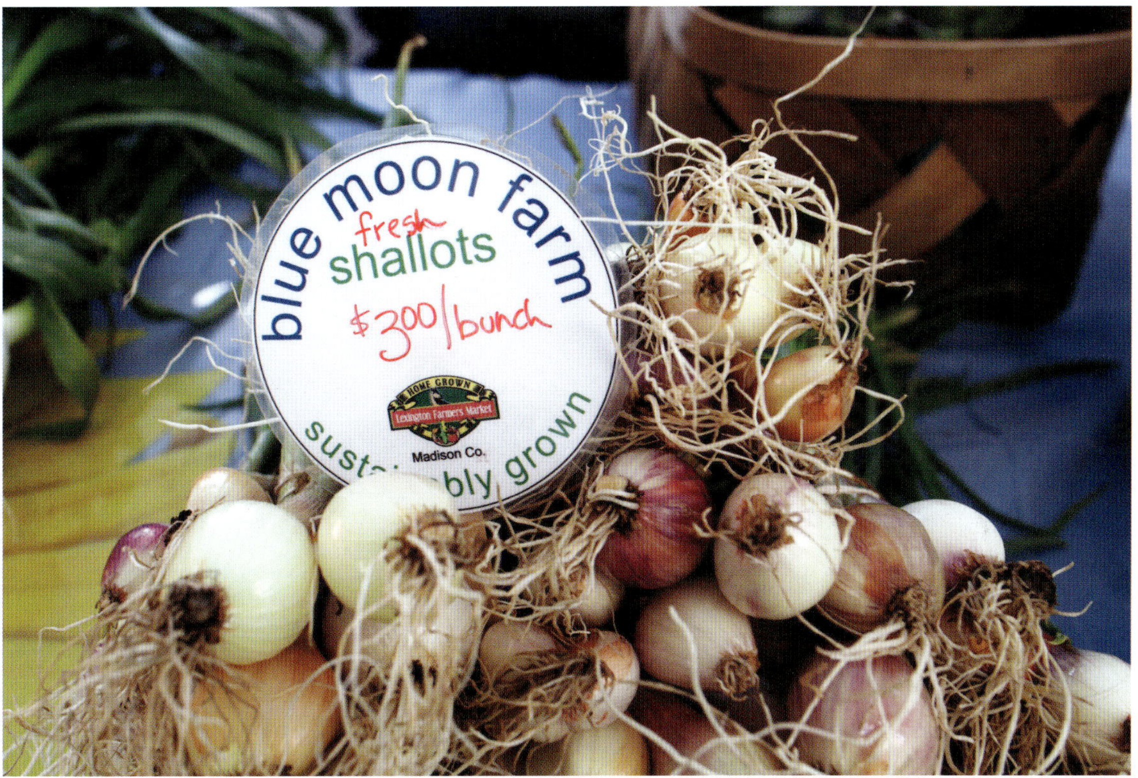

Blue Moon now sells shallots and many other vegetables, meats, cheeses, pastries, herbs and spreads at the Lexington Farmers' Market. *Sarah Jane Sanders.*

While they taught central Kentuckians how to make zestful food with garlic at each of its growth stages, Leo and Jean steadily expanded their farmers' market table holdings with new crops from their farm, such as shallots, as well as other trusted Kentucky producers' foods. Now the customers who wait in clumps at Blue Moon's booth on Saturdays and Sundays can buy a whole meal's worth of Kentucky ingredients that will only be made better with garlic: frozen Colcord Farm beef or Stone Cross Farm pork, Cloverdale Creamery cheese, Vibrant Greens and Sunrise Bakery breads and sweets—even a distinctive garlic chocolate chip cookie.

Several years ago, at the urging of a fellow Lexington Farmers' Market grower, Leo began approaching restaurants to offer fresh, locally grown products from Blue Moon and other farms. "J. Woods had a lot of peas one year, and he said, 'Why don't you try selling these to restaurants?' I did that. And then the restaurants would say, 'What else do you have?' I found restaurants that were able to take advantage of what we were all growing."

Kentucky Proud Restaurant Rewards Program

From the Kentucky Department of Agriculture website, www.kyagr.com: "The Kentucky Proud Restaurant Rewards program is open to any Kentucky Restaurant that is purchasing Kentucky Proud products that have direct Kentucky farm impact, and promoting the use of Kentucky Proud products and agriculture. Depending on how proud you are to serve your customers Kentucky Proud products, you can receive up to 20% of the value back."

Now, a lot of Leo's work involves brokering and delivering foods to restaurants year-round. "New restaurants are buying our foods. Long-time restaurants are changing what they buy, but they keep buying. A lot of them work to take advantage of the Kentucky Proud Restaurant Rewards program. It's a magic time. I'm glad I got to it before I'm on a walker."

Colonel Newsom's Country Ham, Princeton (Caldwell County), Kentucky

Nancy Newsom Mahaffey says her family probably began curing hams not long after reaching Virginia in 1642. Both the pigs and the meat-curing knowledge likely were there. Many accounts say Sir Walter Raleigh brought pigs to Jamestown, Virginia, in 1607, and that Native Americans cured venison long before that. While the exact origins of country ham are a bit misty, a member of Nancy's family set down a processing method in a will in the late 1700s. Nancy follows that process today to produce her acclaimed hams.

Her customers benefit from a recipe and set of practices her Newsom ancestors perfected and followed for more than two hundred years. The salt and brown sugar rub that begins the cure includes no nitrates or nitrites. Long, repeated exposure to cool hickory wood smoke adds color and flavor while boosting the hams' keeping powers. People-friendly molds, particular to the Newsom smokehouse, help preserve the hams and give them flavor. Long hanging in circulating outdoor air—ten months at least—means the hams go through summer heat, which further concentrates flavor and influences texture.

More than thirty years ago, Jeff Bradford, who wrote for the *Hopkinsville New Era*, reported that out of three nationally acclaimed country ham producers in the Pennyrile, a large physiographic region that includes parts of western Kentucky, "The hams of Colonel Bill Newsom in Princeton are the only ones of the three that are still cured in an old-time smokehouse. These hams might not be as pleasing to the eye as others, but as Col. Bill says, 'I don't cure for looks, but for taste.'" And Colonel Bill's daughter Nancy keeps hams in an old smokehouse, not out of nostalgia, but because that's where the great molds and microbes live. The smokehouse holds the secret to the flavor and particular goodness of Colonel Newsom hams, providing a good example of the ongoing use of proven, timeless techniques for producing fine food with spectacular flavor.

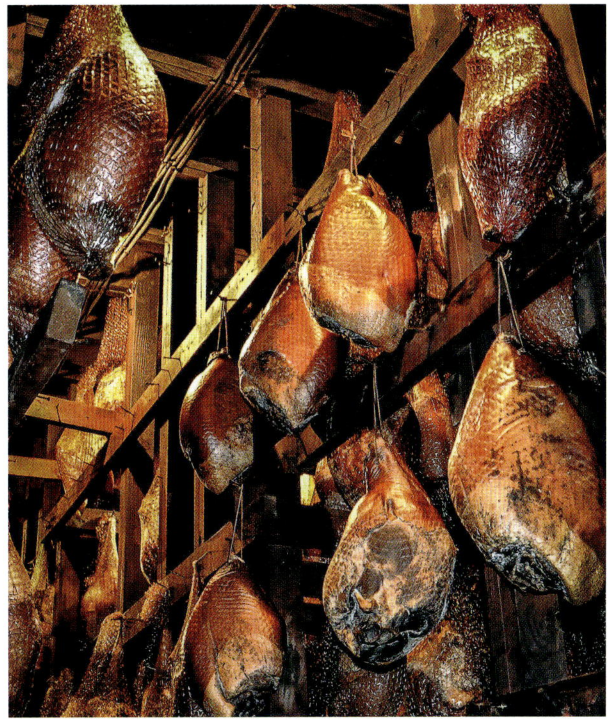

Colonel Newsom's Country Hams age in place in Princeton. *Anita Baker*.

At one time, so many people in Kentucky raised their own hogs and cured their own hams and bacon that these were not big sale items at the Newsom family store. Nancy said, "In the early days, beginning in 1917, there was no market for cured hams in my grandfather's store. Everyone cured their own." Nancy's father, Colonel Bill Newsom, took over the store in 1933, when he was eighteen, and began curing and selling hams in a limited way. The quality of his hams and the movement away from self-sufficiency on many farms led to significant ham production and sales by the 1950s.

Legendary American cookbook author and teacher James Beard found Colonel Newsom's ham in 1975; he championed it for the rest of his life. This began Colonel Newsom's connection to chefs and food leaders, a tie that remains crucial to Colonel Newsom's survival, Nancy said. Kentucky chefs, including Chefs Edward Lee, Laurent Giroli, Kathy Cary and Michael Paley, feature Colonel Newsom's ham in special menus at their noted Louisville restaurants.

In 2014, Zingerman's Roadhouse, a quality-focused restaurant that belongs to the family of businesses in Ann Arbor, Michigan, featured Colonel Newsom's ham—and Nancy herself—in a spring "Bacon Ball," a "special dinner centered around bacon, ham and all things good that come from the pig." Food magazines, culture magazines, men's magazines—all have featured the engaging Nancy Newsom Mahaffey and her family's hams. Perhaps the hams' most prestigious notice came when a Newsom ham became the first from the United States to become a museum exhibit at the Museo del Jamón de Aracena, a museum dedicated to cured ham in Spain, where jamón has been central to food and culture for centuries.

Each year, Nancy and a small, dedicated crew of skilled workers do the heavy lifting and delicate decision making that yields one more harvest of splendid Kentucky country hams, cured as they have been for hundreds of years. The process they follow and the passion they bring to their work serve as a truing tool for people committed to sustaining Kentucky's food heritage and cuisine.

Smoked, Cured, Idolized: Pork in Kentucky Smokehouses

Smokehouse pork, cured with salt—and sometimes a few add-ins—and browned from the smoke of hickory or another fine-scented wood, must be among the top-five ways to create Kentucky flavors on a plate. The flavors of bacon made by curing and smoking pork belly or pork jowl or the bones and trimmings of a cured, smoked, aged upper hind leg—ham—may have seasoned more Kentucky food than any substance other than salt.

Authentic cuisines from any part of the world begin with the foods that grow well in a certain place, with particular concentration on preparations of those foods that sustained life across seasons and years. Cured, smoked pork—add in aging, too, for hams—probably came onto the North American land mass shortly after pigs arrived with the earliest European settlers. According to the Pork Fact Book of 2002–03 produced by eXtension, the online information resource of Cooperative Extension, Columbus brought pigs to Cuba in 1493; Hernando de Soto brought pigs to Tampa Bay, Florida, in 1539; Hernando Cortéz brought them to what is now New Mexico in 1600; and Sir Walter Raleigh introduced pigs to the Jamestown Colony near the Atlantic Coast in 1607. No wonder we like bacon!

Settlers placed high value on pigs and the pork they yielded. Pigs eat nearly anything and so are fairly easy to raise. They multiply quickly, with each sow averaging ten piglets per litter, and many sows littering twice in a year. Their meat can be processed on a farm and then cured to help feed a family across a year or more. As eXtension noted, "As the seventeenth century closed, the typical farmer owned four or five pigs, supplying salt pork and bacon for his table with surpluses sold as barreled pork."

Salt-cured pork had sustained Asians and Europeans for millennia before Europeans came to the New World. It is possible that Native Americans' experiences with curing and preserving venison influenced the newcomers' ways of handling pork. In any

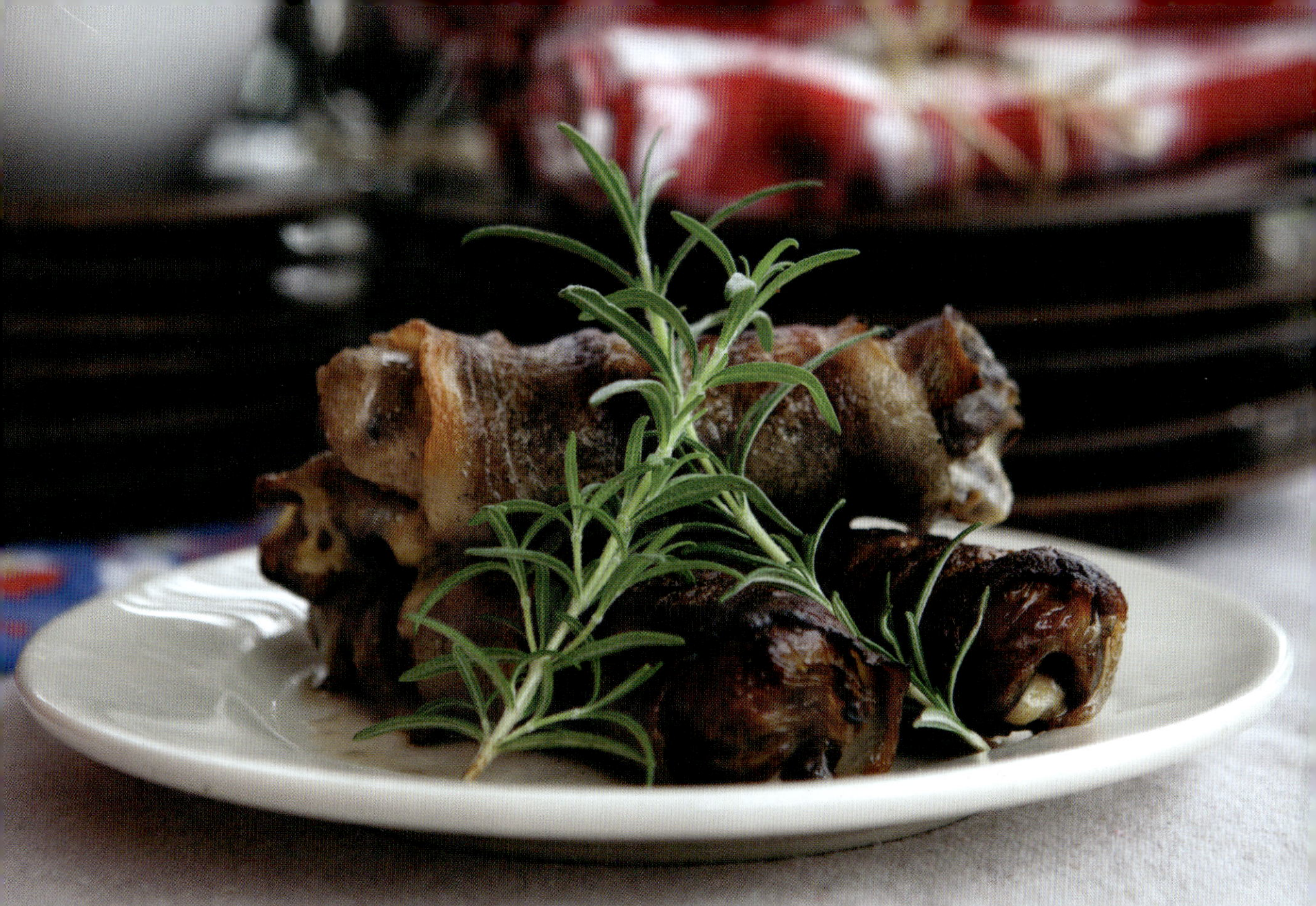

Hood's Heritage Hogs bacon wraps a Hood's sausage that's split and filled with cheese before being slow cooked to melty, crusty perfection. *Sarah Jane Sanders.*

case, salting, curing, smoking and, for some cuts, aging have been practiced in this country since shortly after hogs were introduced, likely over three hundred years ago.

Bacon currently enjoys a "treat food" status that might have surprised the cooks and eaters in most Kentucky households before the 1940s. Nearly every meal likely contained dishes made more delicious by the addition of bacon or ham scraps or perhaps country sausage, smoked sausage, lard or drippings saved from any previously cooked pork. Usually these meats flavored other dishes rather than being served as stand-alone entrées. The flavors of smoked pork amounted to the flavors of food itself, certainly on the Kentucky table.

Prior to the mid-twentieth century, when each farm household raised, cured and ate its own pork, no one needed to use the term "country ham." Just "ham" sufficed. Once new types of ham curing and cooking became available, the term "country ham" began to apply to "uncooked, cured, dried, smoked-or-unsmoked meat product from a single piece of meat from the hind leg of a hog," by eXtension's definition.

The term "country ham" appeared in the 1940s, and it may have caused some unwarranted trouble. For his 2014 book, *Country Ham: A Southern Tradition of Hogs, Salt, & Smoke*, Steve Coomes interviewed many of the living masters of the craft of country ham production. Most describe the tension between country ham as a delicacy that chefs in elite white-tablecloth restaurants have embraced and country ham as food their neighbors think should be inexpensive survival food. Coomes quotes Charles Gatton Jr. of Father's Country Hams in Bremen, Kentucky: "Country ham making is not a high-profit business. Part of that is because there's a limit to what you can charge, to what people will pay for bacon and ham." Coomes quotes Nancy Newsom Mahaffey of Colonel Newsom's Country Ham in Princeton, Kentucky, on the difference in the amount of respect Europeans

Hood's Heritage bacon tops slow-cooked, from-scratch Really Amazing Baked Beans. *Sarah Jane Sanders*.

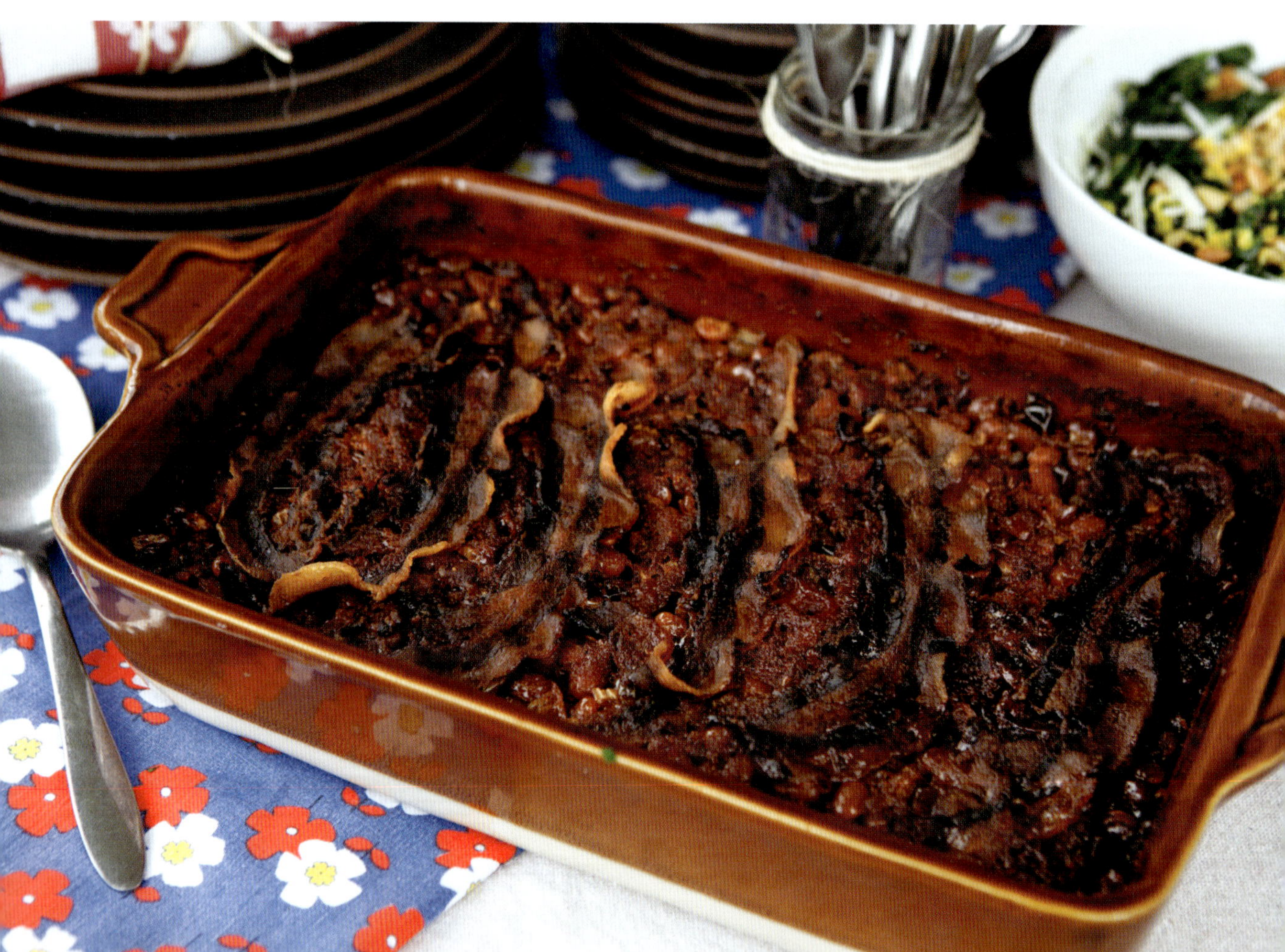

and Kentuckians hold for prized, high quality hams: "The prices they get there [Spain] are so high end! You see *Ibéricos* here for $1,500, and I'm selling my two-year-old hams for around $125."

One way some of the master ham crafters and nearly all their noted chef customers see to change public views on country ham involves serving it like European prosciutto or other cured meats: uncooked, sliced paper thin, with proper accompaniments. To many Kentuckians this may sound almost as strange as biscuits made without flour. We are a plucky lot, though. We try, taste and learn. We'll soon be seeing paper-thin slices of charcuterie-style country ham on appetizer platters in restaurants in our hometowns, and soon after, we'll serve ham this way ourselves—if we can get our knives sharp enough.

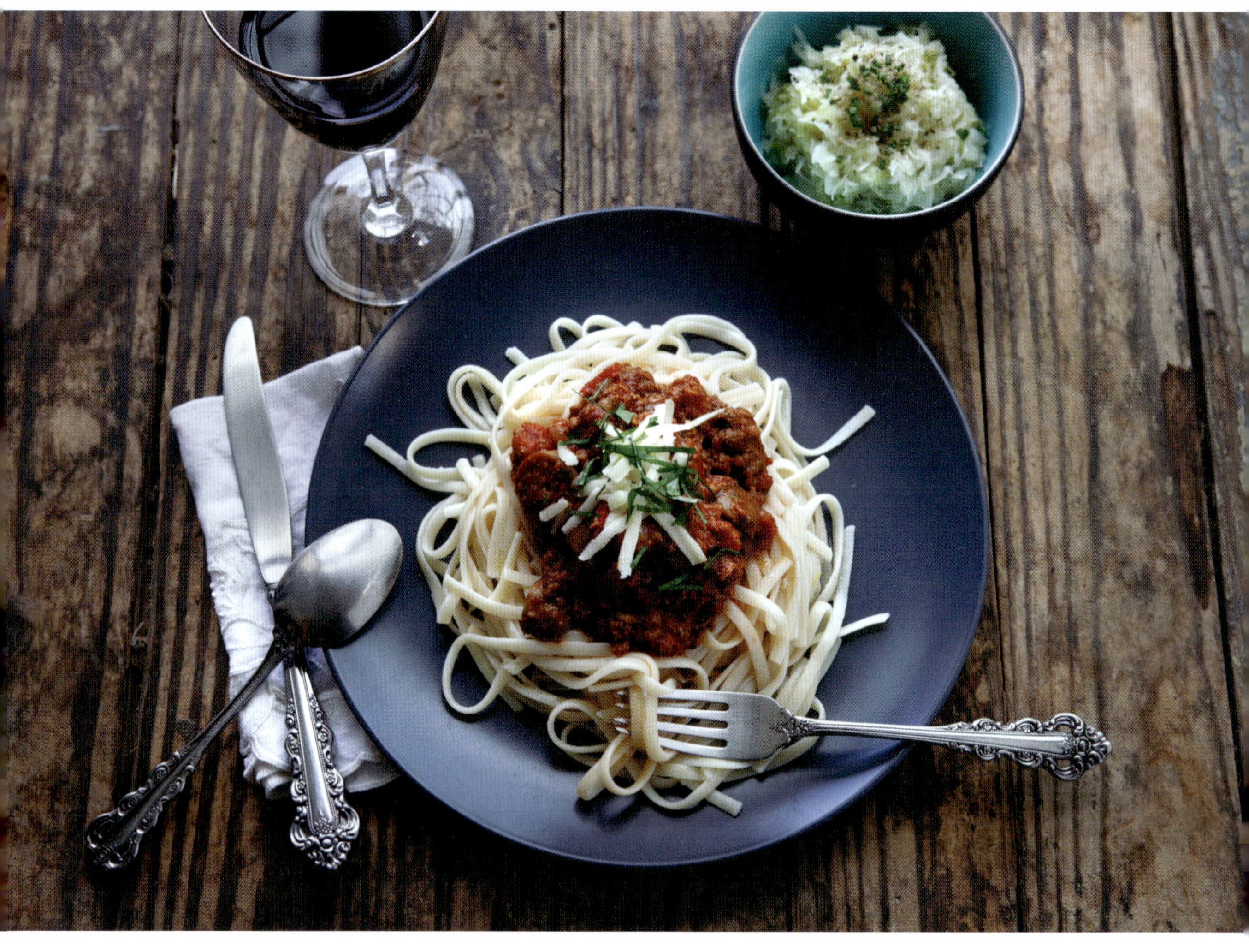

Bonus meal: With sauce from the freezer or vegetables fresh from the garden, Kentucky's own Lexington Pasta makes it easy to cook homemade dinner in minutes, any day of the week. *Sarah Jane Sanders.*

Meal 6
BONUS

PASTA

The answer for the days or nights when a meal has to appear in minutes? Pasta, of course. Pasta, noodles or spaghetti would not have seemed like Kentucky food in the long-ago past, but Lexington Pasta Company now makes fresh pasta available in the central part of the state, and the company uses local ingredients when it can.

Grocery store pasta tastes good, too. Delicious gluten-free pasta options have become more widely available.

Good topping options can be utterly simple and quick:

- Blue Moon garlic slices sautéed in Maysville-based First Fresh olive oil, pasta, salt, pepper, a bit of Kentucky cheese. Done.
- In summer, chop ripe, fresh tomatoes and toss without cooking onto hot pasta, drizzle with olive oil, salt, pepper, a bit of cheese and maybe some torn basil or parsley. Done.
- Chopped crisp Kentucky bacon, lightly beaten eggs tossed quickly with super-hot pasta, Kentucky Parmesan, parsley: carbonara!

Or spend an hour in advance. Set up a wonderful meat or meat-free tomato sauce in a large stockpot; once it's cooked, tuck meal-size packets in the freezer for nearly instant comfort any night of the week. Visit http://www.savoringkentucky.com/even-more-homemade for links to spaghetti sauces and pasta toppings.

For dessert? Pull out the bourbon balls from Ruth Hunt Candy or other fine Kentucky candy makers. Small, intense, blissful. They may be small, but they are more than enough.

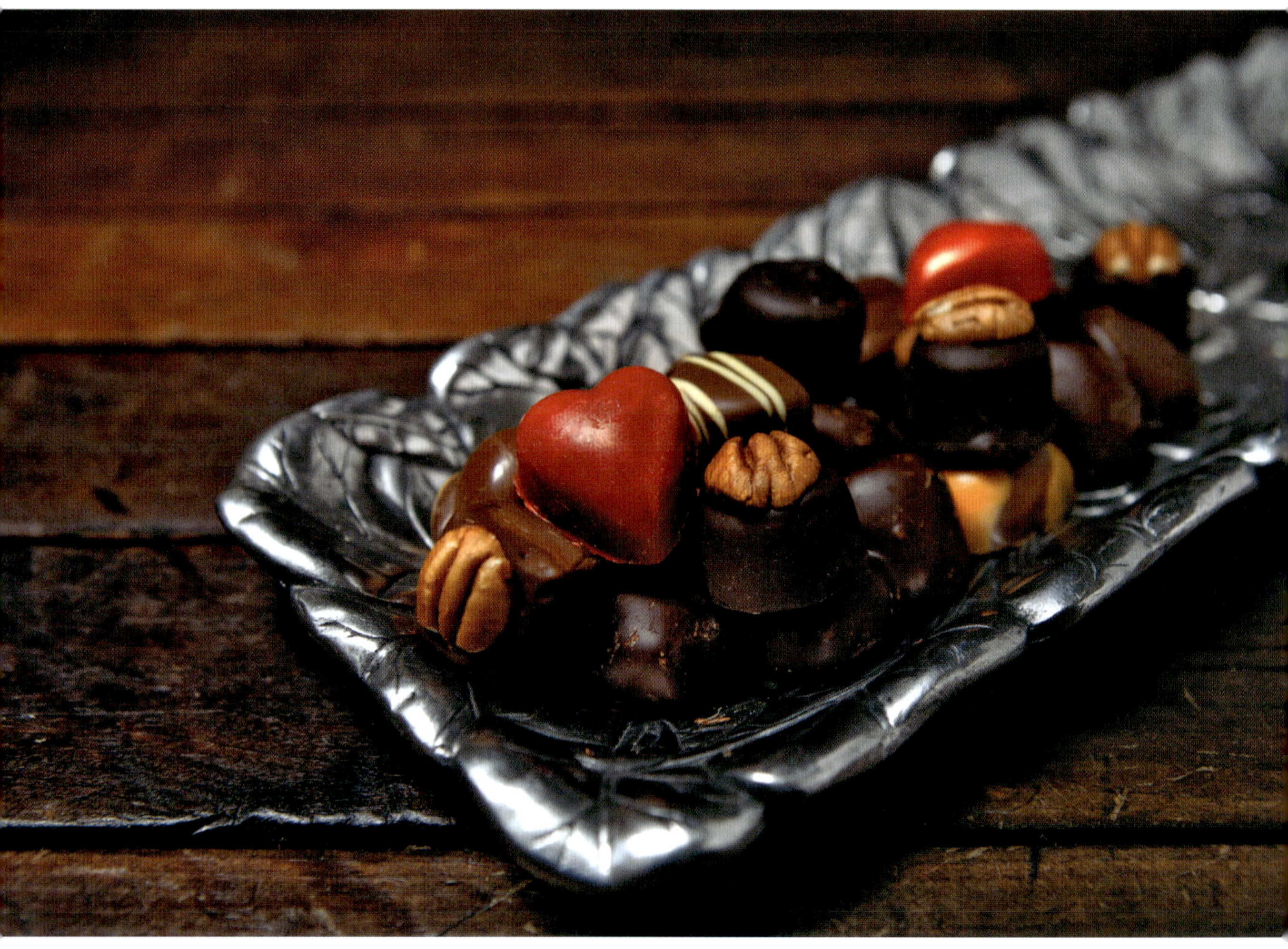

Ahhh, chocolates. Ruth Hunt Candies makes many chocolates, particularly splendid bourbon balls, some with Woodford Reserve bourbon; many other artisan chocolate confectioners also melt hearts in the lucky state of Kentucky. *Sarah Jane Sanders*.

INDEX

ABOUT THE AUTHOR

Rona Roberts hosts Savoring Kentucky, one of Kentucky's longest-running food blogs. Rona speaks and writes about the pleasures of Kentucky food and champions those who produce it. She is the author of *Sweet, Sweet Sorghum: Kentucky's Golden Wonder*. Rona founded Lexington's weekly Local Food Percolator lunch, a forum for connecting people working toward an excellent, self-sufficient local food system. Rona is a native of Wayne County and a veteran of the United States Peace Corps. She and her excellent husband, Steve Kay, are parents and grandparents of a kitchen full of cooks and eaters. Rona and Steve host weekly community Cornbread Suppers every Monday at 6:00 p.m. You're invited.

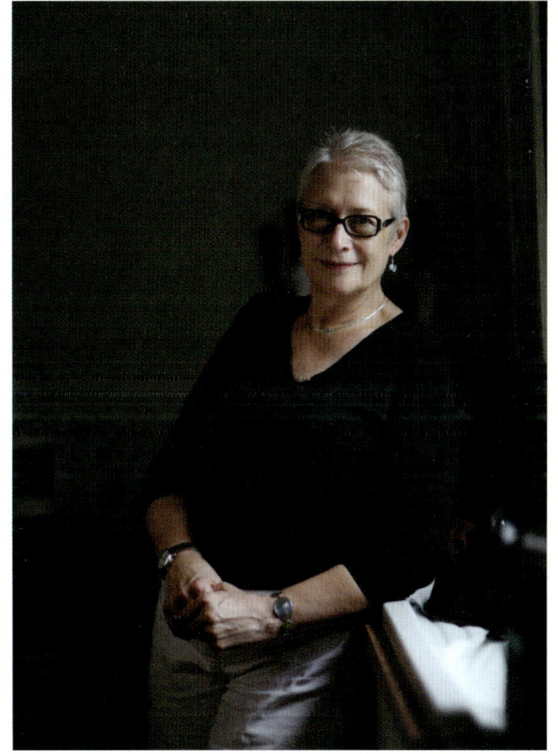

Visit us at
www.historypress.net

This title is also available as an e-book